Risk

Also available from
Bloomberg Professional Library

Mastering Microcaps:
Strategies, Trends, and Stock Selection
by Daniel P. Coker

Market-Neutral Investing:
The Essential Strategies
by Joseph G. Nicholas
(August 2000)

Small-Cap Dynamics:
Insights, Analysis, and Models
by Satya Dev Pradhuman
(August 2000)

And from
Bloomberg Press

Investing in Hedge Funds:
Strategies for the New Marketplace
by Joseph G. Nicholas

A complete list of our titles is available at
www.bloomberg.com/books

Attention Corporations

Bloomberg Press Books are available at quantity discounts with bulk purchase for sales promotional use and for corporate education or other business uses. Special editions or book excerpts can also be created. For information, please call 609-279-4670 or write to: Special Sales Dept., Bloomberg Press, P.O. Box 888, Princeton, NJ 08542.

The New Management Imperative in Finance

Risk

JAMES T. GLEASON

Bloomberg Press
Princeton, New Jersey

This publication contains the author's opinions and is designed to provide accurate and authoritative information. It is sold with the understanding that the author, publisher, and Bloomberg L.P. are not engaged in rendering legal, accounting, investment-planning, or other professional advice. The reader should seek the services of a qualified professional for such advice; the author, publisher, and Bloomberg L.P. cannot be held responsible for any loss incurred as a result of specific investments or planning decisions made by the reader.

Library of Congress Cataloging-in-Publication Data

Gleason, James T., 1952–
    Risk: the new management imperative in finance / James T. Gleason.
        p. cm. — (Bloomberg professional library)
    Includes bibliographical references and index.
    ISBN 1-57660-074-2
    1. Risk management.   I. Title.   II. Series.

    HD61.G57 2000
    658.15'5—dc21

                                99-089745

Edited by Maris Williams

First edition published 2000
1 3 5 7 9 10 8 6 4 2

"Go help to ensure the world allocates its resources wisely."

Hanna Holborn Gray, President,
University of Chicago
Commencement address to the 1982 graduate school of business

Contents

CREDIT RISK MANAGEMENT

RISK IN PORTFOLIOS

DEVELOPING A GLOBAL RISK MANAGEMENT PROCESS

Acknowledgments

Most books on financial risk management have a pantheon of authors and editors. Having just completed a solo effort, I understand entirely too well why this is the case.

This book would certainly not have been possible without the help of the following people.

Jacque Murphy's enthusiastic encouragement got me started. Scott Aguais, Marc Baumslag, Sandeep Bidani, Ottho Heldring, Craig Johl, David Lawrence, Victor Mausch, David Nordby, David Rowe, Emerson Nagle, and Fred Vacelet all provided encouragement and constructive advice on the manuscript.

Jeff Kinneman, Vince Kaminski, and Kal Shah at Enron Capital all helped to create the Enron case study. Brian Ranson helped write the Bank of Montreal case study. He also provided very useful and insightful advice on the whole Credit Risk section. I also thank the many people at Big Auto Company and Big Oil Company who were instrumental in ensuring that complete, accurate, and illustrative case studies of their organizations appear in this book.

Rizwan Kadir, Gino Perina, and Diana Holdsworth were all very helpful researchers. Jared Kieling, Barbara Diez Goldenberg, Maris Williams, David Frank, and Gail Doolin at Bloomberg provided good advice and assistance throughout the process. Nancy Marcus Land provided many word edits that clarified and simplified the presentation.

Special thanks to Dr. Ross Miller for granting permission to use his previously published chart in this book.

Finally, special thanks to my wife Sarah, who graciously created space in our lives for this endeavor even though it took far longer than planned.

Introduction

This book shows how and why *risk* has become the new strategic imperative in financial management. Financial firms, which have traditionally mediated flows of capital through markets, have been squeezed by recent market developments. Greater price transparency, new trading products, and increased competition (resulting from deregulation, globalization, and so on) have tightened these firms' margins. Even worse, electronic markets are reducing the need for any intermediaries at all. This trend is well underway in the most fluid capital markets.

Financial firms' role in capital transfer has diminished, but their role as intermediaries for risk has grown. Derivative products allow them to easily parse and price specific bundles of risk. They can achieve ongoing profits by pooling risks and hedging the net exposures. They can also make ongoing profits by adjusting the risks inside financial deals, customizing them to investor and corporate tastes. Dealers will still be needed in those sectors of capital markets that require transfer of financial risk. To win in these new risk markets, dealers must measure, price, and manage all their financial risks much more efficiently than they do now.

This book describes financial risk management and examines its recent evolution and its impact on financial service organizations. Financial risk management is a set of processes, supported by quantitative methods, that allows firms to know, control, and accurately charge for the financial risks they are taking. These processes and techniques, which I call *global risk management* (GRM), can better align the incentives and activities of everyone in the firm, thereby enhancing returns through wiser allocation of scarce risk resources. GRM is reshaping the management of financial service firms as radically as technology, globalization, and deregulation have reshaped capital markets.

This bold assertion is a straightforward extrapolation of current developments. Risk management processes grew out of valuation models that were developed to price derivatives. As derivative products expanded from the fixed-income markets to cover other markets such as commodities, currencies, and equities, the range and flexibility of valuation models expanded. Frameworks emerged for measuring the risks on a consistent basis, across various markets. Value at Risk (VaR) was the first risk measurement framework that cut across markets and products. An additional framework based on measuring risks in stressed markets is also emerging. These frameworks provide a base for risk-adjusting performance, creating internal markets for risk, and many other ways to optimize firm value.

These risk frameworks have recently been extended to cover credit risk as well. The mathematicians and physicists (rocket scientists) who came to Wall Street and revolutionized the markets with quantitative models have turned their considerable abilities to credit risk. Their results have galvanized credit markets. They have developed models that can measure credit risk, price it in external markets, and allow allocation of capital for it internally (internal pricing). The new credit risk models even provide information about the marginal contribution of each loan to the overall risk/return profile of the credit portfolio.

These models change how banks view loans and how loan markets work. Traditionally, a loan was viewed as an asset that was bought and held to maturity. Now, loans are regarded as a portfolio whose risk-adjusted return should be actively managed. The new credit models and the new perspective have led to an explosion of growth in secondary markets for commercial loans. The major institutions are just starting to manage their credit portfolios more actively.

GRM is currently more a vision than a reality; for example, the techniques for credit risk have not been fully validated. However, forms of GRM are in place at banks and securities firms such as Chase, Bear Stearns, Citigroup, Bank of America, and Nations-Bank. Similar frameworks for risk analysis, called dynamic financial analysis (DFA), have been developed and deployed at insurance companies. The full value of GRM will be seen only over time, but the preliminary results are compelling. The GRM framework is applicable to all financial intermediaries, banks, securities firms, and insurance firms.

How This Book Is Organized

This book contains five sections. The first section lays out the contours of risk and generally charts our journey. The full spectrum of risks that business organizations face is diagrammed, to show where the financial risks fit within that spectrum. The diagram also illustrates key topological distinctions among financial risks, such as the differences in how market and credit risk can be measured and managed. Major changes in the capital markets, which make the use of GRM a strategic imperative for financial intermediaries, are summarized.

The second section looks at market risks and the tools for managing them. After briefly noting the generic tools for managing market risk, this section examines each major market segment: commodities, currencies or foreign exchange (FX), fixed income, and equities. It also tracks how quantitative models grew to describe the fabric and contour of market risks in every market.

The third section examines credit risks and the tools for managing them. A schism exists in credit management, born of historic, market, and cultural differences between the trading and the commercial lending organizations within large commercial banks. We will look at the tools and management techniques, both old and recently developed, that help manage credit risk. The new analytical tools are largely extensions of the market risk models, and, together with those models, they make up a uniform set that covers both market and credit risk. The management implications of this unified set of tools are explored.

In the fourth section, we track the emergence of GRM tools and techniques. The portfolio measures of risk, such as VaR, stress, DFA, and credit portfolio risk measures, are the keys for expanding risk management from a function of control to the broader function of managing and harmonizing activities. As illustrated, features inherent in simulation techniques make them the best tools for measuring the dynamic interactions in risk.

The fifth section discusses the practicalities of building a GRM process. First, we describe the GRM vision and the reality that is quite far from that vision. The GRM development framework is then established. The real initiatives that are examined illustrate how to successfully build pieces of the GRM process and maximize the power each piece has. Finally, the "ten commandments" of GRM development lay down the most important rules for sound GRM development.

Risk Management Transparency

To date, the power of risk as a management tool has been obscured by its complexity. Most risk management texts have required readers to be facile with Greek letters and mathematical formulas. Arcane details and complex math are necessary to describe precisely how risk management works, but they are not needed to see the historic direction and growing significance of risk for financial managers.

Markets for transferring capital have been in place for a long time. The markets for transferring financial risk began with the first currency swap in 1981. The new derivative products greatly facilitate the transfer of risk, just as securities have facilitated the transfer of capital to its most productive applications. The development of markets for risk, and the ability to price it accurately, gives financial firms a powerful yardstick against which they must measure the risks (both on and off their balance sheets) for the returns (both immediate and long-term) that they are getting.

This book shows why it is strategically imperative for financial service firms to develop a global financial risk process to harness this new knowledge. It provides a practical understanding of the issues involved, and it gives real case examples, while going light on the math. It describes how GRM is being implemented today and how it will work in the future.

Risk

THE SPECTRUM

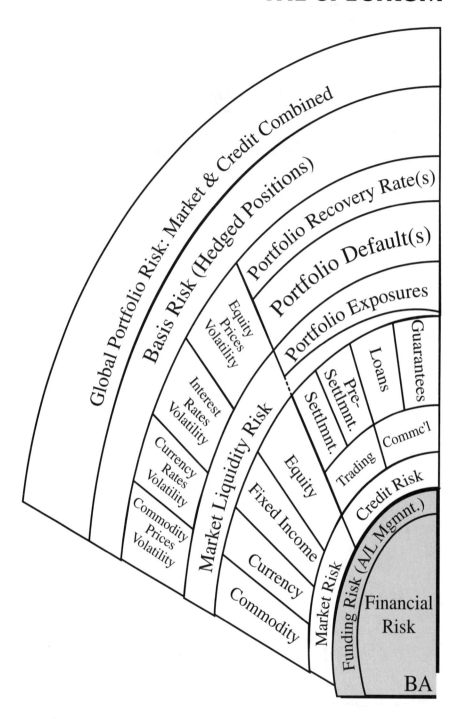

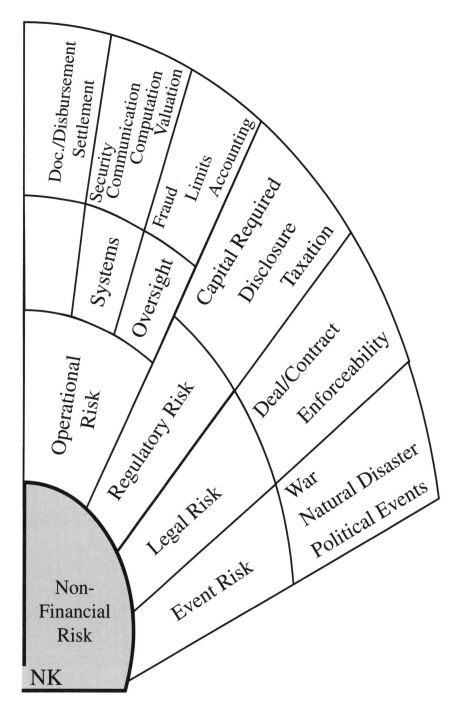

THE RISKS AND
THEIR CONTOURS

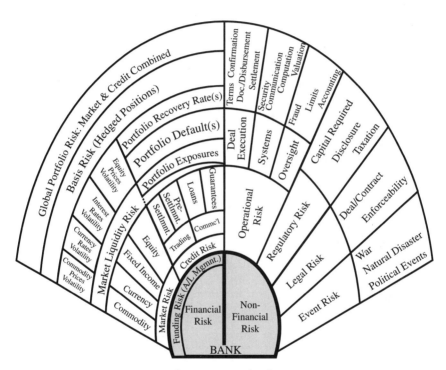

The Spectrum of Risks

Global Risk Management's Emergence

1

The past twenty-five years have seen more changes in capital markets than were introduced in the entire prior history, which spans centuries. Increased global trade is only one factor that has contributed to stepped-up activity in capital markets everywhere. Product diversity in financial markets themselves has exploded. New derivative products, which parse and price specific financial exposures, are brought to market daily. Widespread deregulation has increased competition, narrowed spreads, and lowered barriers to the flow of capital. Tremendous growth in the volume of market trade and product diversification, coupled with falling unit costs, has largely offset the revenues lost from narrower spreads. As transaction costs are driven lower, capital moves more swiftly to the highest perceived yield—risk-adjusted, of course—around the globe. Sovereign barriers to capital movement (particularly, the exporting of capital) are dropping as many emerging market nations compete to attract investment.

The intermediaries in capital markets are feeling pressures from these changes. With greater efficiency a priority, most major financial service firms have launched cost-saving initiatives over the past five years. Some have conducted several rounds of personnel-shedding programs. The raft of mergers of dealers—Citibank/Salomon Smith Barney, BancOne/First Chicago NBD, Deutsche Bank/Bankers Trust, and Bank of America/NationsBank, to name a few—is also attributable, at least partially, to pressures for greater efficiency.

TECHNOLOGY AND COMMUNICATIONS

Advances in computing power and communications have been another major catalyst for the changes in capital markets. For example,

3

each month, 45 million home owners in the United States pay approximately $30 billion in interest on mortgage loans. About half of these payments pass through investment trust vehicles directly to investors. Mortgage-backed securities (MBS), created in 1971,[1] now cover 46 percent of the $5.7 trillion residential mortgage market.[2] Studies show that these securities lower retail mortgage rates by .4 percent to .5 percent, thus providing mortgage borrowers with about a billion dollars in lower interest costs every month.[3]

At the same time, investors are being given another investment choice, which can enhance yield. With no credit risk (because Uncle Sam shoulders it), these securities have yielded between 30 and 250 basis points more than treasuries of the same duration. Investors require a premium because of prepayment and liquidity risk; these securities have less predictable cash flows and less liquidity than Uncle Sam's bonds. The MBS market is one of the largest segments in the U.S. fixed-income market. However, these securities would be impossible without the technological capacity of computers to keep track of the thousands of accounts in each pool of mortgages, individual borrowers, investors, interest, principal, and prepayments.

The development of electronic trading is another example of how technology facilitates markets. Pit traders and trading specialists are expensive, slow, and error-prone, compared to the computers. Exhibit 1.1 shows Nasdaq's trade volume versus NYSE's trade volume over time. Nasdaq obtains electronic assistance to discover price and trade; NYSE continues to rely on specialists to set market-clearing prices and facilitate trading. Neither of these markets is as efficient as electronic communication networks (ECNs), which can determine price and match trades without any human intervention, at a fraction of the normal cost.

Dinosaurs, move over! It's just a matter of time before the specialists and pit traders join you. All the growth in trading is occurring in the electronic forums, where buyer and seller can discover price, and trade much more cheaply. The automation of markets is reducing transaction costs and facilitating increased trade. Electronic markets are rapidly dominating trading of the most homogenous products, such as equities and foreign exchange (FX).

A subtler benefit of technology—cheaper data storage and faster, cheaper communications—accrues to the dealers and providers of

Exhibit 1.1 Nasdaq versus NYSE Trade Volume (Average Daily Share Volume)

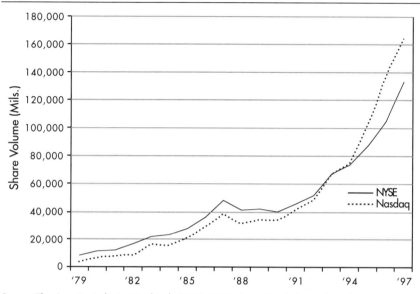

Source: The Security Industry Yearbook 1997–1998, Securities Industry Association.

liquidity in these markets. Thanks to these developments, they can capture and save extensive price histories relatively cheaply. These logs of time-series of prices are used in statistical models to better understand how markets behave. That information allows improvements in valuation models and increased trading profits.

Technology developments enable GRM as well. The new tools and techniques for financial risk management require massive data storage and computing requirements. Until recently, computing and communications speeds were too slow to support measuring risk globally. Memory, storage, and computer processing time were constraints to broader and more extensive use of quantitative risk measures.

QUANTITATIVE MODELS

Another trend that has led to change in the capital markets is the increased quantitative rigor that accompanies activities such as pricing, trading, investment, lending, and portfolio management. Before they deal, virtually all financial managers today run series of quantitative tests that help clarify the risks and returns of each transaction.

The specific analysis varies from market to market. For example, the valuation and portfolio models for equity are quite different from the ones for fixed income. There are also variations among institutions: an insurance company's quantitative analysis differs from that of a securities firm. With growing demand for data and for the analytical tools to interpret them, a large and specialized financial information industry has blossomed in the past ten years. Companies like Reuters Group PLC and Bloomberg L.P. provide the latest data, along with analytical functions, to all market participants.

Academia corroborates this trend. Twenty years ago, my alma mater, the University of Chicago, had several courses in statistics, regression analysis, and financial models such as the capital asset pricing model (CAPM) and the Black–Scholes option-pricing formula. It was in the vanguard with a requirement that all students take a minimum set of quantitative courses. By contrast, the 1999 curriculum contains over fourteen courses within the financial management field that cover quantitative financial analysis. These new courses carry titles like "Futures, Forwards, Options, and Swaps: Theory and Practice," "Theory of Financial Decisions" (versions I through IV), "Fixed Income and Asset Pricing," and "Financial Engineering: Mathematical Models of Option Pricing and Their Estimation."

Risks encountered in capital markets are similar to risks seen in gambling. Attempts to understand dice and other games of chance have yielded some of the formulas that underpin risk analysis today.[4] Probability models were adopted most readily in the insurance markets, where the statistical frequency, timing, and severity of events drive insurance value, premiums, and profitability. There were no comparably useful analytical tools in capital markets until the early 1970s. Two key theoretical developments—portfolio risk and option valuation—formed the foundation for the emerging GRM process.

Portfolio Risk

First came the concept of portfolio risk and its offspring, the CAPM. In 1952, Harry Markowitz, then a graduate student at the University of Chicago, wrote his Ph.D. dissertation, "Portfolio Selection."[5] It introduced the concept of portfolio diversification, which has become the mantra of stockbrokers and investment advisers around the globe. Markowitz noted that the variance of return for a portfolio is typically less than the variance of individual holdings within the portfolio, and he suggested that an investor's performance should be measured by both the portfolio risk—that is, the variance of return—as well as the returns achieved. This breakthrough led to the capital asset pricing theory, which links the value of an asset with its risk/return profile in relation to the total market risk/return.

Gold, for example, has very low historical returns but a higher portfolio value, because of its contribution to total portfolio risk/return. Its value, historically, has been negatively correlated with most other asset values (e.g., when all assets lose value, gold increases in value). This feature, as a portfolio counterweight, makes gold and other countercyclical assets more attractive than their historical return alone would predict. In mid-1999, during the protracted bull market, gold was losing its luster. Conventional wisdom no longer views gold as a store of value and a portfolio counterweight. Perhaps market paradigms have shifted and gold is no longer needed as a store of value in troubled times. However, it is equally plausible that prolonged good times have led us to forget the value gold provides.

The full impact of portfolio theory on capital markets is clear now, because it is so widely applied. Consideration for risk was folded into asset managers' practice and jargon. Talk of total return gave way to discussion of risk/return and portfolio diversification. Markowitz and his colleagues explained a great deal more about observed market behavior than their predecessors. This development has affected all portfolio managers, but its impact in equity markets has been deepest. Virtually all portfolio analysis done today is based on the insights provided by Markowitz, who was awarded a Nobel prize, somewhat belatedly, in 1990.

Recognition may have been slow in coming because the practical application of Markowitz's theories had to wait for more computing power. The theory was largely complete by the early 1960s, but the computers at that time could not run with it. It takes a powerful computer to digest the reams of price-history data and calculate the correlations among individual assets. Each new asset adds a row and column to a grid that relates the new asset's price moves to the price moves of every other asset in the grid. In the late 1960s and early 1970s, computers gained enough speed and power to begin measuring risks and returns in portfolios. In the years since then, technological developments have made possible ever-more-sophisticated and quantitatively rigorous measurement of risk and return. Quantitative models that had outstripped computers became practical as technology caught up. The synergy between the analytical models and computing power has yielded a far greater impact than developments in each field alone could have produced.

Option Valuation

A second quantitative breakthrough occurred in 1970, when Fischer Black and Myron Scholes collaborated to develop the option-pricing model that carries their name. Robert Merton also helped with key aspects. Ironically, their article describing this breakthrough was rejected several times before it finally went to press in 1973.[6] Their formula allowed European options to be valued in terms of five variables: (1) strike price, (2) current price, (3) volatility, (4) time to maturity, and (5) the risk-free interest rate. This model won a Nobel prize for its developers in 1997. The prize is well deserved; the model's impact on financial markets has been enormous. Its variations and descendants are used to value almost all assets that contain options. Equities, for example, can be viewed as an option on the residual cash flows of a business, and the model has been applied to them.

A host of other new analytical tools has significantly affected financial markets. Some, like option adjusted spread (OAS) analysis, have greatly assisted in valuing securities with options embedded in them. Others determine the term structure for interest rates, which is a key for consistently valuing many securities. Collectively, quantitative models have changed the way all markets determine value, and have influenced how securities trade.[7]

DEALERS IN FLUX, TOO

The forces that have changed capital markets are reshaping the intermediaries as well. Since improved technology and quantitative models have allowed financial service firms to know much more precisely the risks they are taking, their immediate, reflexive response has been to control the risks with limits. The more sophisticated and effective response is to use the firm's knowledge of risk to improve allocation of scarce resources. This response takes a lot longer to build because it is much more complex than a limit process. GRM is the emerging discipline to meet these changing needs.

MAJOR MESSAGES IN THIS BOOK

This book contains major messages regarding the fabric of risk, new tools and techniques, simulation, infrastructures, and the effect of risk on markets and dealers.

Fabric of Risk

Financial risk, in most markets, can now be measured and quantified. Risk models capture the threads that connect prices in every market—the fabric of risk. In some markets, physical connections link prices. For example, pipelines and other modes of transportation connect oil and gas prices across geography and through time. In other markets, the fabric of risk is less tangible but still very real. For example, interest rates connect the forward foreign exchange rates of various currencies.

This book illustrates how the fabric of both market and credit risk can now be measured with a consistent and related set of quantitative models. This is the foundation for GRM.

New Tools and Techniques

 Markets have developed numerous quantitative models that help participants to understand risks and to value them both individually and in portfolios. Derivative products that parse risk, and allow it to be traded, developed in close conjunction with these new measurement techniques. Throughout this book, the new tools and techniques that serve as the basis for GRM are identified by this icon whenever they are discussed.

Simulation Captures the Dynamics

Simulation is the most complete, albeit most complex, way to measure and manage financial risk. Most other techniques cannot capture the dynamics involved. For example, certain products, like options, have return profiles that cannot be portrayed by static models. Similarly, portfolios evolve through time and are not static. Market and credit risks, moreover, are not independent; they are woven together by economic conditions. Simulation, though computationally intense and very challenging to build, is the only way to capture the dynamic interplay of risks and activity through time.

Infrastructure

The biggest barriers to implementing GRM are organizational and operational impediments. GRM sits at the nexus of technology, complex quantitative models, and firmwide operations. Intense support from all three is required to build GRM successfully. Most risk projects focus on the first two elements, to the detriment of the third. Significant resistance to change is hidden in the organizational fiefdoms that typically exist at financial service firms today. Regional managers are not eager to have precise measures of the risks they are taking available to all. They are quick to spot the shortcomings and problems, and unlikely to appreciate the new insights that GRM provides. Significant data and process challenges are also inherent in the spaghetti bowl of systems and redundant data flows that is served up at most global firms. As issues around the models and the technology are resolved, the problems with systems infrastructure and political issues become apparent.

Efficient Markets, Efficient Dealers

GRM is a strategic imperative. Ever-more-efficient markets will foist efficiency on the intermediaries. As margins narrow and products become more standardized, operational efficiency is the first yardstick for competitive advantage. Dealers in these markets have to become as efficient in their use of risk as they are in their use of capital, or they will become extinct. In some capital market segments, the development of electronic markets will eliminate the need for intermediaries, no matter how efficient they are. Electronic forums can bring buyers and sellers together and discover price for pennies a trade. Intermediaries can no longer compete in the most liquid markets, where high volumes of homogenous products create the capital flows.

Dealers are still needed to hold and manage risky positions. Electronic exchanges cannot handle these parts of the market, because they transfer significant risks that are unique to each deal or trade. The winners in these market segments will be the dealers who measure, price, and manage their risks better than others do. GRM is a survival imperative for dealers.

WRAP-UP

- Capital markets have undergone great changes in the past twenty-five years.
- Developments in technology and communications have combined, creating synergy with new quantitative models, a much deeper knowledge of risk, and new markets and prices for it.
- Electronic trading will eliminate dealers from the deepest, most liquid capital markets.
- Dealers are still needed for mediating risks, but they have to be more efficient than the markets. GRM is their vehicle to the requisite efficiency.

The Full
Spectrum of Risks

2

Being prudent and risk-aware professionals, we will plan the path of our investigation. The lay of the land, the contours of risk and risk management, will guide our planning process. Exhibit 2.1 represents the spectrum of risks that business organizations face. This particular spectrum covers the risks that a commercial bank has, but is largely

Exhibit 2.1 The Spectrum of Risks. Appendix I contains a definition for every financial risk noted in this spectrum, along with examples of how the risk can hurt or even mortally wound an organization.

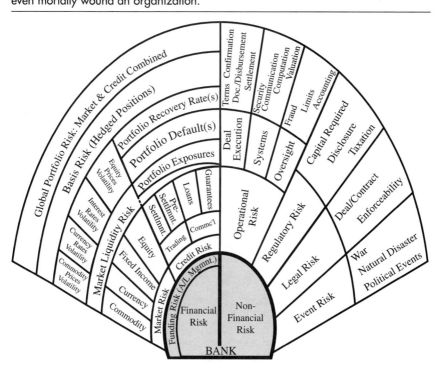

applicable to securities firms as well. The distinctions between banks and securities firms, while still significant, are shrinking.

This spectrum can easily be adapted and extended to other service and manufacturing organizations. The largest changes would probably occur in the area of operational risk. The risks shown include the proper execution of dealing or trading. Other organizations would have to revise this portion of the spectrum to match the risks inherent in their activities. Some organizations may want to move portions of the spectrum around. For example, property/casualty insurers may find it prudent to move the event risks over to the financial side of their spectrum, since they insure against events and have a financial stake based on what occurs. They would also want to divide the natural disaster portion of the spectrum into more specific sets of events, such as flood, fire, storm, and earthquake. For them, event risks are a market risk.

Let's look at the organizing principles of this spectrum. The spectrum splits down the middle, differentiating the two basic categories of risk, financial and nonfinancial, that organizations face. Major risk aggregates wrap around the firm at the core of the spectrum. Moving out from the center, these aggregate risks are broken down to finer levels. The splits can be seen where spokes radiate out from the center. On the financial risk side of the spectrum, we see risks that cut across the spokes; arcs like liquidity risk lie across several of the spokes. This layering of risks is a major reason financial risks are so interesting—aside from the fact that a lot of money is involved.

The arcs on the financial risk side include funding risk, market liquidity risk, basis risk, and global portfolio risk. Also, three arcs are stacked at the top of the credit risk portion of the spectrum: portfolio exposures, portfolio defaults, and portfolio recovery rates. Perceptive readers have, at this point, noticed the importance of portfolios to credit risk, and the multiple arcs in the credit risk slice of the pie.

In the market risk section, the spokes are more dominant, but major arcs are cutting through them. In the next chapter, we will explore this major topological difference between credit risk and market risk, and then finalize the itinerary. Features on the financial side of the spectrum will be explored fully throughout the rest of the book.

OPERATIONAL RISK

The nonfinancial risks most closely linked with financial risks are the operational risks. Operations are a vital part of financial institutions' activities. Financial institutions require high levels of technical and operational support to deliver information and analysis to their traders, brokers, and lenders for structuring and pricing deals. The same high level of operational support, including computing and technology, is needed to follow through on the dealing, for example, to confirm, account for, settle, and manage the deals and portfolios. Entities on the buy side, such as mutual funds, insurance companies, and pension funds, require significant operational support as well.

Many risk managers, inspired by the concept of charging capital for risk, think it can be applied to all operational risks, just as it is being applied to the financial risks. They claim to have developed measures that track the frequency and size of exceptions that occur in operational processes. They quantify the losses that occur with each exception. They are also developing risk measures from managerial reviews, such as internal audit ratings and scores. Some banks have converted these measurements into projections of loss, including measures of both frequency and severity. They then assign capital to cover those loss projections.

This development is appropriate and laudable for parts of the operational risk spectrum. Operational risks should be measured, where possible, with more quantitative rigor than is now common. The deal execution and systems sectors are particularly tractable to this analysis.

Will the measures developed so far protect firms from their operational risks? Exhibit 2.2 lists the largest publicly known losses from operational failures. They are among the most significant losses financial institutions have ever reported.

Common threads can be seen across all these losses. First, the losses took years—and in one case, over a decade—to achieve. Perhaps risk managers can take comfort in how hard it is to lose billions of

Exhibit 2.2 Table of Losses from Operational Risk

Organization	Approximate Loss $ Millions*	Primary Cause	Time Period of Accumulated Losses
Sumitomo Corp.	1,800	Fraudulent trading	10 years
Orange County	1,600	Fraudulent trading	1–2 years
Barings Bank PLC	1,200	Fraudulent trading	4 years
Daiwa Bank, US	1,100	Fraudulent trading	12 years
UBS	689	Incorrect option models	At least 2 years
NatWest Markets	110	Incorrect option models and fraudulent valuation	2 years
Kidder Peabody	100	Incorrect accounting	At least 1 year

* Managing Financial Risk, Yearbooks 1996 through 1998, Charles W. Smithson, Ed. CIBC.

dollars overnight, particularly in the operational risk arena. Some corollary to Murphy's Law must be at work here; traders smart enough to circumvent operational controls take a long time to achieve massive losses.

Second, lax oversight was a key contributor to every one of these losses. Too much control was concentrated in one individual, usually the trader. Segregation of duties would have precluded each of these losses, or at least made them much more difficult to achieve undetected. Traders should never be involved with middle and back office functions, such as deal confirmation, administration, settlement, revaluation, and accounting.

Third, and most important, these losses are not very tractable to quantitative measures. None of the operational risk measures promulgated so far would have uncovered these problems while they germinated over the years. Yet, clear segregation of duties and full independent review/revaluation would have revealed them. The lesson is: The risk management function must be independent from the business function. This is true for financial risks as well as for operational risks.

No metric covers oversight risk as well as tried and validated control techniques that are qualitative. Qualitative measures provide clear trading rules, complete segregation of duties, and supervision that includes frequent revaluation from independent sources. I believe that the trend to stick a risk number on everything has distracted operational risk managers from their primary responsibility, which is to ensure independent oversight.

We will discuss operations a great deal more in this book, but not operational risks or the tools to measure and manage them. The seamless integration of operations with all of the firm's dealing activities is a vital prerequisite for viable GRM. Effective and consistent management of financial risks requires a fully integrated operations infrastructure. Increasingly, the hardest part of GRM is building that infrastructure.

OTHER NONFINANCIAL RISKS

There are three other major categories of nonfinancial risk: (1) regulatory, (2) legal, and (3) event. From a risk management viewpoint, these three warrant a much smaller proportion of concern than the space they take on the spectrum. I give them a proportionately small amount of ink.

Regulatory Risk

The regulators trail the pack they are supposed to regulate. On the banking side, in 1988, a supranational bank organization (Bank of International Settlements, or BIS) published controls intended to ensure capital adequacy for credit risk at banks.[1] It then took over eight years to develop and implement uniform capital requirements to cover market risks.

In the meantime, regulators have fallen woefully behind on the credit risk side of the spectrum. The banks have developed derivative products that effectively circumvent the capital requirements for credit. Regulators agree, almost universally, that their capital requirements for credit are obsolete and inappropriate. They discuss openly how banks flout capital requirements by converting loans with corporate clients, where an 8 percent capital charge is incurred, into credit risk with other banks in developed countries (OECD banks), where a 1.2 percent charge is incurred. Yet, in the next breath, they predict that it will be years before changes can be developed and implemented.[2] They are making progress. BIS recently issued a discussion draft for revising the 1988 accord.[3] Yet, the needed reforms are still years away.

Economic forces, rather than regulatory prudence, will continue to drive this revolution. The regulators explicitly acknowledge their reliance on market discipline in the latest proposed revision to the 1988 accord. However, concerns have been expressed about systemic risk from increased interbank trading and from the increased leverage of credit risk.[4] Both of these developments create, in global financial markets, a vulnerability that is very hard to measure. The regulators' laissez-faire policy, and perhaps also their ponderous bureaucracy, will be viewed quite harshly should global financial markets collapse, as they nearly did in September 1998. We have to hope the regulators continue to be effective at handling the crises—such as arranging the bailout financing for Long Term Capital Management—that their policies might be helping to create.

Legal Risk

The legal risk that financial intermediaries face most frequently (and that has the largest consequence) is contract enforceability. Most legal actions seek to nullify trades that have led to significant losses. Case law is beginning to provide some clear guidelines for institutions to follow when they are determining whom to trade with and how to structure their trades.[5] The guidance includes where and how to book trades. The International Swap Dealers Association (ISDA) provides documentation standards and training seminars that help institutions minimize legal risk. Most financial organizations establish an ongoing link between their legal departments and their policy departments, in an effort to ensure appropriate, legally enforceable dealing.

Event Risk

Event risk may be somewhat predictable, but it is not controllable. For example, in the late 1990s, Chase saw the problems in Southeast

Asia. By curtailing its activities in those markets prior to the series of crises in mid-1997, Chase avoided significant losses. Similarly, some institutions, through good foresight, curtailed activities and avoided significant losses when Mexico devalued the peso in 1994.

Insurers make a market in event risk by providing protection against adverse outcomes. The options that they sell work on the same principles as financial options and are valued the same way. As standard tools and techniques evolve, there is greater crossover between the event markets in which the insurers operate and the financial markets where securities firms and banks have operated. Insurance companies are treading into financial market territory, selling options for specific adverse financial events.

The nonfinancial risks on the right side of the spectrum will not be discussed further in this book. The tools for managing them are based on different paradigms. The exception to this observation, insurance against event risk, is already noted.

Wrap-Up

- Risks can be viewed in a spectrum that illustrates their relation to the firm and to each other.
- There is a major divide between financial and nonfinancial risks. Financial risks are interrelated and require a unique set of tools to measure and manage them. This tool set is just emerging.
- On the nonfinancial side, operational risks are a key component at financial service firms. Quantitative tools to capture and manage operational efficiency are appropriate. Applying those tools to the oversight function is risky business.

The Contours
of Financial Risk **3**

As tools to model both market and credit risk have evolved, the contours of financial risk have emerged. The latest analytical tools cover all financial risks and start to model the complex interactions between them, through time. Examining the development of these tools against the backdrop of this risk spectrum provides a view of their power, limitations, and managerial implications.

FUNDING RISK—THE PRIMAL ARC

Funding risk is the primal arc. It is the risk that current obligations/liabilities cannot be met with current assets. It is primal because it deals with the solvency of the organization. It spans both market and credit risk by being inside the institution. The financial arm of all business organizations concerns itself with this risk. Each determines capital needs for its business, what returns that capital will achieve, and how those needs for capital will be fulfilled. This funding or asset/liability function is the institution's internal financial market, where internal uses for capital are assessed, selected, and matched with external sources for capital, debt, and equity.

Throughout the 1960s and 1970s, savings and loan companies (S&Ls) rode positively sloped yield curves to a comfortable, complacent position. They took in deposits paying interest that floated with short-term rates. They used those deposits to make mortgage loans, generally at 30-year fixed rates. This mismatch between assets and liabilities was a cash machine, so long as long-term rates remained higher than short-term rates. The mortgages typically earned 2 to 3 percent more than the deposits required. When the yield curve inverted in the early 1980s, the S&Ls suffered billions in losses. Their cost for funds significantly exceeded the fixed rates they were charging for their mortgages. This is the textbook example of asset/liability or funding risk.

Financial organizations have unique and special concerns with funding risk. The timing and size of cash flows, on both the pay and the receive sides, can be interest-sensitive. Many assets and liabilities have embedded options that can shift cash flows considerably. These options, coupled with the leverage that banks and securities firms have, can create problems. Salomon went through a perilous liquidity crunch following the bond trading scandal that caused its chairman to resign in 1991. Warren Buffett stepped in as temporary chairman to steady investor concerns, and backstop facilities were tapped to ensure liquidity.

This liquidity risk relates closely with the outer arc, global portfolio risk. It is best to look at it after the full spectrum of financial risks and tools is understood. It requires portfolio-level consideration, and some consideration of credit risk.

MARKETS AND RISK

Moving beyond a firm's internal funding risk, we see the major split between market and credit risk. Within the market risk quadrant, we see four spokes, one for each major financial market sector. Starting on the left with basic commodity and currency markets, we climb higher on the market risk ladder into the debt/fixed-income market and the equity market. Commodity and currency markets are just as complex as the debt and equity markets, but they deal in tangible items and are thus easier to explain and understand.

Commodities

Commodity markets cover all parts of the production value chain. From the raw materials, through various processes to finished products, one business's finished product is the next business's raw material. Carmakers require large quantities of various metals—aluminum, rolled steel, and so on. They are structurally short all these materials. On the flip side, aluminum smelters and steelmakers are long those same materials and structurally short the ore. Similarly, cereal makers are short and farmers are long various cereal grains. Commodity markets cover these value chains down to the smallest links,[1] right down to the market for skinned, boned chicken breasts.

Currencies

Currency markets are where businesses with activities in various countries convert currencies as needed. The development of easy and relatively low-cost currency markets, including forward prices that span years, has occurred in an efficacious cycle with globalized trading and globalized capital flows. Increased global trade has led to increased foreign exchange (FX) activity, which has lowered transaction costs, thereby encouraging more trade, and so on.

FX trade volumes have also grown from the linkages that have developed between capital markets. Many international companies now tap into all available capital markets, regardless of currency. They issue debt where costs are lowest (including any needed currency conversions). This corporate arbitrage of capital markets has contributed to FX volume growth as well.

Fixed-Income Markets

Fixed-income markets are those in which investors provide capital in the form of debt, e.g., loans or securities. These huge markets have many variations and contain many segments: government, high-yield and convertible, municipal bonds, and mortgage-backed securities. There is also an increasing variety of product structures (loans, pass-through securities, simple debt securities, and so on) accompanied by a large set of derivative products that further adjust the risks. This is almost exclusively an institutional market. There are no exchanges. The buyers, sellers, and dealers are all large institutions.

Equities

In equity markets, investors provide capital to firms in exchange for shares of stock. These are huge markets as well, but do not have as many variations as the fixed-income markets. Almost all equity trading is mediated through exchanges, although big blocks of stock move via institutions. The investors are both institutional and individual.

Market Spokes

These four major markets' spokes divide into finer and finer niches, primarily along product, market, and geographic lines. For example, in commodities, there are mining/extraction, agricultural, and energy submarkets, to name a few. Each of these is further divided. There are diverse conventions for operating out at the tips of all these market branches—for example, how buyers and sellers meet, determine price (including how prices are quoted), and settle trades. The regulatory or legal framework also varies by market niche; each is largely based on historical precedent. These market variations create an interesting potpourri. This diversity of market standards is a major contributor to the perception that financial markets are extremely complex and specialized. However, there are strong unifying forces at work that will certainly reduce this diversity. Technology, deregulation, and globalizing markets are forcing more efficiency, transparency, and a uniformity that will eventually help to standardize major market niches.

Common Denominators

Variation across the markets obscures the three basic risks they all share: price, volatility, and liquidity.

Price   Price risk is the primary common denominator. It is the risk of loss or gain from market fluctuations. Most markets provide a price now and into the future. There is a simple linear relationship between the value of an investor's position and the market price. Change in value equals change in unit price times number of units held. A "+" or "−" is applied to the units held, depending on whether one is short or long. No mathematicians needed here, except for those positions that do not have market price quotes. For these instruments, that trade infrequently, value is determined with mathematical models. The current value of a position is determined by marking it to market or marking it to model; MTM in both cases.

Volatility Volatility is the second common denominator. It is a measure of how much the price could change, up or down, over a given period of time. Its impact on the value, while secondary to price, is important. Accurate predictions of volatility allow position holders to determine how much they can expect to lose/gain from holding positions.

Here is where we find work for the mathematicians. Price risk and volatility are easy to grasp conceptually, but price is easier to measure than volatility. Price is provided by markets most of the time; volatility is not. It can only be estimated, and those estimates fluctuate with each market move. Sudden shifts in price cause the estimates of volatility to increase, and steady prices cause the estimates to decrease. Estimating volatility accurately is important because it is a key determinant of value for many derivative trades. Mathematicians are employed to provide the best possible estimates from market data.

Liquidity Liquidity risk is the *market* piece of market risk. It is the risk of loss from being unable to adjust or change a position because of market inefficiency. Price and volatility focus on the value of the item/position. Liquidity risk considers how value can only be realized through transacting in a market. Although the spectrum shows liquidity arching across all markets, it is typically a feature of each market segment and niche. Occasionally, in stressed situations, illiquidity can spread across financial markets.

Liquidity is probably the most slippery element in risk management. There are many relative measures of liquidity but no precise ones. For example, trading volumes, both notional and unit, and spreads' average bid/ask differential are indicators of market liquidity. More volume and narrower spreads indicate more liquid/efficient markets. Like volatility, liquidity moves with each move in the markets. Indeed, there is some correlation between volatility and liquidity. When markets suffer big losses, volatility rises and liquidity generally goes way down. On October 19, 1987, most New York-based equity markets became quite illiquid during the highest volatility ever experienced.

Note that the spectrum shows widening in the credit quadrant. In the past ten years, secondary markets for credit risk have grown from virtually nil to billions of dollars.

We should look at these common denominators of risk in every market. Although each market may have different mechanisms that drive price and volatility, the measurement techniques and the hedging tools across all markets are similar. This is what is driving the revolution.

BASIS RISK

Basis risk is the risk of loss from differences between a position and the hedge or balancing position. These differences may cause the value change in one position to not exactly offset the value change in the other position.

One of the larger mortgage companies originates the most non-conforming residential mortgages in the country. These loans do not fit within the guidelines established by various government-sponsored agencies that back several mortgage loan security programs, so they can't be securitized in those programs. The loans remain on the originator's books until enough have accrued for a special nonconforming MBS issue, which occurs about every two months. If rates rise, these fixed-rate assets fall in value; if rates fall, they increase in value. The originator wants to hedge this interest rate exposure until the assets are securitized and moved off his books.

There is no forward market for nonconforming mortgages, so they can't be hedged directly. However, there is a relatively liquid forward market in conforming mortgages in the United States. Value changes in conforming mortgages are similar, but do not exactly match the value changes in nonconforming loans. The mortgage company hedges less than perfectly by selling conforming loans to offset the nonconforming loans it originated/bought. The risk from this difference in basis is small compared to the overall interest rate protection the hedge provides. This is the most cost-effective hedge for this particular exposure.

Basis exposure comes from any difference between the two positions, such as maturity dates/times, underlying item, reset dates, and so on.

ALTERNATIVE VIEWS AND INSIGHTS

Other ways to look at these markets provide additional insights. For example, it is useful to note that developed markets have more volume, liquidity, and statistical predictability than emerging markets, where events tend to drive major market shifts. The resulting risk measurement tools and management techniques in these two types of markets are different. Statistical measures predominate in the developed markets, and stress-related measures tend to predominate in the emerging markets.

Another distinction is exchange-traded versus over-the-counter (OTC) markets. Equity and commodity markets are predominantly mediated through exchanges, whereas currency and fixed-income markets tend to trade OTC. Perhaps history has shaped this difference. Commodity and stock markets started in town squares, where individual buyers and sellers participated. These markets grew into exchanges. Currency and fixed-income markets grew up inside institutions. The banks mediated currency exchange, which grew into FX markets, and various institutions—banks, securities firms, insurance companies, pension funds, and mutual funds—built the OTC fixed-income markets.

Derivative trading that has recently blossomed in all these markets is predominantly OTC. There appear to be two major reasons that OTC trading has predominated in derivative markets:

1. OTC markets provide more flexibility for structuring, pricing, and settling. OTC deals can be molded to the exact risks being mediated.

2. OTC trades don't require margin for collateral. Margin/collateral is a fixture for controlling credit risk in exchange-traded markets.

NEW MEASUREMENT TOOLS AND MANAGEMENT TECHNIQUES

 Here is the source of the revolution. The quantitative measures of risk, and the development of financial products to parse and trade that risk, started in this market risk quadrant. The seeds of the revolution were sown with the breakdown of the Bretton Woods agreement in the early 1970s. This agreement had controlled interest and currency rates. Banks and securities firms eventually learned, painfully, that they were now exposed to rate fluctuations in these two key markets. To protect themselves, they developed measurement techniques and instruments to parse and trade the financial risks. The first swaps occurred in the late 1970s. By the early 1980s, they were an established feature in the debt/fixed-income markets. Swaps' ability to parse and exchange pieces of risk assisted their rapid expansion across currency and commodity markets. More recently, they have boomed in the equity and credit loan markets.

In every major market niche, new quantitative techniques can help to accurately measure the risks (particularly price and volatility risk), and new derivative instruments are available to parse and trade the risks. This revolution has helped both the natural position holders (e.g., suppliers and buyers) and the market intermediaries to better manage their market risks. An interesting feature of this revolution is that most of the management and hedging of market risk occurs at the disaggregated level, out in the specific market niches. In the mortgage origination example, we saw how the most appropriate hedging instruments are typically in the same market niches where the exposure is being generated. Hedging typically occurs position by position, largely without consideration for broader portfolios.

CREDIT RISK

Credit risk is more complex and requires analysis at a portfolio level. There are two somewhat conflicting definitions of credit risk. Each is valid for the group that uses it, but the two definitions are an example of the clashing concepts and turmoil that credit risk and credit markets are going through. The mathematicians and derivative product designers who started the quantitative revolution over in market risk have turned their focus to credit risk and have stirred up the staid world of commercial credit.

Trading versus Loans

Traders measure credit risk as the spread above a risk-free yield curve. It is the premium that the market demands for holding instruments that may default. Traders are concerned with whether the spread or credit risk premium will widen, lowering the value of the debt they hold. They assume that there is a liquid market for credit risk; in fixed-income markets, where these traders deal, that assumption is largely true.

On the other hand, traditional bank loan officers view credit risk as the risk of loss due to failure of a counterparty to perform as contracted. It is the loss that will occur when a loan defaults or a trading counterparty fails to settle. Loan officers are concerned with how the bank will get repaid. They assume loans are bought and held to maturity. Holders of this view (in the world of commercial loans, it is the prevailing position) are less concerned about the market value of a loan. However, market forces and the market perspective are encroaching.

Eventually, a hybrid perspective will evolve, based on how liquid the loan markets eventually become. However, default events will continue to create precipitous changes in value, no matter how liquid the markets are. Also, liquidity in credit markets will always be tenuous. In times of stress, credit markets will be the first to freeze, and holders of the risk may be forced to retain it until it matures or defaults.

Credit Complexities

Several other characteristics of credit risk make it difficult to measure. Default is a low-probability event, but with big consequences—very large losses. With the probability of default being so small (sometimes fractions of a percent), very small shifts can lead to a big shift in loan value. Also, the time period over which these events must be forecast, the tenor of the loans is typically years. Such long tenors complicate any effort to test or validate a new quantitative model. Most validation techniques use many actual observations to confirm that predictions are accurate. When an observation period spans years, it is difficult to obtain a lot of them. Also, credit deals contain built-in features that reduce the risk. Loans can contain collateral agreements, material adverse change clauses, cross-default clauses, covenants, and so on. Swaps and other derivative instruments can be subject to closeout netting and to margin collateral calls (for either a downgraded credit rating or when net market value of the deals moves above a threshold). The impact of these features on the credit risk complicates quantification. Retail credit is easier because the product is more homogenous and no single default is going to radically alter the portfolio return.

The most important complication is that credit risk can be measured only in portfolios. Credit defaults tend to happen in concentrated flurries. The prospects of whole industries or geographic areas rise and fall together. Falling prospects can yield a host of defaults at one time. The last big collective portfolio debacle in U.S. markets hit commercial real estate in the early 1990s. More recently, the market perturbations in Southeast Asia have reaped a full harvest of defaults. Everyone knows qualitatively that credit trouble comes in bunches and can be traced to economic factors, monetary policies, and business cycles. However, quantitative methods to capture defaults in credit portfolios—that is, how defaults are bunched (correlate)—did not exist until very recently. The speed with which methods have developed and have been disseminated is quite impressive.

The Contours of Credit Risk

Similar to market risk, credit risk has two spokes: traditional credit and trading activities. However, that is where the similarity ends. Within each side of the split, risk measurement and management are quite different. They both must determine portfolio measures of exposure, default, and recovery, but features within the two markets force them to do it very differently.

Loan Credit Risk

Credit risk from traditional lending is pretty straightforward. The institution has loaned money (or is committed to loan money) and is concerned with how the loan will be repaid. The exposure of the loan amount is fairly static, so the concern is primarily over default probability, with a secondary concern about recovery. Lenders focus on what might cause the borrower to default, and how much of the loan they can recover in default. The loans are typically extended to corporate customers and frequently contain clauses related to issues of seniority or collateral that help ensure significant recovery. Similarly, contingent credit risk, like letters of credit and guaranties, result in a known loss if a default or series of defaults occurs.

Trading Credit Risk

Credit risk from trading is a little more complicated. It comes in two flavors: presettlement and settlement. The complication is that the exposure component is not static; it varies over time as markets move.

Settlement risk is the risk of loss from a party's defaulting at deal settlement: you've transmitted your side of a trade, and the counterparty fails to transfer the other side of the deal because of insolvency. This risk is also known as Herstatt risk, named for the 1974 default on FX payments by the German Herstatt bank, which resulted in major disruptions and near gridlock in the interbank payment systems. This served as a wake-up call for regulators and banks. It helped all FX market participants realize how vulnerable their payment infrastructure was to settlement failures. Chapter 10 provides more details.

Presettlement risk is the risk of loss from failure of a trading counterparty before the trade reaches settlement. Suppose the participant in a six-year deal defaults after three years. The other counterparty, to keep his or her portfolio balanced, would have to go into the marketplace and replace the defaulted deal. The cost to replace a deal depends on the market prices and factors at the time of the default. The first big challenge for presettlement risk is measuring how large the replacement cost might become. We can determine the current market value—the replacement cost today. However, given varying market conditions like deal amortization, where might this exposure move in the future? The most accurate measure of this exposure is made at the portfolio level. The diversification from natural offsets and other credit features (like closeout netting and collateral/margin agreements) significantly reduces presettlement exposure. Once the exposure profile through time is known, default and recovery considerations can be applied, as they are in loan portfolios.

Another major difference in credit risk from trading comes from the counterparties involved. Corporations are a minor part of the trading market. Most trading activity occurs between the largest over-the-counter (OTC) liquidity providers: banks and securities firms. Default of any one of them is unlikely, but the correlation of default among these providers could be quite high.

In the chapters on credit risk, we will explore the customers, traditional products, risks, emerging techniques, and new credit derivative products. This preview illustrates that credit risk is difficult to measure exactly, and its measurement and management can only occur at a portfolio level.

PORTFOLIO RISK

Until recently, the major consideration for measuring market risk on a global level was asset/liability management in banks, and similar actuarial functions in insurance companies. Because most market risks have been managed on a decentralized basis, out in each of the niches, global market risk has not been as important from a manager's perspective. Indeed, when market risks are aggregated to global portfolios, the total risk is less than the sum of its parts. Diversification dilutes the market risks for the total portfolio. In financial portfolios, size does matter. The portfolio diversification effects that Harry M. Markowitz describes in *Portfolio Selection: Efficient Diversification of Investments* help firms with large diversified portfolios.

OUR JOURNEY

By now, our path is pretty obvious. It starts in Section II, at the source of the revolution, market risk, and moves on later to the more complex and less fully converted credit risk. Within the discussion of market risk, the more straightforward markets (commodities and currencies) provide clear insights before we tackle the more complex capital markets (debt and equities). In each of the markets, we will explore the fabric of risk; that is, what mechanisms drive price and volatility and what instruments are available to manage them?

Section III describes some of the math wizards who turned their considerable skill to credit risk. Many examples of how new quantitative tools and techniques are being applied to traditional loan portfolios will be reviewed, along with how they are yielding a very different view of where the credit risk is. We will also see what is driving the boom in credit derivatives, which parse and trade credit risks. In credit risk for trading, we'll take a look at how projections of portfolio level exposure are being created and used to manage incremental trading activities.

Section IV expands on the portfolio considerations already established, especially in the credit section. GRM is based on using these new firm-wide measures of portfolio risk to guide decision making.

The final segment, Section V, addresses how to build the global risk management process. These initiatives are themselves fraught with risk. The key features that successful initiatives share are noted, along with the most common challenges and pitfalls.

This journey will allow us to see how the unifying set of measurement and management tools matured, and how they are radically altering how financial intermediaries, both banks and securities firms, manage themselves.

WRAP-UP

- ▪ Risk has fabric and contours that are consistent across all markets.

- New tools to measure/value risk have grown simultaneously with products (derivatives) that parse and trade risks.
- These tools and techniques started in fixed-income markets, but they have rapidly expanded to all markets, and have even extended to credit risk and risk in large portfolios.
- Many firms are rushing to build comprehensive global risk management processes—an extremely difficult task.

This book will follow, approximately, the same development path.

MARKET RISK MANAGEMENT

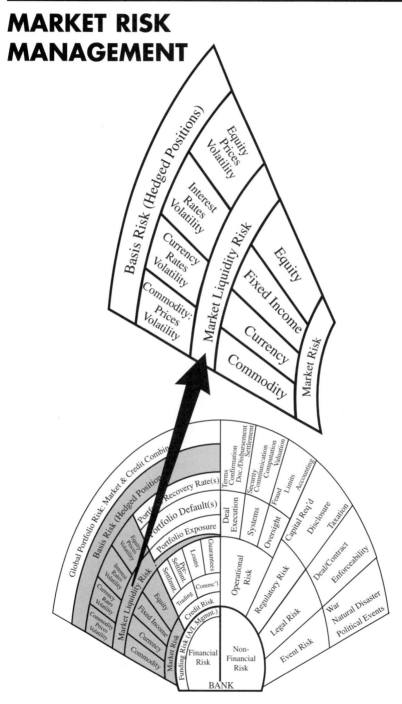

The Market Risk Spectrum

Market Risk: Tools and Uses

There are three basic tools for adjusting market risks: (1) forward purchases/sales, (2) swaps, and (3) options. This tool set is fundamental and applicable in all the markets, but there are many variations in how the tools are applied in each market. They can be combined (for example, an option to enter into a swap), and they can have structural variations, such as exotic options, with different payout structures. The three tools themselves are quite straightforward; the many ways they are applied or combined yield the complexity.

These tools are used to hedge, to arbitrage, or to speculate. Hedgers use them to offset existing position(s). Arbitrage traders try to remain risk-neutral while extracting a profit from temporary market price disequilibriums. Speculators use them to take or increase position(s). Examples offer the best way to illustrate the tools and their uses.

HEDGE EXAMPLE

Tastee ZeeWheets is one of the top breakfast cereal manufacturers in the country. It forecasts a need for 100,000 bushels of wheat, its largest raw material, for each of the next twelve months. It is chronically short of wheat and is vulnerable to a rise in wheat prices. The company would benefit, however, if wheat prices fall. Shareholders and managers like to see a steady income, so insurance against wheat price fluctuations is worth something to the firm.

Forward Purchase/Sale: The "Lock-It-In" Defense

The Chicago Board of Trade provides a forward market in wheat, as do markets in Kansas, Minneapolis, and Canada. Each market facilitates

37

the exchange of wheat both immediately, at spot rates, and at specified dates in the future. Tastee ZeeWheets can go to these markets
and lock-in wheat cost by purchasing, going long, as required.

Given the forward market in Exhibit 4.1, Tastee ZeeWheets can
insulate itself from price variations by purchasing wheat as noted.

The markets don't provide prices/delivery at the exact times
Tastee would like. Tastee has to either stock up in certain months or
retain a forward seller who will deliver every month as needed. Typically, it would find such a seller in the over-the-counter (OTC)
market. If it buys ahead, it will incur extra storage costs for carrying
wheat forward in certain months. However, Tastee has locked in the
cost of its wheat. Assuming a negligible time value to money, and no
storage/carry costs, Tastee will pay $3.212 million, or an average of
$2.6766/bushel, for its wheat. Done! *Hedging through forward markets
will result in a higher average cost than buying at spot. Each business must
determine what extra cost it is willing to incur to protect itself against adverse price moves. Risk management provides firms with information about
their market risks, the costs to hedge, and the most cost-effective hedges.*

Forward purchases/sales provide a first line of defense against
price fluctuation. They are frequently the cheapest and most common method for hedging price risk. They work best when the requirements can be precisely defined, and where the suppliers and
buyers can easily meet. Through forward markets, suppliers can
lock-in predictable revenues, and purchasers can lock-in costs. With

Exhibit 4.1   Tastee ZeeWheet Forward Purchase Program

	Purchase (Bushels)	Forward Price ($/Bushel)	Purchase Cost (Dollars)
Dec.	300,000	2.45	735,000
March	200,000	2.50	500,000
May	200,000	2.67	534,000
July	200,000	2.82	564,000
Sept.	200,000	2.91	582,000
Nov.	100,000	2.97	297,000
			3,212,000

Note: The exchange does not provide purchases in Jan., Feb., April, June, Aug., and
Oct. Tastee ZeeWheet needs to buy extra in other months.

this tool, all three market risks—price, volatility, and liquidity—are replaced with counterparty or credit risk. Tastee is dependent on its counterparty to deliver wheat as contracted, and the counterparty is dependent on Tastee to pay. Market volatility and liquidity may affect its ability to perform, but Tastee is no longer exposed to the market risks.

A major caveat for forward markets is how closely buyers and sellers must match on amount, quality/grade, and delivery dates. Any mismatches produce basis risk, which neither counterparty wants because it reduces the effectiveness of the hedge.

These deals result in an exchange of the material. In reality, most exchanges have mediators between the buyer and sellers, and trades with physical delivery are a small proportion of the total trade volume. In this example, the mediators are typically grain co-ops and agricultural conglomerates. They sit between the suppliers and buyers. In many cases, the biggest forward purchases/sales do not occur via exchanges. Instead, they take the form of long-term contracts directly between major suppliers and major buyers.

Swaps: The "Switch-Out-of-It" Defense

Tastee can also swap out of its wheat price exposure. Suppose Tastee buys its wheat on the first day of every month, paying the spot rate at that time. Tastee can swap its exposure to those twelve monthly spot rates (which float) onto a fixed rate. Tastee contracts to receive whatever the floating spot rate may be each month, in exchange for paying a fixed monthly rate. Tastee then uses the floating rate it receives to buy the wheat it needs. The net effect is to pay a fixed rate and receive its wheat allotment each month. If it can obtain a fixed rate of $2.6766/bushel, Tastee's position is *similar* to the forward purchase alternative.

Tastee didn't remove all its market risk; it retained liquidity risk. Tastee still has to go out and buy the wheat at spot rates each month. In extreme market conditions, Tastee may not be able to obtain the wheat it needs at the quoted spot price. Also, Tastee really minimizes its basis risk with this deal. The swap is tailored to offset Tastee's exact risk, which is the price of wheat on the first business day of each month. Forward markets frequently introduce timing, quantity, or quality mismatches—basis risks, which dilute the protection the hedge provides.

The key similarity is that Tastee now has credit exposure with its counterparty. It depends on receipt of the floating rate each month. All deals that hedge market risk introduce credit risk with the counterparty. Credit risk in exchange-mediated deals works differently from credit risk between two independent counterparties. The exchange becomes the counterparty for all trades, and it calls for collateral to be posted on trades for which the market value grows to exceed established thresholds.

 Swaps facilitate risk transfer for hedging because exact matches between the suppliers and the buyers are not required. The intermediary customizes swaps to each side, removing the basis risk that each hedger has to take. Various basis risks accrue to the intermediary, who is better equipped to measure them, to offset them with other trades, and otherwise to efficiently manage them—in other words, to run a dynamic partial hedge. It is easy to understand how swap structures have grown to conform to customers' specific needs. Concomitantly, it is easy to understand how swap activities in each market naturally gravitated to the major dealers in those markets. They were best equipped to pool, measure, and manage the resulting risks.

Swaps are predominately an OTC rather than an exchange-traded activity, because customers do not want basis risk. They want hedges that exactly match their risk. Exchange-traded swaps have to be packaged in standard quantities, standard qualities (where relevant), and standard tenors/dates. To be traded on exchanges, they need uniformity that precludes them from conforming to specific customer risks. The OTC markets let the customers shape the swaps exactly their way. So, OTC trading has predominated swap markets, even in commodities and equity markets where the underlying item is most frequently traded on exchanges. Swaps markets also gravitated to OTC trading because of the credit exposure they generate. Exchange-traded products obtain credit protection with margin requirements and calls for collateral when the market value of positions exceeds specified thresholds. OTC markets do not have these administrative and capital-burning burdens.

Options: The Cap/Floor Defense

Tastee's final way to reduce its risk is to put a ceiling on it. It can purchase an option to buy, or "call" the wheat it needs each month at a given strike price. This effectively puts a ceiling on how much the wheat will cost. Suppose Tastee purchased calls for 100k bushels of wheat for $2.70/bushel in each month of the year. In any month when the spot price exceeds $2.70/bushel, Tastee will exercise its call option, and in each month when the spot price is below that strike price, Tastee will not exercise its option. It will buy at the lower spot price. This call puts an upper limit on the wheat cost, but still lets Tastee enjoy the gain from a fall in prices. Note that Tastee has to pay a premium to buy those call options. Insurance policies cost money.

Frequently, commodity buyers like Tastee pay for the ceiling they purchase by selling a floor, a "put." In effect, they put a collar around their price exposure with a sold floor and a purchased ceiling. The tightness of the collar can be adjusted as Tastee wishes. Tastee can put a loose collar with a ceiling of $3.00/bushel and a floor of $2.36—that is, a wide price range—around the current price. Another possibility is a tight collar with a narrower range of price exposure. OTC dealers will provide Tastee with the full range of collar options, all of which are self-financing; the sold floor will pay for the purchased ceiling.

 Options are another line of price defense. They provide selective insurance against specific price moves. Like swaps, they contain a great deal of flexibility in terms of both structure and payout. They are also the most challenging to value and can have the most complexity. Many individuals and families protect themselves from extreme losses by buying put options (insurance) for their high-value possessions, such as a house, a car, health, and life. More complex options have been developed in which the payout is determined by the path that prices take. These exotic options are most commonly used by sophisticated financial intermediaries to hedge specific exposures to arbitrage, or perhaps to speculate.

The Tastee example shows how all three tools can control or reduce the market risks, particularly price risk. Also, all three create credit risk; the hedger is dependent on a counterparty to perform. We also caught a glimpse of how the development of swaps radically altered all financial markets.

The three tools are related; options can synthetically create a swap, and the prices for swaps and options should remain centered around the forward price line. Arbitrage ensures this.

ARBITRAGE

Suppose we squeeze the price range in the collar down to 0. As the collar gets narrow, we find the strike price where Tastee's purchased ceiling has a value equal to the sold floor. When the strike of these two options converges, the result is a swap. A put and a call option can synthetically create a swap.

What does this say about the prices of these instruments? The price where the collar will converge must be near the swap fixed price and the average forward price noted above. If prices for any of these instruments get out of line with the others, an opportunity to create arbitrage profit exists. Suppose you can use a swap to lock-in a price of $2.68/bushel and can use options to lock-in a price of $2.75/bushel. Sell the option-based trade at $2.75 and buy the swap at $2.68, locking-in a .07/bushel profit. Keep hitting this arbitrage until the prices move back into equilibrium. There are, in all the markets, lots of arbitrageurs patrolling the prices to ensure any disequilibrium is corrected through a trading profit for them.

 The flexibility inherent in swaps and options to parse and trade specific financial risks makes them useful for all sorts of arbitrage. The first swaps were transacted to circumvent a tax that the United Kingdom charged on converting pounds sterling to foreign currency. The tax was levied to discourage capital from moving overseas. British companies that wished to invest in subsidiaries overseas found it was cheaper to arrange currency swaps than to pay the tax.[1] Swaps can also be used to arbitrage fixed and floating interest rates.[2]

These tools are more than just another line of defense against price fluctuation. Swaps and options facilitate arbitrage of market price anomalies. *Swaps and options, because they are such low-cost*

arbitrage tools, have forced all the markets to finer pricing and greater efficiency.

SPECULATION

These three tools can be used for speculation, too. Tastee can make bets about the markets as easily as it can hedge its natural position. Derivative products facilitate speculation, just as they facilitate hedging and arbitrage. The loss scenarios that prove this statement generally fall into two groups:

1. Aggressive corporate counterparties, such as Procter & Gamble, Gibson Greetings, and others, which started to use their treasuries as profit centers.
2. Various fund managers (pensions or general), mostly for state and county funds (like those in Connecticut, Florida, Wisconsin, and Orange County, California).

Some of the contributing factors across all these losses include aggressive derivative sales teams, lax oversight of the buyers, naïve and unsophisticated buyers, and, sometimes, fraud.[3]

WRAP-UP

- The three tools for managing financial risk are:
  (1) Forward Purchase
  (2) Swaps
  (3) Options.
- These tools greatly facilitate hedging, arbitrage, and speculation.
- Arbitrage has forced more efficient pricing in all markets.

Commodity Market Risk Management

5

The company in our first case study is one of the larger carmakers in the world. We will examine this commodity end-user's exposure to metal, its risk management (RM) response, and some of the specific deals it transacts to hedge its exposures. Next, we will study an intermediary. The Enron story is quite remarkable. The company had the vision to become the market intermediary well before its competitors and even before the market existed. The successful execution of that vision and the resulting dominance in natural gas markets have made this a classic business case. Besides illustrating the risks in commodities and the concurrent market dynamics, these specific cases identify the fundamental features of risk and management in all markets.

CASE STUDY: BIG AUTO CO.

Since cars are largely made of metal, carmakers around the world are exposed to metal price changes. Let's look at these exposures metal by metal. An average car weighs 3,300 pounds. Steel makes up about 55 percent or 1,800 pounds. So exposure to steel price fluctuations is significant. However, car companies do not work with raw steel, but finished steel products. (Their steel requirements are quite customized; they need customized shapes with surface treatments to prevent rust.) The next metal, by weight is aluminum with about 7 percent or 236 pounds per car. Most of the aluminum goes into cast pieces like engine blocks. In the pursuit of lighter, environmentally friendly cars, aluminum has recently claimed an increasing portion of car weight. Methods to mass-produce aluminum bodies are in development, but are not currently cost-effective. Carmakers typically have additional minor price exposure to other base metals like copper for electric cables, lead for batteries, and zinc for rust treatment. They also have price exposure to certain precious metals, notably platinum and palladium for catalytic converters. While the requirements for these precious metals is measured in ounces rather than pounds, the price is high and volatile, so price risk for them can be significant.

Price Exposure

Let's examine the risk for each metal by quantifying how much it could change the base material costs in an average car. Three parameters create this risk: quantity used, current price, and price volatility. In Exhibit 5.1, we map these parameters and the resulting price risk to each metal.

Price Risk in this case is the product of volatility, price, and quantity. An overall measure of price risk could be the sum of individual price risks (e.g., $107.43). This is a straightforward, albeit rudimentary, measure of risk; it does not consider how these prices move in concert. When summing up the risks to specific metals we are assuming that the price changes across all of them move in lockstep (e.g., have a correlation of 1). More sophisticated risk measures

Exhibit 5.1 Price Risk for Metal in Cars

Metal	Quantity (lbs. per car)[1]	Price[2] ($/lb.)	Cost/Car	Volatility[3] (1 month)	Price Risk
Steel	1,802	.1951[4]	$351.69	16.8%	$59.08
Aluminum	236	.6538	154.29	21.4	33.02
Copper	46	.7568	34.81	36.3	12.64
Zinc	12	.5144	6.17	27.3	1.69
Lead	15	.2247	3.37	29.8	1.00

[1] *1999 Ward's Automotive Yearbook,* Ward's Communication, 1999, p. 49.
[2] TheFinancials.com, Commodity Market Reports, August 16, 1999.
[3] TheFinancials.com, Commodity Market Reports, August 16, 1999.
[4] Cold-rolled steel, the largest component of the many forms of steel that go into cars.

like VaR, quantify this risk measure more rigorously and include consideration for how these prices do not all move to the worst case together.

Getting back to the autos, we can see how all three parameters drive the risk. Steel contributes the most risk because each car consumes eight times more of it than any other metal. Aluminum is next largest because of its relatively high quantity and high price. The risk seems to become inconsequential after copper until one considers that Big Auto Co. produces more than five million cars and light trucks each year, creating an annual exposure to lead prices of more than $5 million.

Volume Exposure

Carmakers don't know exactly how many cars they will produce each month or each year. Production volumes fluctuate. Accurate forecasts are, of course, a vital requirement for hedging. However, most carmakers are reasonably certain of their production schedules and requirements for the next six months. They also have general forecasts for the longer term. They can forecast their requirements, particularly their immediate ones, but cannot predict them exactly.

Linear Gain/Loss

Carmakers' exposure to each metal is linear. This means that each change in a metal's unit price results in a gain or loss exactly proportional to that price change. The gain/loss equals the price change times the quantity required. Exhibit 5.2 shows this linear gain/loss profile for 90 million pounds of aluminum, which is a typical average monthly requirement for a global carmaker. We can see that the linear relationship applies, no matter how big or small the price change is. Financial products in some markets have convexity: The gain/loss is *not* linear in relation to the underlying driver of value. For commodity exposures, we are blessed with an exposure proportional to price.

To complete this description of exposure, we need to consider time. Carmakers have this exposure profile, or something similar to

Exhibit 5.2   The Linear Gain/Loss Profile

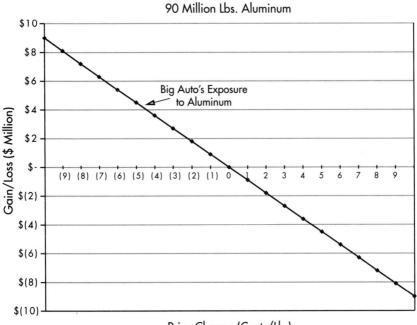

it, for each metal, for each month into the future. The specific profile in each month depends on the metal and the forecast volume. The zero gain/loss point for each month's profile is centered on the forward price of each metal. We know that, generally, the forward price is higher than the current spot. The exposure for each metal can be visualized as a series of these monthly profiles, centered on that metal's forward price line.

Risk Management Response

Big Auto Co. is one of the top ten automakers in the world. It produces over five million cars and light trucks per year. Its exact exposure each month depends on production schedules, which fluctuate with seasonal and market shifts. How the company manages this exposure demonstrates many "best practice" elements. This study focuses on the oversight and operations. Other significant aspects, such as accounting and legal concerns, are not included.

Direction and Oversight   A group within the company's treasury department performs commodity hedging activities. This treasury group coordinates its activities quite closely with the purchasing staff. A risk management committee comprised of individuals from senior management, including the chief financial officer (CFO) and the chief economist, guides the treasury group. Senior representatives from the audit and accounting departments sit on the committee as well. This committee has responsibility for oversight of all hedging activities, including exposures in currency, debt, and commodity markets. The committee:

1. Establishes risk management philosophy and policies.
2. Oversees risk management activities, including a regular review of performance versus benchmarks.
3. Meets quarterly and covers hedging at a strategic level.

Reporting to the risk management committee is the metals steering committee, composed of senior members from the treasury and purchasing departments. This committee meets monthly to:

1. Review results, including market movements, hedge performance, and net exposure changes.
2. Specify subsequent adjustments to hedge positions.
3. Review policies/procedures, counterparties/limits as guided by the risk management committee.

The metals steering committee provides guidance at a more tactical level.

Hedging Activity

Big Auto Co. can handle its exposure to steel and other metals by locking-in long-term fixed-price contracts directly with suppliers and through vertical integration, which means taking an equity interest in the metal supply chain. Every major automobile maker uses various "lock-in" solutions.[1] Such agreements bring significant economic value to both the suppliers and end-user. Long-term agreements insulate suppliers and buyers from large earnings swings that occur with market price fluctuations. These agreements go beyond reducing earnings volatility; they help both sides achieve longer-term objectives. The seller, with a major supply contract in hand, can more easily justify the significant capital expenditures that are required to ensure that supply. In this case, it might be mining equipment, processing plants, and similar resources that are purchased. The buyer, with a supply contract in hand, has more latitude in planning the usage of the material in its product. With some metals and prices effectively hedged in the purchasing arrangements, the treasury group concentrates on the remaining metal exposures.

Hedge Measures Big Auto Co. summarizes its hedge activity with one number, called coverage, which describes approximately what percentage of the exposure is protected. Coverage is defined as the notional amount of all hedge positions in place for that time period/month. Zero coverage means that no hedges are in place. Fifty

Exhibit 5.3 Gain/Loss with 50% Hedge

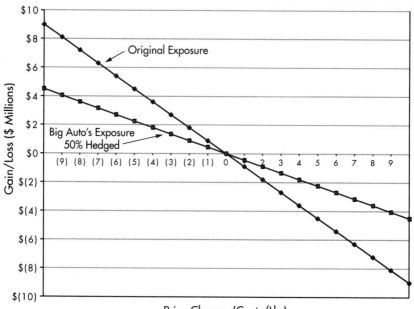

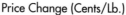

Price Change (Cents/Lb.)

percent coverage means that hedge contracts are in place for half the notional monthly requirement, and about half the exposure is covered. With 50 percent coverage, a price increase will generally result in only half as much loss as the unhedged position. On the flip side, a price decrease will result in half as much gain. In essence, the 50 percent coverage has flattened the slope of the gain/loss line, as illustrated in Exhibit 5.3. Coverage is a simple and straightforward concept; it is also the best single summary statistic of how the risk is hedged. Let's go to the next level of detail to get a more complete risk picture.

Coverage counts a swap for 45 million pounds exactly the same as a collar for 45 million pounds. We know that swaps and collars, especially loose collars, yield a different gain/loss profile. Exhibit 5.4 shows how the gain/loss profiles for a swap and a loose collar, cap/floor at 5 cents, are quite different, even though the coverage for each is 50 percent. The swap shifts the whole gain/loss line; the collar shifts only the portion that is above the ceiling and below the floor strike prices. Exhibit 5.5 provides a scenario that accentuates

Exhibit 5.4   Gain/Loss with 50% Swap versus 50% Collar

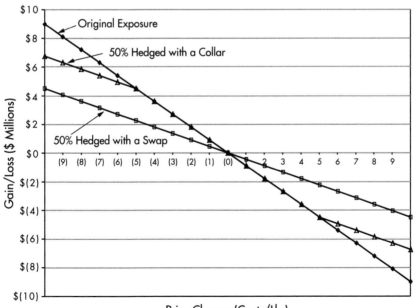

Exhibit 5.5   Gain/Loss with 100% Hedged (Swap versus Collar)

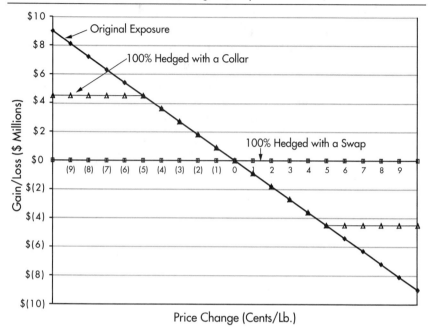

this difference by raising the coverage to 100 percent. This level of coverage implies that exposure to price change is minimal. However, 100 percent coverage using a wide collar leaves the hedger exposed to multimillion-dollar gains or losses within the ceiling and floor.

We see that coverage is an adequate descriptor when swaps are used to hedge, but if there are options, more information is required to communicate the net position and exposures. Big Auto Co.'s reports to both the metals steering committee and the risk management committee provide a much more complete picture. The reports are essentially grids and graphs that show the net gain/loss in each metal due to various price moves, at different points in the future. Coverage is the first approximation, followed up with a lot of detail.

The general lesson here is that risk management requires consideration of many aspects. No one number can adequately describe the risks that exist along many parameters—time, price, volatility, volume—in each market. *To fully understand the risks and hedges in each metal, Big Auto Co. relies on a series of standard reports that show the risks along each parameter.*

Every general rule has an exception. The compelling power of Value at Risk is that a single number, computed by using a consistent methodology, allows risk comparisons across markets and positions. The limitations of these numbers must be clearly understood and impressed on users and managers. Just as Big Auto Co. has one summary number, the market intermediaries have a set of summary numbers to characterize their risks to senior levels. But, like Big Auto Co., they have a host of other parameters along which they measure and manage risks in each market.

Big Auto Co.'s specific hedging decisions reflect its viewpoint on market conditions. For a chronic buyer like Big Auto Co., the golden trading rule, "Buy low and sell high," becomes "Buy low and *wait when high*." Big Auto Co. will increase its hedging coverage when the company analysts believe prices are at or near a low point. They will lock-in the prices before they go up. They will not put on hedges when they believe prices are at or near a high point. "Don't buy now, because tomorrow it will cost less."

Hedge Patterns   Other general patterns of the company's hedging activities are notable. These patterns are typical of all end-users— that is, the chronic buyers and sellers—and are driven by economics. Hedging activity is most intense in the near term. The farthest time brackets get much less action and, generally, much lower levels of coverage. The second pattern is that the hedge activity shifts as time moves the longer-tenor exposures to more immediate ones. In the long time frames, Big Auto Co. obtains partial protection against extreme price moves with collars that have a wide spread. Using these loose collars, Big Auto Co. bends or flattens the outer edges of its exposure profile. As the exposure becomes more immediate, it increasingly hedges the whole gain/loss profile, not just the tails.

Four factors drive this behavior, and they are generally applicable for all hedging activity:

1. It is more expensive to hedge the long-term exposures. The market demands a bigger risk premium, which is built into the forward price that the swaps and collars orbit around.

2. In the longer tenors, the cost variation among hedge products becomes significant. Exhibit 5.6 illustrates how swap

Exhibit 5.6   Long Tenor Transaction Costs

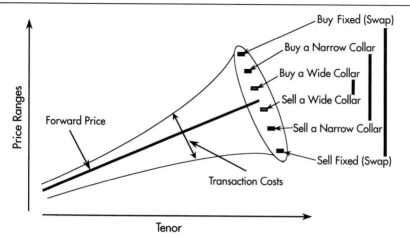

transaction costs widen out more than collars. This cost differential is similar to lowering an auto insurance premium by accepting a higher deductible.

3. There is less certainty about the exact long-term commodity requirements. In this specific case, there is uncertainty about Big Auto Co.'s overall sales volume and product mix. Which models will be hot?

4. There is more opportunity to pass cost changes along in the value-added chain—in this case, to dealers and consumers.

The first and third factors encourage a hedger toward partial coverage in the long tenors, and the second and fourth factors encourage a hedger to choose wide collars instead of swaps in the long tenors.

Consistent with best risk management practice, Big Auto Co. has approved a specific set of products to be used for hedging. They vary slightly by metal, but they are essentially vanilla swaps and collars. Other strategies, generally involving more exotic products, could be included in a hedging program. Some of them are touted to lower overall costs of hedging while still providing commensurate levels of coverage. These claims, which have not been proven, become questionable when all the extra costs (more complex valuation models and systems, and the potential of less liquidity) are considered. Best-practice hedging programs clearly state their strategy, the allowed hedge products, the purpose of each product, and the valuation methods used. In Big Auto Co.'s case, the standard set of vanilla swaps and collars is prescribed.

The important concept here is that simple hedge tools like swaps and options/collars are used to selectively flatten portions of the exposure or gain/loss line. The flattening process generally works the outer edges first and the whole profile later. Let's now look at some specific exposures and hedges.

Hedge Details   Generally, most metal purchase contracts are based on the average daily price quoted on one or another specific metals exchange [the London Metals Exchange (LME), or COMEX (CME) in New York]. The contracts typically purchase established quantities of the metal from a given supplier each month, at a price equal to the average daily price that occurred in the prior month, as quoted by a given exchange. To minimize basis risk, traders obtain hedges that match this specific price exposure. Because many metals are priced on monthly averages, the corresponding hedge market is well developed. There is a fairly deep and liquid OTC market for swaps and collars that are based on the monthly average of daily prices.

Big Auto Co.'s specific metals purchase contracts are generally consistent with this industry standard. Hence, the matching hedges can be obtained quite easily. However, some purchase contracts are not based on the monthly average at a given exchange. These contracts determine purchase price using something other than the calendar month—say, for example, two months of daily prices. The purchase price may apply to a different purchase period as well: two or more months instead of just the following month. For these unique purchase agreements, there are always compelling business reasons based on supplier and Big Auto Co. economics. The result is an unusual exposure to hedge. If Big Auto Co. were to hedge with contracts based on the monthly average, it would create various basis risks that could be considerable. Fortunately, a host of metals dealers will provide swaps and collars that exactly match Big Auto Co.'s specific purchase exposures. Big Auto Co. can obtain, via competitive bid, exact hedges with no basis risk, at a competitive price. The intermediaries take on the basis risk by providing hedges that are customized to Big Auto Co.'s needs.

This example illustrates one of the main reasons why OTC markets for swaps and options have grown much more rapidly than exchange-traded markets. Like many buyers and sellers in these markets, Big Auto Co. has specific and unique market exposures resulting from its procurement contracts. Big Auto Co. cannot find the tailored, specific hedges it needs in the general forward markets or among the exchange-traded derivatives that are available. Only OTC derivatives can be shaped to match each end-user's specific market exposures.

Best Practice

Several groups promulgate best practices for risk management, especially for the intermediaries in these markets.[2] Exhibit 5.7 distills the best practice features from these sources and cites how Big Auto Co. compares.

Although it is a corporate end-user, Big Auto Co. has developed a process consistent with best practice. The process appears quite advanced; it even comes close to the best practices of intermediaries.

CASE STUDY: INNOVATIVE ENRON

1978 was a watershed year in the U.S. natural gas industry. Since the early 1950s, gas prices had been fully regulated. In the post-oil-embargo years, 1975 to 1978, the oil price escalations led to significant increases in demand for natural gas as an oil substitute, especially as the regulated prices remained steady. Like any commodity for which the price is held artificially low, a significant gas shortage occurred. In the regulated U.S. interstate market, delivery amounts were trimmed and new hookups were discontinued. During this same time, we note, no shortage occurred in the unregulated intrastate markets. The interstate shortage, in concert with the oil price run-up, led to the enactment of the Natural Gas Policy Act in 1978. This federal legislation established a phased deregulation of gas wellhead prices. Essentially, the Act allowed the price of all new gas discoveries to float. Expectations were that new gas supplies would enter the market and meet the high market demands. The existing gas reserves were to remain at the regulated prices.

Exhibit 5.7   Risk Management at Best Practice and Big Auto Co.

Best Practice Feature	Big Auto Co. Practice
1. Senior Management Involvement • BOD approved committee to over-see risk. • Set policy consistent with risk goals and establish specific policies regarding derivatives. • Review and approve procedures. • Meet regularly to oversee activities and ensure compliance with policies.	• Risk Management Committee with BOD membership oversees risk, sets policy, and meets quarterly. • Steering committee meets monthly to review results and ensure compliance with policies. • Clear policies and procedures regarding authorized products/trades, authorized counterparties including limits, competitive pricing (e.g., bid procedures).
2. Control Processes • Independence and segregation of duties. • Frequent mark to market and other risk assessments (e.g., market risk, credit risk).	• Segregated front and back office activities. Independent risk management function. • Independent MTM valuations and risk assessments daily, including system generated VaR and credit risk assessment.
3. Operating and Information Infrastructure • Build operational processes and systems to support all trading activities, based on nature size and complexity of activities. • Build systems and process that capture all significant risks on a timely basis.	• Significant investment to build an integrated trading and risk management system in treasury • Single system supports operational aspects like trade pricing, trade entry, confirms, accounting, and settling as well as risk aspects, VaR, Credit Exposure across all trades (e.g., financial and commodity trading activities).

What happens when a little bit of free-market activity is introduced into a controlled market? Essentially, the free market pressures shred the regulated portions of the market, eventually yielding a deregulated process from wellhead to consumer. In the gas markets, it has taken a little while: twenty years. Here is how it played out. The bill was enacted to spur new exploration and discovery, and it was so effective that the market price for gas fell below the regulated well-head prices. Dealers in the regulated markets were losing money. Demand for regulated gas at high prices was quite low. Regulated utilities developed an acute supply surplus of high-cost gas, purchased under long-term, fixed-price contracts. This led, in the mid-1980s, to additional legislation that effectively deregulated all wellhead prices.

Next, the pipeline or transportation services came under competitive pressure, as their wellhead supply became unbundled from their transportation service. In 1993, the Federal Energy Regulatory Commission (FERC) opened up excess pipeline capacity to competitive market forces. While still regulated, the transportation services are under competitive market pressures as an increasing proportion of their capacity is used at rates established by bidding for leases on pipeline capacity.

The market pressures have moved downstream to the local (gas) distribution companies (LDCs). These companies originally had geographic franchises for distribution and sales of gas to consumers, bundled at regulated rates. Sales of gas to consumers have also been unbundled from local distribution, putting on LDCs the same competitive pressures that the pipeline companies experienced. Gas marketers now market gas directly to consumers. The marketers purchase it at wellheads or various concentration points, and transport it to the consumers via leased pipeline capacity.

Enron's Start, Strategic Direction, and Execution

How did Enron, formed in 1985 through the merger of two troubled regional gas utilities, become the world's preeminent gas intermediary? It did so by riding the wave of gas deregulation that moved from wellhead to consumers. Kenneth L. Lay, the CEO of Enron, had a vision that was quite different from that of traditional pipeline companies. He set a strategy that leveraged on the pending deregulation, rather than fighting it or hiding from it in the sheltered, regulated area.

Like other pipeline utilities at the time, Enron was heavily in debt and was burdened with the take-or-pay long-term contracts to buy gas at high fixed prices. Unlike other utilities, Enron aggressively negotiated out of these contracts. More importantly, Enron set up several separate unregulated businesses to buy gas, transport it, and sell it. Lay staffed these unregulated entities with outsiders, including commodity traders and other market dealers. They understood the new forces shaping the gas wholesale market. These nimble traders enlisted significant investments in technology to support their market-making activities. The unregulated entities studied, built, and used sophisticated gas valuation models as the market developed. By the late 1980s, Enron had developed the gas trading skills to become the premier gas wholesaler.

Prices in Deregulated Markets   Enron positioned itself to understand the dynamics of deregulated pricing across the 75,000 gas wellheads, both onshore and offshore, throughout Texas and Louisiana. With deregulation, each well became a price point for both current and future prices. Each of these price points is woven into a web of prices, physically connected by pipelines. These price points are connected to key concentration points, like Henry hub in Louisiana or Waha and Katy hubs in Texas.

Enron was the first company to understand how arbitrage trading ensures that the fabric of price remains tight. When the price at a given wellhead or location ranges too far above the price levels nearby, arbitrage traders sell it and buy an equal amount from the surrounding wells. Enron was the first to understand and use this basis risk in its trading activities. Also, Enron understood how all the prices in the field rise and fall in concert with the prices fetched at the *concentration points*, where the wholesale gas prices connect with the demand side of the market. Henry hub and other concentration points are the maestros; each move of the price baton at Henry ripples out across all the wells in all the fields.

In 1998, the coastal waters of Texas and Louisiana were lashed by a series of tropical storms in the span of three weeks. On September 10 to 12, tropical storm Frances charged up the Texas coast and on into Louisiana. An earlier storm had already disrupted production. Frances caused some offshore production to "shut in," using the industry jargon. Two weeks later, Hurricane Georges stormed ashore at the Mississippi–Louisiana border. This major storm had formed in the Atlantic Ocean. Its impact on production was predicted well in advance of its arrival. It shut in about 70 percent of offshore production for a week or so.[3] Overall, offshore gas production makes up about 50 percent of the total Texas–Louisiana output. Production figures for September 1998 are not available but were well below normal, primarily because of Hurricane Georges.[4]

The market impact of this supply disruption is shown in Exhibit 5.8. The daily spot price at Henry hub, which had been trending downward through July and August, spiked in early September. Traders scrambled to replace lost offshore supplies by pushing up prices. The prices did not revert to prestorm levels until mid-October. Other factors may have contributed to this spike, but the gas trading professionals attribute the price jump almost entirely to the storms and the resulting supply disruptions. This sequence illustrates how gas prices are wedded to the pipelines and the flow of gas through them.

Enron, the Gas Market Intermediary

 Enron had positioned itself not only to understand the deregulated markets, but also to provide its customers with the sale and purchase options they wanted. It established gas purchase programs that included pricing alternatives and

Exhibit 5.8   Daily Gas Prices through the Hurricanes of 1998

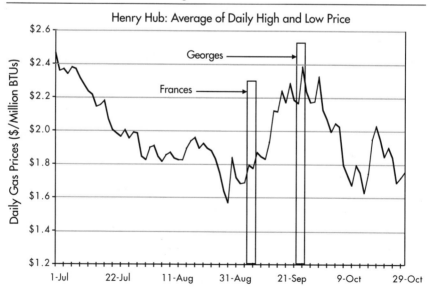

financing alternatives. Gas developers/suppliers could sell to Enron under contracts in which delivery could vary each month, and pricing could vary (sell at spot or spot within a collar or fixed price, and so on). Enron's extra innovation was to combine these purchase packages with financing alternatives. Given Enron's size and creditworthiness, it could frequently offer to prepay its purchases from the suppliers at financing rates they could not obtain themselves. By offering a diversity of sales and financing alternatives, the gas suppliers were able to create a package that best suited their needs, and Enron was able to build a substantial market share of the gas supply.

Enron provided similar services to the gas consumers through various gas marketing programs. Gas buyers could customize quantity, price, delivery, and settlement terms within the contracts they negotiated. Delivery amounts could be tied to heating degree days (a standard index that reflects how much energy is required to heat an average home), and pricing could be tied to a given index or spot. It could be capped or it could be locked-in fixed. Enron also established various partner programs that would enable retailers to optimize their delivery capability with the ability to finance storage capacity, and so on. Enron provided buyers and sellers with the alternatives they wanted, but how did they manage all the market risks that accrued to them?

We shouldn't be surprised that Enron Capital and Trading Resources, the unregulated side of Enron, organized its activities the way most market intermediaries do—by channeling the specific market risks to desks where each is pooled and the resulting net exposure is managed. In gas markets, the major risks are transmission/delivery, price, basis, storage, and index. Each purchase-and-sale contract is broken into its component pieces of market risk, and each piece is then parceled to the desk that manages it. For example, a long-term fixed-price gas purchase gets broken down into price, delivery, basis, and index risk components. The price risk needs to be matched with the corresponding long-term sales or balanced through swaps and options. Similarly, each other market risk component of the deal gets netted, and then the desk manages the residual market exposure.

In this way, the spokes prevail within the market risk spectrum. The exposures from market trades can be broken down and managed according to their component pieces. In this specific example, the component gas exposures accrue to specific desks where they are pooled and managed on a net basis. The desk, the nexus for exposure and management, also becomes the focal point for incremental exposure. The desk provides prices that reflect its own appetite and, ultimately, the overall market's appetite for additional trades. This organizational pattern prevails across the market risk spectrum.

Beyond Gas Intermediation

Enron has leveraged the intermediation and finance skills it developed in gas by applying them to closely related markets. In the early 1990s, it leveraged its gas/energy acumen and its financial strength to become the leading sponsor of energy projects around the world. More recently, it has expanded its intermediation activities into the electricity markets, which are undergoing deregulation. The electricity markets are approximately three times larger than the natural gas industry,[5] so Enron has ample opportunity for continued growth.

Enron's ability to leverage its strengths and to adapt and expand into new markets has won it numerous management accolades. A *Fortune* survey has deemed it the most innovative company four years in a row (1996–1999). McKinsey cited it as a "petropreneur."[6] *Harvard Business Review* noted how it uses its financial engineering skills to control gas price volatility for its customers.[7]

COMMODITY MARKET FEATURES

Commodity markets span a very diverse set of products. The markets for exchanging these products are equally diverse. However, some common features about the risks are notable. These are physical items—typically, materials in the production chain. The pricing models capture tangible risks and costs. They include, in many cases, transportation and storage costs. These markets typically involve large notional quantities of a homogenous product. These markets also have relatively high volatility from fluctuations in supply or demand. For example, agricultural commodities markets balance fluctuations in supply (which are largely weather-dependent) with fluctuations in export demand—for example, if Russia or China has a bad crop. Occasionally, these markets, because of their volatility, may not be as liquid as other major markets.

Our case studies have shown that the gain/loss in these markets is linearly related to price change. Hedging occurs using the standard tools, such as forward purchase, swaps, and options with large notional amounts. Most commodity markets are typically exchange-driven, yet the derivative activities are OTC-driven. There are significant reasons why swap and option activity gravitates to OTC venues for all markets. The primary purpose for these markets is to hedge price risks. There are speculators and investors in commodity markets, but the difference is not easy to discern. Finally, in Enron, we saw the dynamics at work. As natural gas emerged from regulatory controls, the company developed intermediation skills to match the evolving competitive market.

WRAP-UP

- Commodity markets contain a fabric of prices that span across geography and time.
- The links connecting these prices are physical (pipelines).
- Derivatives can parse market risks into component pieces for precise pricing and management.
- Buyers and sellers in these markets have specific exposures that are most effectively hedged with customized deal structures in OTC markets.
- Market intermediaries, who provide these customized deals, accrue most of the market risk and then pool it and manage it professionally.

Currency Market Risk Management 6

In ecology, there is the concept of biodiversity. The colder, higher latitudes of our planet contain relatively few species, but those species occur in great quantities. The ecosystems near the frozen arctic region contain vast tracts of boreal pine forests populated with a similarly limited set of fauna. In the temperate latitudes, we encounter more species (diversity) and more dependencies among the species (complexity). The tropical latitudes are home to an incredibly diverse set of species, each occupying specific ecological niches, in systems vastly more complex and interrelated than in the higher latitudes.

Market systems show a similar progression in product diversity and complexity as we move from boreal commodities through temperate currencies to tropical capital markets (fixed-income and equity). Commodity markets consist of large-volume trades in a relatively limited set of basic products, and there is limited correlation between product groups. Some groups of commodities rise and fall together—energy, base metals, precious metals, and grains. However, those groups are relatively independent of each other. In the currency markets, there is more diversity both from the multiplicity of currencies and from a slightly more extensive set of traded products in each currency. There is also a much more extensive set of dependencies across the whole market.

This chapter examines how currency markets, and the changes in them over the past twenty years, have contributed to the globalization of capital markets. Currency exchange is the channel for capital to flow between various capital markets around the globe. Over the past decade, many of the impediments to currency exchange—regulatory constraints, transaction costs, transaction speeds, and liquidity—have become minimal. The reduction of these barriers has contributed to phenomenal growth in the foreign exchange (FX) markets. Various capital markets around the globe have become more closely linked through these currency flows.

MARKET DYNAMICS

Until the early 1970s, most major currencies adhered to the Bretton Woods agreement, signed by forty-four nations in 1944. It established controls over currency exchanges, yielding stable rates. The early 1970s marked the beginning of the current currency market regime. At that time, the U.S. dollar was removed from the controls and allowed to float in value. Other major currencies followed suit as the agreement broke down. Since then, multiple schemes for currency exchange have evolved. Some economies, such as Hong Kong, have maintained a system of fixed exchange rates. Others have adopted systems in which the rate is controlled but, over time, is allowed to move. Most of the major currencies have adopted systems in which the exchange rate floats. This has led to a notable increase in exchange rate volatility. Banks that had the franchise for foreign exchange saw their market expand rapidly as institutions exposed to FX volatility sought to hedge it.

In 1974, the volume of FX transactions settled each day was approximately $1 billion. In 1994, the daily settlement amount had grown more than a thousandfold to $1 trillion.[1] In the same period, transaction costs have moved much lower. This increase in market efficiency has contributed to more market liquidity, creating a benefit spiral. Lower barriers and costs bring in more market participants, yielding more trade volume, lower transaction costs, and so forth. Other factors contributed to this growth as well. The reduction of sovereign and regulatory barriers helped. The growth in global trade and global investment has fueled the FX market volumes, and technology has greatly facilitated the expansion. The development of electronic fund transfers and cheap global communications has reduced the settlement costs.

This growth led to tremendous profits for banks, which saw their FX earnings peak in 1992 and 1993.[2] More recently, the development of electronic brokerages, where buyers and sellers establish price and trade without human intermediation, has "profoundly changed the profit equation for banks."[3] Two competing trading systems, one from Reuters and the other from a consortium of thirteen global banks, now handle around 60 percent of the London spot market.[4] Margins have been drastically squeezed. "The typical fee for a Deutsche mark trade used to be $14 per million; it is now about $3.50."[5] Since that quote as 1996 ended, margins have shrunk even further. Today's levels were entirely unthinkable ten years ago.

The creation of the euro has hurt FX earnings. Foreign exchange volatility among the European currencies dropped, from 1997 through 1998, as their rates converged on the euro targets. Profit opportunities in these currencies declined along with the volatility.

Trading—both dealing and settling—has become highly automated, and trade has migrated to the institutions that have the lowest processing costs. About two-thirds of all FX trading takes place among the bank dealers.[6] This concentration of trade, coupled with the increase in volume, has also led to an increase in risk among the dealers. The payment/settlement system for interbank currency trades is especially outmoded, and, because of timing differences in the payments, it leads to settlement exposures that are a large multiple of the net value being exchanged. This settlement risk is a form of credit risk and is discussed in Section III.

VALUATION AND RISK MECHANICS

In Chapter 5, we saw how natural gas prices at each wellhead are interlinked by the pipelines. A similar mechanism connects the exchange rate of currencies forward through time. For the major currencies, which float in value, interest rates dictate what the forward exchange rates will be. Interest rates are the pipelines connecting the value of each currency. If the forward exchange rate between two currencies does not fully reflect the difference in earning power that each currency has—that is, the interest rates—an opportunity for arbitrage profit exists. This rule, called *interest rate parity*, is best illustrated with an example. Suppose the US$–Japanese yen exchange rate is 100 yen to the dollar, and the risk-free one-year interest rates are 5 percent in the United States and 1 percent in Japan. If the one-year forward exchange rate is anything other than 96.1905 yen to the dollar, a profit can be made. Exhibit 6.1 illustrates the interest rate parity principle.

How do we make a profit when this rate isn't 96.1905? Suppose the forward exchange rate is exactly the same as the current spot rate: 100 yen to the dollar. We borrow 100 yen at 1 percent interest, exchange it into $1.00, and invest it at 5 percent. At the same time, we enter into a one-year forward exchange of $1.01 for 101 yen at the current forward rate. At the end of the year, we've earned $1.05. We convert $1.01 of those earnings back into yen to repay the loan, and pocket the 4 cents as profit. Banks and other well-heeled organizations, of course, tend to transact high notional amounts when they arbitrage.

Now suppose the forward rate is off in the other direction, say 90 yen to $1.00. We reverse the flow of funds, borrowing dollars, earning a small yield in the yen market, but converting back to dollars with yen that have appreciated. The 101 yen we have at the end of the year, using the 90 yen/$ rate that we can lock-in now, converts

Exhibit 6.1   Interest Rate Parity in Forward Exchange Rates

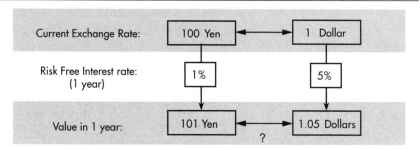

The Forward Rate implied by interest rate parity is:
101 yen/1.05 dollars = 96.1905 yen/dollar

back to $1.1222. We can pay the loan balance due, $1.0500, and still pocket a tidy 7.22-cent profit. For any forward rate other than 96.1905 yen to the dollar, we can lock-in a profitable position. The profit margin gets smaller as the forward rate in the market gets closer to the rate dictated by interest parity.

This principle of interest rate parity applies across all currency pairs, and across all time periods. The linkage for these values is not as tangible as a pipeline connecting wellheads, but it is just as compelling. It covers all floating currencies, and there are many more interconnections (complexity). With close to a hundred floating currencies, each with a series of forward time periods/prices, this activity converts into thousands of currency pairs that are woven into the price parity fabric. Arbitrageurs correct any mismatch between actual forward rates and the rates implied by interest parity.

If trading were really this simple, we could all be highly compensated FX traders. Some of the complications FX traders must deal with are in the dynamics. Spot exchange rates fluctuate. Interest rates fluctuate. Expectations of where these rates are moving change. Transaction costs, liquidity risk, taxes, and credit risks enter into the mix. In addition, some pretty powerful communications and computing systems are needed to analyze the markets, and some pretty hefty capital must be lined up to enter the game. However, the basic message is that interest rates drive the relative values of all floating currencies. Economic factors and fiscal/monetary policy are the biggest factors contributing to spot rates, but then the interest rates in each country dictate where the forward FX rates should be.

We have seen some big differences between currency and commodity market valuations, but it is important to recognize what they share. Each has threads or links that connect values across the market. Each specific price in each market is linked to the other market prices around it.

Let's turn now from the threads of currency value to how they are woven together into a fabric, and how the contours of risk are measured in that fabric. There is a great deal of variety in how sovereign entities have institutionalized the controls over their currencies. Some smaller currencies have coordinated their monetary and fiscal policy to align with a major currency. For example, prior to

1999 and the euro, the Dutch guilder was engineered to closely match the value of the German mark. Similarly, the Hong Kong dollar has been effectively engineered to be pegged to the U.S. dollar. Significant benefits from a steady and predictable currency value have accrued to their economies. Other attempts to control currency fluctuations have not been as successful, as we saw throughout Southeast Asia in 1997 and 1998. Smaller countries' efforts to dampen the volatility of their currencies have had varying degrees of success. The creation of the euro removed FX risk across many European countries while providing (hopefully) a stable currency to compete with the U.S. dollar.

When we start to examine the risk in currencies, just as with commodities, we immediately look to the volatility of each individual currency. Volatility is the first measure of how much we could gain or lose by taking a position. We look next at how each currency's value correlates with other assets—mostly, other currencies. This provides a measure of what hedges are available, aside from the currency itself. Prior to the euro, the Dutch guilder, by aligning itself with the stable German mark, dampened its own volatility, and because it was so highly correlated, provided a hedging extension to the much deeper and liquid Deutsche mark market. A trader long Deutsche marks and short Dutch guilders had a less volatile portfolio than when holding just one of those positions.

This effect leads, quite naturally, to portfolio volatility. We start with the volatility of each currency/position and then link them together through correlation to yield the overall portfolio volatility. Although we also have to consider the liquidity, we will see this same progression in every market. Many of the tools for market risk measurement/management are the same across all markets, even if the underlying drivers of value are different.

RISK ILLUSTRATIONS

There is nothing like a major market perturbation to help uncover risks. Three recent currency market earthquakes, and the risks they exposed, provide illustrations of how the market is moving. These examples have been picked to illustrate some specific currency market trends rather than to teach a lesson.

1. In September 1992, the Bank of England, in the face of tremendous market pressure, had to abandon the linkage of the pound to other European currencies and allow it to devalue. Although George Soros has been lionized or demonized in the popular press as the man who broke the Bank of England, the reality is a little different. Perhaps Soros made the most money by betting against the pound, but he was just one of a host of traders who decided that the underlying economic fundamentals were more relevant indicators of the pound's value than the monetary engineers' actions and proclamations. This event showed that the central banks alone can no longer directly engineer the value of their currencies. The markets have grown to a point where it is difficult for them to control prices through direct market intervention. They still have a very full set of tools to influence currency values and, when they cooperate, they have the wherewithal to fend off speculative attacks.[7]

2. Mexico devalued its peso on Sunday, December 20, 1994. There were many deep repercussions, and a minor side story was played out at Chemical Bank Corporation. On the Friday before this devaluation, a currency trader at Chemical failed to close out his long peso position, which he had established during the day. This failure cost him his job. It also cost Chemical Bank $70 million in pretax losses.[8] Trading operations have changed dramatically since that time; now, there is a much greater chance that this exposure would be caught and corrected the same day. A more automated operation creates closer and more timely monitoring of activities. In this specific example, today's automatic deal entry, paperless trading, and same-day confirmations of trades make it far more difficult to hide trades. Stuffing tickets in a desk doesn't work anymore.

   The sovereign entities also have other forms of direct intervention available to them, as Malaysia proved, in September

1998, when Prime Minister Mahathir Mohamed put capital controls on price movements of the ringgit, and limited stock trades. The long-term price of these controls will only be revealed over time, when we can see how Malaysia's economic development fares and whether foreign investment is permanently chilled.

3. The Thai baht devaluation occurred in July 1997. This event showed us a dark trait of globalized markets—namely, global contagion—but it also illustrated two trends that were more parochial. The devaluation immediately threw a number of Thai corporations and banks into insolvency. Many Thai businesses carried a currency mismatch on their balance sheets—another form of basis risk. Their assets were in Thailand and were valued in baht, and most of their liabilities were loans denominated in U.S. dollars. They believed this was safe because the currencies were pegged. The rapid devaluation of baht (20 percent) inflated their U.S. dollar loans in baht equivalents. Few firms, especially highly leveraged ones, can remain solvent after an immediate 20 percent inflation of their debt. The problem was compounded by a run for the exits. All firms with dollar liabilities sought to balance their position by buying dollars. Within months, the baht was driven to less than 50 percent of its former value. It has recovered considerably since then, but this is one of many examples where balance sheet mismatches have been fatal to a business or group of businesses. Asset/liability management, which has remained somewhat autonomous in financial institutions, is becoming much more fully integrated with other risk management functions, such as market and credit risk.

The Thai baht devaluation certainly had ripples. Part of the tsunami hit a series of derivative contracts between J.P. Morgan and some South Korean counterparties. In early 1997, J.P. Morgan had provided financing to a South Korean venture that involved investment in Thailand. Within that financing package, several South Korean counterparties provided J.P. Morgan immunity from a baht devaluation. SK Securities, the party with the most to lose in the transaction, filed in Korean courts to block payments to J.P. Morgan, even though the contracts and payments were with other counterparties. SK claimed that J.P. Morgan had not properly explained the risks associated with the contracts. This sounds similar to the Gibson Card greetings and Procter & Gamble suits against Bankers Trust. However, these contracts were between supposedly sophisticated financial institutions that should have known the risks they were taking. J.P. Morgan filed countersuits in New York against the three counterparties and one guarantor in its contracts. Around $500 million is in dispute. The matter is not yet settled but appears to be moving toward resolution.[9]

This example illustrates how progress is being made in derivative law. Each major market shift that triggers major payments provides examples of how to clarify the contract/agreement language. The occasional legal dispute provides more clarification about the responsibilities and rights of various counterparties in these agreements. Derivative trade agreements are becoming standardized, and trade is migrating to countries whose legal systems help to ensure their enforceability.[10]

END USERS

 Currency risk management is not the exclusive domain of large global corporations. Any company, even a small one, that generates a significant portion of its revenue in a foreign currency is a candidate for hedging currency risk. For example, *RISK* Publications is a relatively small, U.K.-based firm that generates over half its revenues in foreign currencies. It is vulnerable to a strong pound, which would devalue its foreign currency receipts, deflating its annual revenues. In the spring of 1996, it hedged against this risk with an average rate, dollar put/sterling call. The hedge option finished well in the money and significantly reduced the revenue reduction that resulted from the pound's rise in value.[11]

Global corporations create different FX exposures with their various activities. Each activity has strategies associated with it that can ameliorate the FX exposure.

Revenue/Cost Mismatches

The most persistent—and, frequently the greatest—vulnerability comes from income mismatches—situations in which a corporation's costs are based in one currency and its revenues are based in another. Any shift in the exchange rates can lead to unplanned gains or losses. This mismatch within the income stream is similar to the balance sheet mismatch noted above, and it can have a similar impact. When profit margins are thin, a currency-induced shift in expenses or revenues becomes huge.

The first and easiest defense is to adjust the selling price to match whatever shift has occurred, but the market conditions constrain corporations' ability to use this defense. In markets where price elasticity is high and competitors have the same situation, this strategy works. The gasoline market is a good example. Underlying costs are denominated in $US (the base currency for crude), and hits all the suppliers fairly uniformly. Prices at the pump move quite quickly in response to all shifts in the underlying costs, including shifts in currency rates. The market conditions for other industries, such as cars and computers, disallow this defense.

Another defense is to correct the mismatch operationally. Some companies can transfer their cost base to more closely match their revenue base. During the 1980s, Japanese carmakers developed production capacity in the United States to more closely match their dollar costs with dollar revenue. This immunized them from a strong yen, which would have inflated their costs measured in dollars. This defense requires long lead times. It takes years to build a production plant, and build an efficient process in a new country. Japanese carmakers were also quite concerned about whether the American workforce could produce cars to their quality standards.

The last defense is to use the FX market when it is feasible and adjust with expectations when it is not. For example, a high-tech software company, with its costs firmly based in U.S. dollars, generates over 60 percent of its revenue in foreign currency. Its earnings are vulnerable to a stronger dollar, but neither of the defenses above is viable. The foreign markets in software are less tolerant of volatile price changes, and the human talent required for software development does not exist in the various revenue-generating countries. Corporations like this use FX markets to convert foreign revenues when they are predictable or certain. These firms also work hard with the investor community to clarify their FX exposure and how they manage it.

For end users, there is a strong linkage between FX risk and operational/financial decisions. The FX management programs at international firms are adapted to the specific operations and finance/accounting situation at that firm.[12]

Capital Markets Arbitrage

Foreign exchange markets increasingly influence end users on the debt side of the ledger, too. The FX markets have greatly contributed to arbitrage across capital markets. Currency swaps convert financial flows from one currency to another. They are the key transaction cost to this form of arbitrage. The FX markets' growing efficiency and liquidity have reduced this cost, allowing corporations to consider many capital markets as funding sources and to find the one with the lowest overall cost. The dealer community frequently includes these FX conversion services in the integrated, financially engineered solutions it provides to corporations.

INTERMEDIARIES

Like the commodity dealers, the FX dealers are organized into desks where the various market risks are pooled and managed. Typically, there is a desk for each major currency, along with desks for groups of minor currencies. The desks have traders for spot, short-term, and longer-term forward deals. Each large bank tends to be strongest in a set of currency pairs. For example, Deutsche Bank has a major franchise in the deutsche mark/U.S. dollar trade. At the FX dealers, the desks for the currency pairs that are the franchise will be near each other.

In FX markets, where the product has become almost completely homogenous, a relentless drive for size, efficiency, and service has developed.

Size Matters

Two features favor larger dealers: (1) risk offsets and (2) scale economies. The FX market risks can be reduced from the natural offsets that occur in pools. The bigger pools typically create more natural offsets. A dealer who can create a large pool of balanced positions has an advantage over one who cannot. Also, scale economies are becoming increasingly tilted toward the large dealers. An increasing component of the costs in this business is fixed costs. It takes a big investment to build the floor, trading stations, communications network, middle/back office, and other trade support functions. The variable costs by trade are small and shrinking.

Efficiency Matters

In FX, the low-cost provider will win. This translates directly into the numerous "straight-through processing" initiatives that are under way. The FX trades that automatically go from initiation to settlement without any human intervention cost a lot less. The FX trading activities are migrating to central locations, partly due to the scale and efficiency considerations. The practice of having each trading location set its own prices has passed, and with it have gone the stories of an arbitrageur's buying Italian lira from Bank A in Italy and selling Italian lira to Bank B in France at a profit. Central pricing is inevitable with electronic markets, high deal volumes, and narrow spreads.

Service Matters

The dealers who wrap the best service package around the generic FX product will win. Banks are selling corporate programs that integrate FX services with other financial activities. They are also providing integrated links to corporate treasuries, including analytical services, and they are facilitating FX pricing/trading and settling.

Risk Management

The FX business has largely become a flow business, except in the long tenors and in the derivatives book. Virtually all trades less than $5 million now move through electronic brokers. When making just the spread on a flow, operational risks rather than financial risks are preeminent. For the spot and generic forward FX products, financial risk from taking positions occurs only in the blockbuster trades. As in equity block trading, the winners are those who can quickly distribute the exposure to buyers.

Financial risk management for FX continues to be important in the less liquid currencies, long forwards, and derivative deals where positions are taken. The use of options, including exotics, has expanded recently in FX markets. The FX middle offices are adopting the sophisticated risk models needed to measure these risks.

WRAP-UP

- The relative values of currencies, both spot and forward, are woven into one fabric.
- Monetary/fiscal policies and economic performance affect spot rates; then interest rates drive the forward rates.
- The FX markets connect capital markets and have grown as all markets have been globalized.
- The products of FX have become commodities with razor-thin margins. Operational efficiency has become critical.
- The FX markets are in the financial temperate zone of complexity and diversity.
- Foreign exchange has a simpler product set and a simpler set of price drivers than the products we will see next, in capital markets.

Fixed-Income Market Risk Management   7

We are now entering the tropical jungle of capital markets. Fixed-income or debt markets are the largest single class of markets. However, the variety of products they offer makes it difficult to regard them as a single entity. "Fixed-income," by the way, is a misnomer that remains with us from earlier and simpler times, when all debt securities carried a fixed rate of interest. The fixed-income market, as discussed within this book, covers all contractual arrangements, including public securities and private loans, that relate directly and tangentially to borrowing money and then repaying it over time. The tangential contracts are largely derivative deals like swaps, options, and credit guarantees.

MARKET DYNAMICS

Within that broad market, over the past twenty years, there has been tremendous growth in market size, product diversity, and sophistication. Let's review developments in the U.S. markets and then cover the variations in other countries, both Organisation for Economic Cooperation and Development (OECD) members and developing nations. Exhibit 7.1 provides the size, growth, and trends of the various major sectors of the U.S. fixed-income markets, which cleave naturally along the groups of debtors that obtain capital here.

The champion of U.S. debt markets is the U.S. government, which has $5.6 trillion outstanding. Our government achieves quite easily the dubious honor of being the biggest single debtor on earth. This debt has grown the fastest as well. Uncle Sam's debt was about 23 percent of the market (as defined above) in 1979 and is now over 30 percent. It rivals the debt of all U.S. home owners, collectively.

Exhibit 7.1   U.S. Fixed Income Market Sectors: Size, Growth, and Trends

Sectors Debtor or Group of Debtors	1978 Outstanding Balance (Billions)	Annual Growth Rate (%)	1998 Outstanding Balance (Billions)	Trends	
				Product Developments	Market Developments
U.S. government[1]	$789	103	$5,614	Options STRIPS Inflation bonds	More foreign investors
Home mortgages[2] (MBS) subset	1,172 88	8.3 18.5	5,782 2,631	Securitization REMICS/CMOs Standardized mortgages	Specialized firms for risk data and analysis
Corporate: Securities[3]	448	10.1	3,067	Securitization of assets	More institutional investors
Corporate: Loans[4]	360	5.5	1,040	Syndication and asset sales	Secondary markets Liquidity Special firms for risk data and analysis Measures of portfolio default risk
Consumer credit[5]	310	7.6	1,332		Securitization of many portfolios
States & local governments[6]	295	7.3	1,199		More institutional investors
Total	$3,374	8.7	$18,034		

[1] Internet source: http://www.publicdebt.treas.gov/opd/opd.htm
[2] Table 1.54, Mortgage Debt Outstanding, *Federal Reserve Bulletin,* Volume 85, Number 6, June 1999 and Table 1.56 Mortgage Debt Outstanding, *Federal Reserve Bulletins,* Volume 65, Number 8, August 1979.
[3] Board of Governors Annual Report, *The Federal Reserve System,* 1997a, 1997b, 1997c, 1997d, Table L.5.
[4] Ibid.
[5] Table D.3 Debt Outstanding by Sector, *Federal Reserve Statistical Release,* Flow of Funds Accounts of the United States, March 12, 1999.
[6] Ibid.

The most notable trend in the mortgage debt sector is securitization. Assisted by several quasi-government agencies—GNMA, FHLMC, VHA, and so on—the mortgage-backed securities (MBS) market has grown from virtually nothing in the late 1970s to over $2.6 trillion today. Corporate debt is the third major debt sector; the total outstanding is just over $4 trillion. The notable trend in this sector is the disintermediation of banks. Corporations obtain debt capital through two channels: (1) directly from debt markets by issuing public securities, and (2) from financial institutions, such as banks and insurance companies that provide loans, private placements, and so on. Exhibit 7.1 illustrates how banks' market share of corporate debt has shrunk over the past fifteen years.

Consumer and municipal credit sectors round out the total debt market. Retail consumers have certainly contributed to this market, although they are not commonly considered with the other, largely institutional, debtors. They are included here because they are a major source for the pools of assets that are securitized. The numerous forms of receivables that consumers create—such as debts from credit cards, car loans, and home ownership—provide a predictable cash flow that is frequently securitized. Within these fixed-income market segments, changes in the customer mix and product mix have also occurred, as noted.

TIME MATTERS

Compared to the trading activities we have examined so far, capital markets allocate resources through time much more extensively. These exchanges of value are balanced only over time. Investors contribute capital now, and expect repayment at specified future points. They demand a premium for use of the funds through time. This is a key difference in capital markets. Consideration for use of resources over time must be incorporated into the valuation and risk metrics in these markets. Most fixed-income analysis deals with the time value of money, or options to adjust the timing of payments.

 In our brave new world of derivatives, the divide between a swap and a loan can be blurred. Swaps can be structured so that a transfer of significant value occurs at the outset and is balanced over time with a series of unequal value transfers back. They can even be structured to reverse amortize loans: Start with neutral market value, build to a significant value through a series of unequal transfers, and then obtain a large balancing payment at the end.

These "loans inside a swap" come on the books with either significant mark-to-market values (the amount loaned at the beginning) or very significant potential future value (the loan builds up to a big repayment at the end). At most institutions, these "out of market" deals require special review and approval, but this practice is not universal. Sumitomo clearly didn't have this policy in place when one of its copper traders, Yasuo Hamanaka, used swaps to obtain financing. In mid-1999, Sumitomo Corporation filed suits against Chase Manhattan Bank and UBS AG regarding transactions they made with Sumitomo. While amassing $1.8 billion in copper trade losses, Mr. Hamanaka obtained $750 million in financing from these two banks (loans hidden inside copper swap contracts). In the suits, Sumitomo alleges that these two institutions knowingly aided the fraud that Mr. Hamanaka perpetrated on Sumitomo.[1]

Derivatives

Despite questions posed by situations like those with Hamanaka, derivatives have altered markets in some very positive ways. Their arrival has changed how both the end users and the intermediaries operate. The risks that an issuer of debt wants to sell are no longer inextricably bundled together in specific packages that the buyers must take. Financial engineers can use derivatives to create a custom menu for both the users and the providers of debt. The end users, both investors and borrowers, can obtain a customized risk profile at the lowest possible cost. The risks that the debtors sell can be teased apart and repackaged into bundles of risk that are more palatable to various buyers. By customizing risk profiles to more closely match end-user utilities, the overall costs can frequently be lowered on both sides. The dealers, by providing risk intermediation services to buyers and sellers, provide economic benefits to all.

Derivatives also allow hedges for the risks that accrue to intermediaries. As dealers providing liquidity to the market, they frequently have to own a significant portfolio. Derivatives allow them to hedge the financial risks in such a portfolio.

The fixed-income market is where derivatives first took root. It is also where derivatives have achieved the greatest maturity and diversity. Fixed-income derivatives can be used to hedge price exposure, lower the cost of funding/capital, adjust or balance asset/liability mismatches, lower the cost to take a position, arbitrage, synthetically create trading positions more cheaply than buying the actual positions, and speculate. Financial professionals almost universally recognize the economic benefit that these instruments bring, despite the many examples of misuse. The high-profile cases of misuse have allowed the popular press to demonize derivatives. However, derivatives' rapid expansion and beneficial adaptation into all financial markets clearly show that they are here to stay.

Securitization

Home mortgages were the first class of assets to be extensively securitized. Exhibit 7.1 shows how securitization now covers almost half of all home loans, having grown from less than 8 percent in 1978. The federal government created a set of quasi-government agencies that greatly facilitated this securitization process. These agencies sponsored the pooling of loans to be sold to investors. As part of the sponsorship, they frequently set underwriting standards to be followed in originating all loans placed in the pool and, backed by the full faith and credit of the U.S. federal government, they immunized investors from all credit risk in the pools. In 1971, when these mortgage-backed securities were first issued carrying no credit risk, they yielded over 2 percent more than their risk-free cousins, government bonds. Over five years, that spread subsequently narrowed to around 50 basis points. Aside from providing very tangible benefits to home buyers in the form of lower mortgage costs, MBS have contributed to standardized underwriting rules, increasing the efficiency of mortgage market origination. Investors have also benefited with a richer set of risk/return choices.

It didn't take long for firms with predictable cash flows to consider securitizing them. The markets have seen all sorts of cash flows become securitized, but receivables predominate. Credit card receivables, car loans, car leases, and medical bill receivables are all candidates for securitization. When corporations or financial service firms securitize assets, they free up capital to redeploy toward higher returns, or to return to equity holders. Recently, there has been a groundswell of banks' securitizing their commercial loan portfolios. This trend allows them to finesse current banking regulations that require them to hold inappropriate levels of capital for credit risk. The same level of capital is required for all commercial loans without regard for the creditworthiness of each counterparty. Banks end up holding too much capital for loans to their most creditworthy customers and perhaps too little capital for loans to their least creditworthy customers.

Technology has made securitization economically feasible. Without cheap and fast computing, securitized assets simply cannot be processed. Each month, securitization requires, at a very high level:

- Tabulating and totaling receipts from thousands of sources within the pool.
- Reconciling those receipts and creating appropriate ledger entries. This requires:
  - Calculating and distributing the cash receipts to individual investors in the pool (frequently, thousands), on a pro-rata or other specified basis.
  - Reconciling and reporting to various legal entities and to the government, as appropriate.

The computer engineers who created low-cost, fast ways to account for these pooled assets, and the legislators who provided the legal vehicles that facilitate securitization, can share in the claim of having provided very significant economic benefits.

Disintermediation

Exhibit 7.1 shows the market share of bank loans shrinking from 45 percent to 25 percent. Most of the growth in corporate lending has occurred in the securities sector, where corporations borrow directly from investors. Disintermediation is not a strong trend in Europe, where bank-lending relationships are much tighter and competitive pricing has not been as important. The switch to the euro is creating competitive forces, which may precipitate more disintermediation.

Market Variations

Developed countries, like the ones in western Europe, have not had government sponsorship of mortgage loans, which facilitated the development of asset-backed securities markets in the United States. However, the asset-backed market is now growing quite quickly in Europe, but municipal securities have not typically enjoyed the tax-exempt status they have in the United States. In the Pacific rim, Japan is the major OECD country. Its protected and highly controlled fixed-income markets have almost no securitization and very little disintermediation. A high proportion of debt remains in the bank loan sector. Some noteworthy economics professionals have claimed that the lack of competition and manipulation in Japan's capital markets has contributed greatly to its current economic woes.[2]

In the less developed, non-OECD emerging markets, the debt markets are predominated by U.S. government-backed securities, Brady Bonds, which were issued in exchange for defaulted commercial bank loans.[3] The last Brady Bond was written in March 1998, but the bonds will continue to mature through 2028.

What Next?

How do we navigate through this dynamic jungle of diverse products and rapidly changing flow of capital? One could easily get bogged down in a morass of detail, for this is truly a vast thicket of submarkets and institutions. As in prior chapters, we'll show the major valuation and risk principles with examples that illustrate the major trends. We will follow the flow of capital from providers through intermediaries to users. Some new risks, unique to these markets, require sophisticated measurement tools and management techniques. However, common risk management principles can still be applied.

VALUATION

The portfolios that dealers/traders hold are quite significant. For example, each major government bond dealer holds hundreds of millions in government bonds. With portfolios this large, tiny variations in yield can lead to big differences in value. This results in a tremendous focus on the value and risk held in the positions. However, you can't look up the latest trade on a screen, as you can in the equity markets. Debt markets contain a huge variety of unique securities. Each is for a specific name, contains a specific seniority, and has a unique set of cash flows and a specific maturity. Only a small portion of all these unique instruments moves through the market each day. Days may have passed since the specific security you want to value actually traded. Therefore, you have to find proxies in the current market. To determine value, the dealers have developed a fair arbitrage-free process for discounting the various cash flows. They also require models to value any options that are embedded in the instruments.

Term Structure

To determine the value of many different securities, we must create a uniform, arbitrage-free way of discounting the various future cash flows. The traditional measures of yield do not work because they capture the average return across all cash flows in the security. Exhibit 7.2 illustrates this problem. Three securities with the same counterparty (U.S. Government) have a cash flow in six months. If we use the average yield of each security to discount those cash flows, we come up with three different current values for that first cash flow. This would create an arbitrage opportunity for our traders. To prevent arbitrage, we need to apply specific discount rates based on *when* the cash flow occurs, rather than the security to which it belongs. We need to apply the zero-coupon discount rate to each cash flow, which means the discount rate that applies to that cash flow and only that cash flow, with no other cash flows/coupons involved.

 How do we determine the appropriate zero-coupon rate to apply to each cash flow? The market gives us the zero-coupon rate for the first cash flow in six months. The

Exhibit 7.2 Cash Flows and Yields for Government Securities

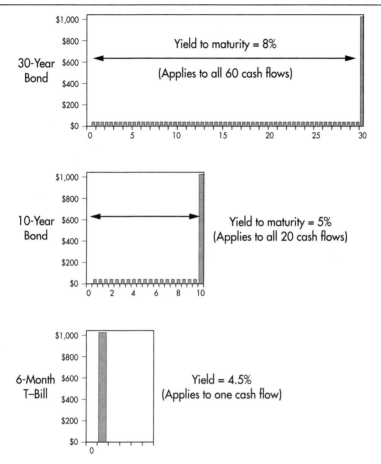

T-bill rate applies to that one cash flow. We can convert this 4.5 percent yield into a discount factor and apply it to all the cash flows occurring in six months. The market also gives us average yields to maturity for many government bonds. If we know the yield of one with just two payments (one in six months, and the next in one year), we can extend our zero-coupon curve out to one year. We have two known items: the six-month zero-coupon rate, and the one-year average yield covering the two cash flows. We can solve for the one unknown: the one-year zero-coupon rate. Once we have the zero-coupon term structure for six months and one year, we can extend it out another six months, using a bond with three cash flows. The mathematics behind this bootstrapping process is quite complex; in fact, there are several possible ways to "bootstrap" a zero-coupon curve.[4] This description shows how the zero-coupon discount rates are linked to market prices and are built stepwise from the shortest tenors to the longest ones.

The term structure for securities that have credit risk can also be bootstrapped, but there are typically fewer points for reference, and the zero-coupon discount rates contain a premium for the credit and liquidity risk inherent in those instruments. The common practice is to meld together information from several markets. For example, to create a term structure for an AA-rated corporate security, practitioners may use LIBOR for the first three to six months, then futures out to one to two years, and then swap yields out to seven or eight years. They use the most liquid instruments for each maturity, and they correct for different conventions of calculation. Many steps are involved in adjusting for different calculation conventions for the various instruments, such as simple vs. compound interest, different interest accrual bases, and so on.

We now have two series of points. One represents the zero-coupon discount rates for risk-free securities, and the other indicates the zero-coupon rates for instruments with a given level of credit risk—say, AA. It is necessary to connect the points before cash flows occurring at any time can be discounted. There are two general methods for connecting the points—linear interpolation or cubic spline. Linear interpolation is a use of straight lines, similar to the simple connect-the-dot puzzles we solved as kids. The cubic spline method is like bending a flexible rod to create a kink-free, smoothly curved line through the dots—a mathematically complex process. Linear interpolation is easier, but it creates problems. Forward rates, which are calculated from this term structure, tend to jump where there is a kink. Volatility—and hence, option valuations—also get distorted by the kinks.

In the past fifteen years, markets have incorporated term interest rate structures and cubic spline interpolation to price bonds. Bond values are now determined by summing the value of each specific cash flow—that is, each payment of coupon and principal. Each cash flow is valued using a discount rate based on the appropriate zero-coupon rate. That zero-coupon rate depends on when the cash flow occurs, and it includes appropriate premiums for liquidity and credit risk. All fixed-income securities that do not have options embedded in them can be valued this way.

Embedded Options

About half the instruments in the fixed-income markets have options embedded in them. For example, all asset-backed securities contain an option for the debtors to prepay their debt. Many municipal and corporate debt issues contain similar prepayment options, typically on specified dates. Another class of corporate securities provides an option to the buyer to convert the debt into equity. Generally, less creditworthy firms provide this option. They obtain lower interest rates on their debt by giving the option to debt holders to share in profits if the firm does well. The value of these convertible bonds, since they are a hybrid of debt and equity, is driven by both debt and equity market factors.

All these instruments need valuation methodologies or models that incorporate the embedded options. An additional set of mathematical methods has evolved that helps to value these instruments. These techniques include option-adjusted spread (OAS) and Monte Carlo simulation. To obtain value, they frequently value the option and security separately and then net them.

Risk Mechanics

We have seen that there is a fabric that binds the values of fixed-income instruments together, in a manner similar to the FX and commodity markets. In the fixed-income markets, the threads of this fabric are made up of various interest rates or yields through time. However, two features that are in the background in the other markets take center stage in the risk mechanics of fixed-income markets: credit risk and time/tenor. In this capital market, there is a very unbalanced flow of funds that is only corrected gradually, over time, with interest to redress the imbalance. Credit risk is a much more important consideration in these transactions, where the payback occurs over time. We'll discuss these credit risk aspects in Section III. The time/tenor aspect is the first risk feature we'll discuss here.

Duration and Convexity

The tenor of a bond is its maturity. This tenor represents the time to the final payment, but duration provides a more robust reference point for bond valuation. The duration of a security can be thought of as the point in time where all cash flows balance. If the cash flows were buckets of water lined up along a plank with heavier buckets for bigger payments and placement driven by payment schedule, where could we pick up the plank and have it balance evenly? For the 10-year bond, it would be about 9.6 years and for the 30-year bond it would be about 25 years. This is simply the duration of these bonds.

Duration provides a first approximation of how much the value of the bond will shift if interest rates change. Changes in value to the 10-year bond can be approximated by treating all the cash flows as a single bullet payment at 9.6 years. Similarly, the cash flows in the 30-year bond can be treated like a single cash flow at 25 years for approximating sensitivity to interest rate shifts.

Simple duration, while conceptually straightforward, is not the best duration measure, because it fails to consider the time value of money. There are several other duration calculations that adjust the weight of cash flows through various discounting schemes. Each form of discounting has its own name (e.g., modified, effective, and Mucaulay). These methods, because of discounting, yield shorter durations than the simple method. They provide an even better measure of value sensitivity to interest rates.

Duration is similar to the gain/loss charts we graphed in the commodity chapter. Unfortunately, in the jungles of fixed-income, the risk doesn't move in straight lines. A small drop of interest rates creates a given increase in value. However, another drop of the same size yields a bigger value increase than the first one. For government bonds, each incremental drop in interest rate helps value more and more. In the other direction, each incremental increase in interest rates hurts value more and more. When interest rates go up, the cash flows get discounted more heavily, creating a bigger loss for each subsequent increase in interest.

This nonlinear relationship between interest rates and bond value is called *convexity*. It is a key risk feature in bond markets. Government bonds are positively convex (e.g., their value goes up more and more when interest rates go down more and more). However, securities that have imbedded call options in them have a negative convexity. When interest rates go down, the issuer may chose to pay off the current debt and refinance it at the lower rates. Any fall in interest rates increases the chance of the put option being exercised, reducing the duration, and the overall value of the security.

With convexity in the risk profile (e.g., nonlinear value changes), options become a more important risk management tool. In Chapter 5, we saw how options can help bend or flatten the linear gain/loss line selectively. Here, they can be used to help straighten the curves in the gain/loss line, converting the risk profile back toward a straight line.

The Greeks

Convexity is also a key feature in option valuations. All options contain convexity that drives each option's value. Options professionals have created a cast of characters from the Greek alphabet to describe the risks in options. The two leading characters, *delta* and *gamma*, describe the convexity. Delta captures the gain/loss that occurs from a small change in the underlying security. It is a measure of the slope of the valuation line. Gamma captures how delta shifts when larger shifts occur in the underlying security. It is a measure of how the slope changes; that is, it measures the convexity. The rest of this Greek cast includes *kappa*, *theta*, and *rho*. Kappa (also sometimes called *vega*) measures the change in option price from a change in volatility. Theta measures the change in option value from the passage of time. Each day that passes moves the option closer to the expiration date, decaying its value. Rho measures the change in option value from changes in interest rate (the risk-free rate). These minor Greek characters do have an impact on the value of options, but the impact is typically smaller than that of the two leading players, delta and gamma. These risk factors are active in all securities with embedded options.

MBS Example

Perhaps no single market contains more of the new and emerging features than the mortgage-backed securities (MBS) market. These securities are derivatives formed from pools of mortgage loans. The loans are packaged into large pools, typically by one of the government agencies, and sold to investors via special-purpose vehicles. These agencies take the credit risk out of these securities with guarantees. The investors buy the monthly cash flows, the principal and interest that are paid each month. These pass-through securities have embedded in them the risk that mortgagors will prepay their loans. The cash flows, and

Exhibit 7.3   MBS Monthly Cash Flows at 50% PSA

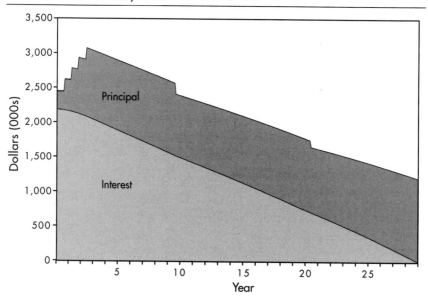

hence the value of these securities, are very sensitive to the prepayment speeds that occur. A basal rate of prepayment occurs due to changes in family situations—promotions, job changes, and births. However, the most important driver of prepayment speeds is mortgage interest rates. When mortgage rates drop, borrowers accelerate prepayments to refinance at the lower rates. Conversely, when mortgage rates rise, borrowers tend to defer paying off mortgages, and prepayment speeds slow down.[5]

Exhibits 7.3 through 7.6 show how a single pool of mortgages can yield very different cash flows under different interest-rate scenarios. Here is a pool of 2,000 loans, all for 30 years, paying a fixed rate. The average original loan balance is $175,000, creating a $350-million pool. The average interest of the loans is 7.5 percent, but .5 percent goes to mortgage servicers for administering the portfolio. So, the rate the securities pay, or the weighted-average coupon (WAC) is 7 percent. The weighted-average maturity (WAM) is 360 months. (In real markets, the securities don't contain brand-new loans like this. They are shown here to show the whole profile of cash flows.)

Exhibit 7.4   MBS Monthly Cash Flows at 100% PSA

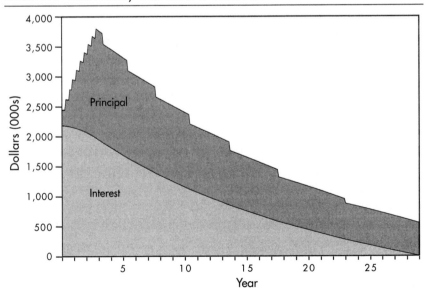

Exhibit 7.5   MBS Monthly Cash Flows at 150% PSA

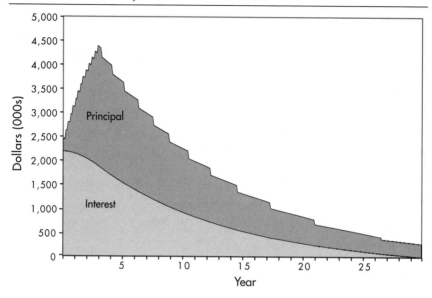

Exhibit 7.3 shows the cash flows (both principal and interest) if prepayments of 50 percent PSA occur. PSA stands for public securities association which has promulgated this standard and widely used measure of prepayment speed. This slower speed is quite likely with a 1.0 to 1.5 percent rise in mortgage interest rates. Exhibit 7.4 shows the cash flows that would occur if prepayments of 100 percent PSA are realized. This prepayment speed is most likely with steady interest rates. Exhibit 7.5 shows the cash flows for 150 percent PSA. This faster prepayment speed occurs when mortgage interest rates drop by 1.0 to 1.5 percent and stay there.

When interest rates drop, the cash flows build up, quite like a breaking wave, at the short end of the time horizon. The more precipitous the interest drop, the more the cash piles up at the short end of the board, as shown in Exhibit 7.6. This cash flow profile is most likely to occur with a 4 percent drop (or more) in interest rates. Similarly, if interest rates go up, the more the cash flow stretches out. The prepayment option embedded in MBS is the key driver for cash flows and value.

Exhibit 7.6 MBS Monthly Cash Flows at 600% PSA

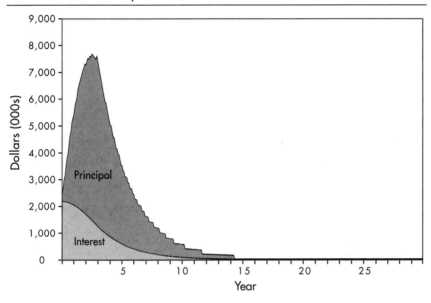

CMOs and REMICs

The financial engineers can do more; in the late 1980s, they went for extra innings. The risks within MBS pools can be further tranched, or carved up, to match specific investors' appetites. Regardless of prepayment speed, a stable area of predictable cash flows emanates from the bottom right of all the graphs. Various financial service firms started a very profitable process of converting MBS pools into collateralized mortgage obligations (CMOs), also known as REMICs (real estate mortgage investment conduits). The firms would purchase several MBS issues with similar characteristics, carve the cash flows into tranches, and sell them piecemeal to investors. These various tranches reallocated the prepayment risk to more closely match specific investor appetites. In sum, the pieces (tranches) fetched a higher price than the original cost of the securities. The CMO/ REMIC business started in 1986 with almost $50 billion issued. It reached its height in 1993, with $325 billion issued. The yields on the safest tranches are typically just a few basis points above treasuries, while the yields on the highest risk classes could exceed 20 percent. Principal is at risk in the high risk classes.

In 1994, mortgage interest rates, which had been dropping steadily for years, suddenly increased 1.5 percent in four months. Prices of various CMO tranches dropped steeply as prepayments for refinancing stopped in the rising-rate environment. The biggest risk takers suffered significant losses in principal, and even the more risk-free tranches suffered losses. The losses were aggravated by a loss of liquidity in the markets.[6] In 1995, the total issuance of REMICs was around $15 billion.[7] Securities backed by commercial loans went through a similar boom that went bust in 1998. These experiments will continue as all participants adapt to the new markets that transfer specific financial risks as easily as they transfer capital flows.

RISK ILLUSTRATIONS

Interest rate swaps could have reduced and perhaps even thwarted the Savings and Loan (S&L) debacle that occurred in the early 1980s. The S&Ls' primary business was largely predicated on riding an upward sloping yield curve. They obtained capital by borrowing at short-term floating rates, and they converted it into mortgages, which were long-term fixed-rate assets. Generally, they had a 2 percent to 3 percent spread between the short-term floating rates and the long-term fixed rate—a tidy profit margin. They also had a significant risk from their asset/liability mismatch. When short-term interest rates rose, they quickly became insolvent. If they had been able to redress the mismatch with swaps or options, they would have remained solvent much longer, and perhaps would have even survived.[8]

By the same token, arbitrage activities can introduce a false sense of security, especially regarding liquidity. The U.S. government bond market, the most liquid market in the world, has specific on-the-run tenors where liquidity is deepest. The most current 10-year and 30-year bonds have the highest liquidity and most trading. Because of the higher demand for these two "on-the-run" bonds, yields for them have been typically 10 to 30 basis points lower than yields for "off-the-run" bonds, or bonds with other maturities.

These discrepancies were seen as an opportunity for arbitrage. When the difference between "on-the-run" and "off-the-run" widened, hedge funds and other trading professionals bought "off-the-run" bonds and sold "on-the-run" bonds. Throughout the 1990s, the differential shrank at a steady pace, fed in part by convergence traders who piled onto this profitable strategy. By the summer of 1998, they had collectively driven the "off-the-run" spread to under 10 basis points for most of the off-the-run tenors.

In August 1998, when Russia defaulted on its bonds and financial markets shuddered around the globe, risk-averse investors flocked to U.S. bonds. However, they went for liquidity and shunned the "off-the-run" bonds. The price differential between "off-the-run" and "on-the-run" bonds rose, handing the convergence traders some whopping losses. The spreads widened even further as these traders sought to unwind their positions into increasingly illiquid markets.

Some reports indicate that this divergence was a primary reason for the Fed's lowering interest rates.[9] It feared that this divergence presaged a liquidity freeze. The differential has narrowed since hitting its peak in September 1998, but it remains well above its historic average. In early February 1999, the 30-year bond yield was 5.18 percent, the 29.5-year bond yield was .09 percent higher, the 29-year bond yield was .19 percent higher, and the 23-year bond yield was .28 percent higher.[10] This illustrates how the difference between arbitrage and speculation is sometimes quite hard to discern. It also shows how liquidity is a key consideration.

CORPORATE USERS

Corporate borrowers seek to obtain the lowest cost funds. Let's look at how that process has changed in the past fifteen years.

Most highly rated corporations go directly to the debt markets for most of their borrowing needs. They have disintermediated their banks. Securities firms still help them tap the markets, and banks still frequently provide commitments for contingent funding, in case the firm's credit rating goes south and investors balk at buying the firm's IOUs.

 Companies with just average credit ratings have new opportunities, too. Interest rate swaps can be used to lower the borrowing costs. There are arbitrage opportunities between the fixed-rate and floating-rate markets. Typically, companies with lower-rated credit find it advantageous to borrow at a floating rate and swap into fixed rates, while borrowers with good credit ratings can move the other way, from fixed to floating. Each group obtains debt that is lower than if it had gone directly to the market for its preferred form of financing. The two groups are arbitraging the market's pricing of fixed vs. floating debt for companies with differing credit risk.[11] They can perform this arbitrage themselves, or, more typically, they can obtain it through an intermediary. Although banks have experienced disintermediation from the lending, they still largely intermediate in the swaps.

Firms that have less than stellar credit ratings and create "junk" bonds have opportunities, too. They are able to lower their cost of funds by making the bonds convertible—that is, providing an option to the bondholders to share in the equity position. This form of funding occurs most commonly in turnaround situations.

Convertible bonds are not new. However, new risk tools and techniques have broadened the span of applications and increased product diversity in the high-yield markets. The divide between equity and debt is less distinct than it was ten years ago. Investors and borrowers have a richer set of product choices in the high-yield arena. They can more closely match their specific needs.

DEALERS

Fixed-income markets are a strange concoction of old and new. The most sophisticated risk tools and techniques germinated in these markets, probably because they contain the most complex set of risks. These new risk tools and techniques have created a broader and more complex set of product choices, and they offer a much broader array of risk/return opportunities to all participants.

The odd aspect is that very little has changed in how deals are done. Fixed-income markets remain a stronghold of trading based on relationships. The market remains almost exclusively driven by institutional investors. Demands for price transparency and smaller margins, which other markets have experienced, are quite muted here—perhaps because of the size and complexity of the risks being intermediated.

Most fixed-income trading is not a flow business. It consists of large blocks of securities moving between institutional investors. A large proportion of it consists of new issues coming into the market. The dealers take very significant position risks (hold inventory) while acting as intermediaries and underwriters. They frequently buy and hold securities, not knowing exactly where they are going to sell them. The risks in these deals are too large and too unique to be handled in more automated ways.

Some fixed-income market sectors—U.S. Treasury notes, and overnight cash, for example—are a flow business. These sectors are moving to electronic forums much more rapidly than the rest of the fixed-income markets.

As with the dealers in other markets, the traditional desk organization prevails; however, the fabric of risk is much richer in complexity here. The desks break out along the product lines noted above: typically, in the United States, there are government, MBS, municipal bond, corporate, and high-yield desks. The risks include interest rate/term structure, spreads off those rates that reflect credit and liquidity premiums, plus convexity and volatility across the whole lot.

Prices and spreads are much less transparent in the fixed-income sector than they are in other markets. The chairman of the SEC very recently chided the industry for its lack of progress in creating more transparency.[12] He is not alone.[13] Perhaps the dealers are guarding their franchise and resisting these pressures. Or perhaps there are genuine roadblocks like competitive situations or technical hurdles that thwart progress.

Risk measurement and risk management in these markets are also carefully guarded. All dealers have very sophisticated models and measures for valuation. They also have extensive tools to measure risks in their portfolios. There appears to be quite a spectrum in how these measures are used in the art of managing dealing activities. Some dealers have created fairly rigid market risk limits and have applied them down to trader levels. Others lean toward more flexible controls, with seasoned managers (typically, ex-traders) to monitor overall positions and market conditions. These seasoned managers direct adjustments guided by their judgment of market conditions. Banks tend to use the rigid control model, and securities firms tend toward the oversight method.

 However, technology is starting to make inroads here. Several major initiatives are under way to create electronic brokering for bond trading.[14] These initiatives will doubtless bring more price transparency to these markets, and will probably reduce transaction costs and perhaps increase liquidity. They will establish a toehold in the most liquid markets first: U.S. Treasuries and short-term commercial paper. Special variations that electronically assist buyers and sellers to negotiate price will probably develop for the less liquid market sectors. When these electronic aids become widespread, more transparency and smaller margins are inevitable. The advent of electronic trading provides end users, both the buy and the sell sides, with opportunities to cut transaction costs. Eventually, they may even disintermediate the dealers.

Dealers will have to adjust to the competitive threat from electronic brokers. As buyers and sellers are increasingly able to meet in electronic networks, the community of dealers will focus on their business proposition. They will have to define the specific services that they provide—analysis, valuation, advice, efficient execution of block trades—and charge according to the value that each service brings.

THE INVESTORS

Over the past twenty years, stock and bond markets have largely supplanted banks as the chosen repositories of value for many Americans. Banks are being disintermediated as the providers of capital and are playing a smaller role as corporate users of capital. The savings account passbooks, bank CDs, and defined-benefits pension plans of yore are being replaced by defined contribution plans, mutual fund investments, and IRAs. As Americans obtained more control over their retirement assets, they have moved them into stocks and bonds. The set of stocks and bonds available to investors has expanded as well. Investors can now procure foreign securities as easily and almost as cheaply as domestic securities.

Three groups have replaced the bankers in managing this investment pool: (1) plan sponsors, (2) asset managers, and (3) custodians. The plan sponsors develop the investment strategy, market the fund, attract investors, and maintain the relationships with the individual investors. The asset managers determine where to invest the funds. The custodians hold the assets safely, execute trades as directed, and provide data about their activities. The asset managers handle the key financial risks, and the custodians shoulder the operational risks.

Investors' Tools and Techniques

Investors are in for the long haul. They are less interested in daily or weekly returns and more concerned with performance over months, or even years. The asset managers' analyses and decisions trace directly to the insights Markowitz provided. Generally, they make specific investment decisions based on the impact of risk and return on portfolio levels over an extended time frame. To get to portfolio levels, the returns and volatilities of all assets need to be considered, along with the correlations of those returns. A side note is that most of the investors' set of risk tools and techniques evolved in the equity side first, and have been adapted for use in fixed income.

This portfolio impact is impossible to measure exactly, but increasingly sophisticated proxies have evolved. The hurdles for exact measurement include incomplete data and significant processing challenges. In fixed-income markets, data for all returns are very hard to obtain. Only a fraction of all outstanding issues move through markets each day. Another difficulty is the size of the correlation tables that would be needed. Markowitz was unable to convert his theory into practice because of this problem. The breakthrough came with the use of betas in the capital asset pricing model (CAPM), which can be viewed as an early form of the factor models in use today.

In fixed-income and equity markets, the first standards for performance came from benchmark portfolios. Indexes containing a standard set of assets were established to provide a benchmark. Asset managers could compare their portfolio to the index, including weightings by sectors and segments within that portfolio. They judged performance and measured risk against the benchmarks.

More recently, factor models have become another tool for measuring portfolio risk/returns and for guiding investments. These models are premised on the assumption that all asset returns are driven by underlying exposures to fundamental factors. They seek to distill the unmanageably large number of returns for all assets down to the manageable set of underlying factors that drive those returns.[15] Factor models can (1) provide the asset manager with a clearer understanding of the risks/returns in a portfolio and (2) facilitate tailoring the risks to match the manager's market view. These factor models were pioneered in the equity markets and were only recently applied to fixed-income markets.

WRAP-UP

- Fixed-income markets are vast and increasingly diverse.
- Derivatives, securitization, and disintermediation have wrought significant changes and greater efficiency for these markets. Arbitrage, facilitated by derivative trading, has increased market efficiency. Derivatives also help institutional investors fine-tune the risks in their portfolios through hedges and through a broader set of investment choices.
- Despite market changes, fixed-income dealing remains a market of institutions and is less transparent than equity trading.
- Electronic brokering is encroaching. Its impact will be very significant.

Equity Market Risk Management 8

If fixed income is the jungle, equity markets are the savanna. There is less variety in the products here, and the risks are more straightforward. The risk/reward premise is quite easy to describe for equities. However, this doesn't make the measurement and management of risks any less challenging. The more direct risk/reward paradigm in equities has helped shape recent trends in the markets. The resulting developments in risk tools and techniques have addressed concerns on the investor side of the market.

A marketplace very different from that for fixed-income securities has developed for the specific risk features of equities. Stocks are a fairly straightforward claim on the earnings of the firm. Because those earnings may rise or fall, this asset class can be quite volatile in value. Unlike with debt, stockholders do not have a fixed schedule of payments they will receive and a fixed rate of interest that their investment will return. Because stocks are riskier than debt, they typically have yielded a higher average return. Over the long run, equities have earned about 7 percent per year more than bonds. However, there is some conjecture that this premium is shrinking.[1]

The risk in holding stock is easier to understand than the risk in holding bonds. Buying a common stock brings you ownership in the enterprise. You share in the enterprise's fortunes, both good and bad, and you have a voice in the management of the firm. The risk you own is the firm's risk, not a promise to repay, combined with a put option.

Stocks are a very homogenous product, which greatly enhances their liquidity. Most issues of equity are for common shares, which divide the firm's ownership and earnings on a simple pro-rata basis. There are variations (preferred shares and voting shares), but common shares predominate the market. When virtually all the stock for a given corporation is homogenous, it is easier to trade. Liquidity is higher. This is considerably different from fixed-income debt, where each issue of debt has unique characteristics: yield, maturity, collateral, seniority level. Liquidity is lowered when each security is unique. Matching buyers with sellers and determining price are both more difficult.

There is also much broader participation in stock markets, which enhances their liquidity. Unlike the fixed-income market, which is almost exclusively institutional, individual investors make up a very significant share of the equity markets. The original roots for equity markets trace back to the time when individual investors predominated. Today, a host of institutions participate too—pension funds, mutual funds, insurance companies, and asset managers—and their participation has increased dramatically in the past ten years.

The final kicker for liquidity is that equities are almost exclusively exchange-traded. Each exchange may provide a different level of liquidity, but all greatly facilitate market efficiency. Recent equity market trends are markedly similar to FX market developments. Trade volumes have grown enormously over the past ten years. Spreads have narrowed, and electronic markets are very quickly moving to dominate trading. Derivatives have become common in this market. However, they are used primarily to refine the risk profiles of investors' portfolios.

VALUATION AND RISK MECHANICS

What is a stock worth? Classic financial theory gives us a clear definition—the discounted cash flow of all future earnings. This creates two questions: (1) What are the future earnings? (2) What is the appropriate discount rate? Each firm is a unique entity, and its prospects for generating future earnings are quite specific. Many equity analysts are employed to discern these prospects and advise investors. They consider many aspects of a company—the management team, market position, balance sheet strength, strategic initiatives, and legal issues—when they predict earnings. An illustrative point here is that analysts specialize in given industries, and they make predictions for industries as well as individual firms within industries. The earnings prospects for a firm are subject to industry and economic trends.

The discount rate must also be considered for valuation. The baseline, risk-free rate is provided by U.S. securities. Earnings from stock assets, which are more volatile than IOUs from Uncle Sam, should certainly be discounted at rates above this base. This premise is borne out in market patterns. If all other factors remain steady, significant shifts in interest rates result in significant and opposite shifts in equity values. When interest rates go up, stocks go down. The firm's future earnings are being discounted at higher rates, and investment funds are being attracted from equity to bonds' higher yields. The appropriate spread for equity risk is an open question.

The easiest way to find a stock's value is to look it up. But that doesn't get you to the underlying risks. Equity valuations move in concert with underlying industry, economic, and individual factors. Barra pioneered the use of models to determine these factors. Asset managers use them to adjust the risk/return profile in equity portfolios.[2]

RISK ILLUSTRATION

In the summer of 1996, Nick Leeson waited in a German prison while authorities in England and Singapore determined who would prosecute him first. At that time, I was conducting a risk review at a major European bank. The memo announcing my review to various bank personnel unfortunately misspelled my last name. It requested all recipients to give risk expert "James Leeson" their fullest cooperation. I enjoyed a lively set of interviews on that engagement.

But let's discuss what Nick Leeson was supposed to be doing while he created losses that sank Barings Bank PLC. He was supposed to be arbitrating the Nikkei Index, which traded concurrently on two different exchanges, in Singapore and Osaka (Japan). Whenever the same item is being traded in two different markets, the opportunity for arbitrage exists. Nick Leeson was supposed to circle above the two markets, looking with an eagle eye at all Nikkei Index future trades on both exchanges. He was supposed to swoop down and pounce when any futures prices moved far enough out of alignment. Nick would buy the future at the cheap price and sell at the rich price, making a small profit, and never taking an open position. This arbitrage helped ensure the two markets remain tightly aligned. Arbitrage trading is a small-return game; it has never earned the huge returns that Leeson reported for several years.

What he really did was take market positions by entering into unmatched trades.[3] The market bets that got him in trouble were straddles—bets that the index would not move above or below a given trading band. In other words, he sold collars, which hedgers buy. When the Nikkei dropped 13 percent in January/February of 1995, Leeson's straddle positions fell out of the money quite a bit. As the Nikkei fell, he kept adding to his long position, expecting to recoup when the Nikkei rose—an outcome that did not occur. Barings' aggressive open positions had been noticed by other market dealers.

He also hid losses from these bets in an error account. He could hide the losses because he had managerial control of the trade process from inception in the front office through accounting and settlement in the back office. This control breached two cardinal rules of risk management: (1) no one independently reviewed and confirmed trading activity, and (2) there was no segregation of duties between the front and back office. The impressive part is that Mr. Leeson was able to hide his fraudulent behavior (and tens of millions in losses) for over a year. He was able to amass a $1.2-billion loss before being discovered. The Simex futures exchange finally tipped his hand by asking Barings' senior management to investigate margin shortfalls on the large loss positions held by their trader in Singapore.

EQUITY DERIVATIVES

Despite the bad press of a few unethical traders who have misused them, equity derivatives have become the most efficient tool for fine-tuning portfolios. Most of the products are designed to serve the investor community. Derivatives can tailor risk profiles of individual stocks, stock indexes, and custom baskets of equities, to achieve the asset managers' goals. Exchange-traded equity derivatives are common for the standard indexes, such as the S&P 500, at standard strikes and maturities. Over-the-counter (OTC) markets prevail for nonstandard products. The equity derivatives take the same product form as those for fixed-income securities, swaps and options, locking-in profits, creating a floor against losses, and swapping out of specific exposure.

Equity derivatives are also helping to blur the distinction between debt and equity. One product, equity-linked debt, lets an investor purchase a debt security with a coupon that blends a regular fixed-interest rate and a rate based on performance of a specified equity (index, basket, or individual stock). The investor can specify the blend he or she wants, that is, how much fixed-interest coupon he trades off for the variable return based on equity. Like debt, the principal is fully repaid but the return is linked to equity. This product provides investors with an alternative to traditional corporate securities.

Another product, an equity forward contract, is a form of borrowing that is repaid by issuing stock. Unlike most equity derivatives, this product is sold to the corporate side. It allows firms to fund projects and pay for them later with stock that they expect to increase in value. This form of financing may not last very long because it unduly levers existing shareholders' interests. If the stock's price drops, shareholders suffer massive dilution from shares issued to repay the debt. Equity forwards have contributed to at least one debacle.[4]

DEALERS AND END USERS

The equity markets are even more of a flow-based business than the FX markets. Only the largest blocks of stock move on a nonflow basis. The rest move through exchanges. Some stock exchanges, like NYSE, establish price through a single floor specialist. Other exchanges, like Nasdaq, have multiple dealers who collectively determine clearing prices. In 1997, an SEC ruling bolstered electronic communications networks (ECNs) as an alternative (electronic) exchange with no human intermediation.[5]

These exchanges incur very little financial risk because they do not take positions, and their mechanisms for settling preclude settlement risk. Dealers (block traders and arbitragers) also are not incurring substantial risk because they are not taking positions, unless they happen to be my ersatz cousin Nick.

Individual investors make up a very significant segment of the equity markets. A very large and prosperous community of brokers has been in place to serve them, but that is changing. Competitive pressures, beginning with the SEC's deregulation of trading commissions in 1975 and culminating with the recent explosion of Internet trading, have radically altered how this market segment does business. The full-value brokerage firms have been disenfranchised. Merrill Lynch's recent and reluctant capitulation to electronic brokering was inevitable. The lower transaction costs and quicker executions now available to individuals have altered their activity, too. "Day trading" has blossomed with a host of popular supporting products like trade stations and Internet chat rooms.

Wrap-Up

- In equity markets, baskets and benchmarks have become the standards for performance measurement. Managers are measured vis-à-vis indexes, for both the risks they take and the performance they achieve.

- Equity managers themselves are increasing their use of "factor models" as a way to measure the underlying risks in their portfolios. Factor models are being used for analysis in the fixed-income markets as well. They have become an investor's tool for analysis.

- Generally, with the theoretical foundation for market risk completed, the theorists moved on to credit risk. The models will certainly undergo refinements and will need expansion to cover large gaps like emerging markets and illiquid or discontinuous markets.

- Big tasks in market risk remain, especially converting practice to fully utilize the new theory. Much of the debate now gravitates around how to build effective processes.

MARKET RISK SUMMARY

 Risk has always existed in markets. What has changed in the past twenty years is our understanding of the market risks. Each market has developed, and now uses, a very extensive set of techniques that delineate and value the specific risks inside all financial deals. New products have emerged in each market to trade the specific risks. This section on market risk management has described this development and outlined how these new tools have provided a clear picture of the fabric of value in each major market.

Derivative trades are based on a zero-sum game. For each deal, when the underlying market moves, someone loses as much as someone else gains. Derivatives don't generate wealth by themselves. Their *raison d'être* is risk intermediation; they allow counterparties with low utility for certain risks to exchange them with counterparties that have more utility for them. Banks and other financial institutions pool the risks, obtaining portfolio offsets. They can trade out of the residual exposures, typically with other dealers in the OTC market.

The spokes prevail in market risk. Across all the markets, most of the risks are managed at the desk or local level. Market risk does not require aggregation to a global level to be managed effectively. However, all the disaggregated dealing for market risk brings us to the credit caveat. For all deals, the firm relies on the counterparty to perform as contracted. The next section examines this reliance on credit, along with the key management aspect of credit: It must be measured and managed globally.

CREDIT RISK MANAGEMENT

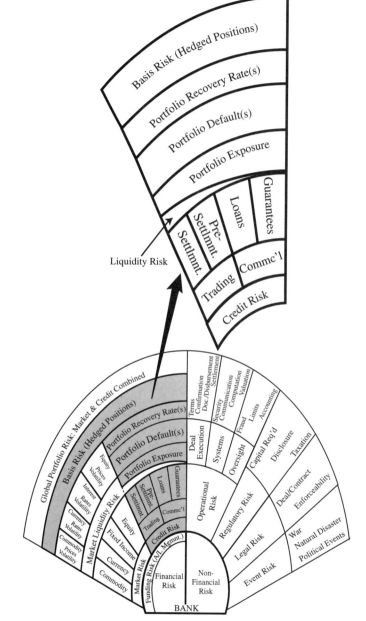

The Credit Risk Spectrum

The Schism in Credit Risk Management

9

Credit risk is currently a hot spot in risk management. The theorists and quantitative wizards who cut their teeth on market risk recently turned their focus to credit risk. Some of the models they built have radically altered how credit risk is measured and managed. These models have even stirred credit markets with new and quite controversial products—credit derivatives. The new methods have also turned the cultural schism between traders and traditional lenders into an open war over how credit risk should be managed. Before we tread onto that battlefield, let's trace the roots of the schism. A brief examination of why credit risk management is harder than market risk, coupled with a review of credit markets' recent evolution will help us understand the current conflict.

CREDIT RISK MANAGEMENT DIFFICULTIES

As noted in our introductory chapters and in Exhibit 9.1, the arcs prevail in credit risk management. Credit risk cannot be accurately measured or managed except in global portfolios. The essential elements of credit risk management are to determine exposures and to apply default/recovery considerations. These elements are incomplete unless they occur at the aggregated portfolio level for each counterparty. This global versus granular requirement contributes to the challenges credit managers face, because they must build processes that gather and analyze credit globally. This is operationally onerous and very difficult to do thoroughly with accuracy and timeliness. However, gathering the transaction data is not the heart of the difficulty.

The biggest difficulty with credit risk is how to measure it accurately. This is where a battle of new theories is clashing with

113

Exhibit 9.1 The Credit Risk Spectrum

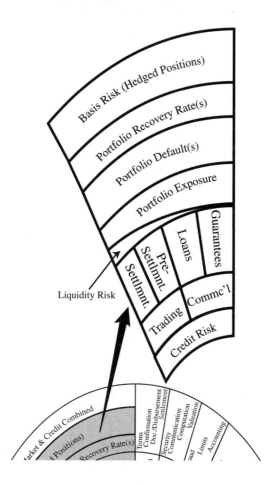

tradition. The old school has lending officers using a committee-based approach that incorporates experience, qualitative analysis, and other nonquantitative considerations. To be sure, their process includes many quantitative aspects, but it is based on a foundation of qualitative analysis. The trader view is that a study of quantitative market models provides a more accurate measure of credit risk. They have developed alternative processes based on purely quantitative foundations, including primarily market prices. To understand these conflicting premises, we need to review some of the difficulties in measuring credit risk, the recent progress in overcoming those difficulties, and changes in credit markets.

One difficulty with commercial credit is the uniqueness of each agreement. Commercial bank loans are not Big Macs™. They are highly customized legal agreements typically negotiated over a long period of time. They are chock full of special clauses and obligations—clauses about material adverse change (MAC, not Big Macs), cross-default, financial covenants, guarantees, collateral pledges, and more—that make the agreements very unfungible. Each debt agreement occupies a unique place in the borrower's capital structure, seniority, security, and so on, and therefore has a unique value/price. While these structural elements do not typically affect default characteristics, they greatly influence the exposure and the recovery profiles and hence impact the value or price of each debt agreement.

There is also the problem of determining default profiles. In the traditional lending world, a credit loss occurred when a counterparty defaulted. While defaults happen rarely, they have a huge impact. The credit loss is typically quite large. It is the infrequency of defaults, coupled with their big consequences that create a significant problem for the quantitative models. Exhibit 9.2 shows how the distribution of credit returns is very skewed when compared with market returns that tend to be more evenly distributed around their average.

This skew in credit returns is well known, but very hard to measure precisely. This graph, for example, is not from actual credit return data. The most important part of this distribution is the loss section, the fat tail on the right of the graph. This is the portion of the curve that has the biggest impact on the price/value of loans. *If credit departments could reliably measure this part of the curve for their counterparties and their portfolios, they would have a significant competitive advantage.* But, until recently, they were unable to. Occurrences of default are sufficiently infrequent to render any statistical method based on actual observations very unreliable. Returns from loans are also hard to observe because, unlike market returns, they last for years and the exposure/return profile is for the whole tenor. These two features of credit risk, long tenor and infrequency of default events, have combined to stymie any quantitative approach.

Exhibit 9.2   Credit versus Market Return Profiles

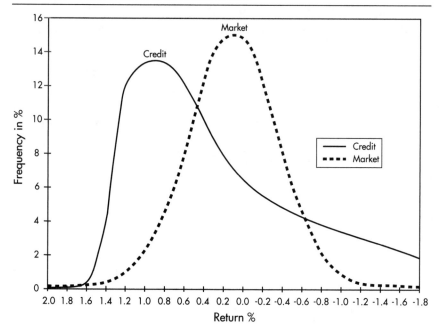

This measurement problem is further compounded by the correlation among defaults. Credit defaults and bankruptcies occur in clumps. Whole industries, geographic regions, and nations rise and fall with the economic conditions that are unique to them. When times are good, everyone makes money and pays debts. When conditions are bad, default becomes a good possibility, not just for poorly managed firms, but across whole regions and industries. Until recently, no quantitative method had a hope of incorporating all these factors and providing better predictions than a seasoned credit officer who understands these relationships intuitively, qualitatively.

A final problem, the paucity of credit data, leads us to a brief market history and the essential question that lies beneath the schism. Credit data is hard to come by. The commercial loan markets enjoyed significant regulatory protection until the late 1970s. In that time, banks' lending profit margin interest spread was sufficiently padded—if the widely cited banking aphorism, 3/3/3 (borrow at 3 percent, lend at 300 basis points, tee off at 3 P.M.), was true—to cushion them from the underlying risks. Tracking data about risk and return in this environment was unnecessary and wasteful.

In the early 1980s, as market pressures replaced regulatory protection and their best most creditworthy corporate customers disintermediated them, U.S. banks started to relate credit risk and pricing much more closely. Banks' profit margins/interest spreads dropped to below 100 basis points, while the risk in their portfolios dramatically increased.

However, out of these trying times came progress. Banks developed the operationally onerous global credit exposure systems that they needed, capturing the full details of their global facilities and outstanding credit exposures for the first time. They were able to examine and more closely manage their portfolio concentrations across industries, geographical regions, and countries. In sum, they improved their methods for tracking and using internal credit data.

Also, external credit data became available as price transparency and liquidity started to creep into the commercial lending market. The emergence of secondary loan markets helped communicate prices, as did various service companies who gathered and published loan pricing data. These service companies provide databases today of price histories, and so on, in a more automated form and are expanding to cover commercial lending in Europe, the Far East, and other parts of the globe. Syndications also experienced significant growth, providing another source for credit prices. In short, deregulation and disintermediation provided a solid push for banks to become more efficient while market forces introduced some price transparency and liquidity into credit markets.

During this same period, OTC markets and interbank trading exploded. In the 1980s and 1990s, while being disintermediated, the biggest banks found balancing growth and profit as intermediaries in the globalization of capital markets. The OTC market increased more than 25-fold since 1987. The exchanges have racked up a paltry ten-fold increase in that same period. This understates the trend, because in the past four years, OTC growth has accelerated while derivative trading on exchanges has leveled off.[1] The majority of OTC trading occurs between the top dealers. The top eight commercial banks hold 95 percent of all banking trades and the top twenty-five hold 99 percent.[2]

There are two sources for the growth. As noted in the market risk section, financial service firms provide hedging and arbitrage services to their corporate clients and then find balancing trades in the interbank or OTC market. They also use OTC markets to manage their own balance sheet and to speculate.

Signs of the pending schism became apparent when derivative deals started appearing next to loans in credit reports on exposure. Initially, credit officers had difficulty understanding exposures that rise and fall with market prices, as these trades do. As derivatives were rapidly incorporated, credit officers' understanding grew. Many credit deals today contain derivatives that engineer the market risks, for example, swapping the floating risk into fixed for the first three years of a loan agreement. Seasoned credit officers remain leery of instruments whose value shifts, especially when those shifts exceed the confidence bands that experts establish as the worst case exposure.

The schism grew apparent with the growth in OTC trading, which created a new and unique portfolio of interbank credit exposure. This portfolio requires a different management process. Exhibit 9.3 summarizes the traditional credit perspective versus the emerging trading view of credit. It shows the differences between the traditional loan and OTC markets.

Exhibit 9.3 illustrates the clash between market-sourced quantitative and traditional qualitative methods. Traders view credit risk as a spread above the risk-free curve; they see a liquid instrument whose value contains a credit component. To them, default is just a point along a continuous spectrum of value. They concede that default is a significant point, because the value of the credit asset undergoes the greatest change at default.

Most traditional lenders view credit risk as an amount that has been loaned to a client and must be repaid. While they pay attention to what value the asset might fetch on the open market, they carry it on their books at par value, with reserves for expected loss applied at deal inception. In this traditional perspective, the current market value of a loan is not relevant. The traditional lender views credit

Exhibit 9.3   The Schism in Credit Risk Markets and Management

	Loans	Guarantees	Trading
Clients/ Customers	Corporations	Corporations and Financial institutions	Banks and other Financial institutions
Products	Term loans Revolving loans Underwriting facilities, etc.	Letters of credit Trade finance Acceptances	Derivatives: Currency Interest Commodity Equity, credit, other
Credit Risk	Loss from a default or a series of defaults		Loss from change in market value including perceived credit worthiness
Analysis	How do we get repaid, deal by deal? • Cash flow • Collateral What are the chances of default? What portfolio concentrations am I generating?		What is my exposure? Where can the exposure move due to: Market price changes? A downgrade?
Features	Relatively static and illiquid exposure		Variable, liquid exposure
Mgmnt. Strategy	Originate selectively, hold to maturity		Originate anything with a good price, then trade out of inefficient assets
Mitigation	Covenants Collateral Cross-default clauses Seniority Guarantees		Netting , margining
Recent Trends	Development of secondary markets More syndications and asset sales More price transparency Credit derivatives to parse credit risk		Growth in OTC markets, increased product diversity
Latest Developments	Better measurement tools: Portfolio optimization—KMV, CreditMetrics, etc. Loan structure has value—KPMG Macroeconomics impact default rates—McKinsey		Monte Carlo simulation to measure net exposure, including natural and netting offsets

assets as largely illiquid instruments that need to be originated very selectively, because they will be held to maturity.

The rift between trading and traditional lending escalated into a war when the quantitative wizards started to model defaults. Using their trading perspective, they uncovered credit default information that resides in market data rather than looking at actual defaults. A small closely-held firm called KMV was the catalyst. It created analytical tools for credit portfolios that have altered the conventional buy-and-hold credit philosophy. In the early 1990s, KMV developed and marketed a model that predicted the default probabilities for 5,000 commercial firms in the United States. This proprietary model used equity prices, historical volatilities, and balance sheet data to predict the probability of default over one year. Analysis clearly showed that this model is better than the traditional predictor, credit ratings.

But KMV was just warming up. While enjoying success from marketing this default predictor, they developed and marketed a methodology that measured the risk/return contribution of individual assets to a credit portfolio. They developed ways to apply Markowitz's portfolio valuation theory to portfolios of credit assets. This process once again used market measures for determining the correlation of default between each credit asset in the portfolio. Other methods have since been developed that measure default probabilities and correlations of default. CreditMetrics™, CreditRisk+™, and a host of others are waiting in the wings.

 These models, which help determine each credit asset's contribution to the overall portfolio risk/return profile, help credit portfolio managers determine which credit assets to hold and which to sell. The new portfolio measures instigate credit-risk trading. The trend toward liquidity in credit markets is clear. The deployment of these models has added impetus to that liquidity as banks sell or swap out of the loans that do not contribute to their efficient risk/return profiles. Only time and perhaps a hard economic downturn can provide a real test of whether these risk-adjusted portfolios are truly more efficient.

While KMV and others have linked defaults with efficient, that is, diversified, portfolios, other model makers have made progress on other aspects of the credit problem. KPMG has created the Loan Analysis System that, among other things, provides information on how specific features within a loan agreement—collateral, MAC clauses, covenants, cross-defaults, guarantees—affect the value and, hence, the price of the agreement. On another front, McKinsey has developed a model/system that links credit defaults and losses with economic conditions. This model/system includes geographic and country considerations as well. These analytical tools are designed to help determine the value of loan assets individually and especially in portfolios. These developments influence the traditional lending side of the table in Exhibit 9.3, where some very significant credit exposures lie.

As a result, the traditional credit process in banks, particularly the biggest ones, is undergoing significant changes. Most have established, or are hustling to set up, credit portfolio management teams. These teams analyze the loan portfolios, determine inefficient assets, and adjust them through asset sales/purchases or credit derivatives. In many cases, these teams are also influencing the origination of new loans. The key question is how much of this trading approach to embrace. These methods are still in their infancy, not having been through a full credit cycle yet, so their validity is not yet proven. Similarly, the newest tool for adding and removing credit assets, credit derivatives, is even more immature and unproven. The market downturn of 1997–1998 in the Far East has provided information on how credit can be structured to improve their enforceability. It also proved the value and viability of credit derivatives. The general consensus is that purchasers of credit protection obtained the insurance they sought.

The trading side of the table is revolutionary, too, because it barely existed ten years ago. The growth of OTC derivative trading among banks over the past decade has been phenomenal. The liquidity providers in these markets have been wrestling just to stay abreast with the growth. In ten years, systems for pricing, confirming, settling, and control/accounting have been developed for the vast and growing array of derivative products. The market risk section illustrated the reasons for the explosion of products. But the growth is abating, and many signs point to a maturing market. Spreads have narrowed and profit margins for most derivative products are now razor thin. Buzz words like "straight through processing" indicate that low costs and higher efficiency are becoming more important.

The growth in credit exposure due to OTC trading is equally phenomenal. Whereas credit exposure for loans is generally static and easily measured, derivative product exposures are neither static nor easy to discern. Most liquidity providers measure their credit exposure to each other by adding it up deal by deal. This grossly overstates the real exposure they are generating. Further growth in OTC trading is constrained by present methods for measuring this credit exposure. It is also constrained by how slowly the participants measure the exposure. Loan exposures don't shift very much and monthly reports were usually sufficient for banks to track these activities. On the derivative trading side, however, even daily measures of exposure are not sufficient, particularly with the shorter tenor instruments.

WRAP-UP

- Credit risk management is hot, with two revolutions going on.
- The explosive growth of interbank OTC trading has forced participants to start measuring global credit exposure on a much more timely basis. The big challenge is that the credit exposure fluctuates. They need to measure it on a portfolio rather than a deal-by-deal basis. Chapter 10 covers this revolution.
- Models that predict default probability and the correlations of default are revolutionizing the traditional credit process. Chapter 11 covers this revolution.

Credit Risk Management for Trading

10

Fifteen years ago, the concept of credit risk for trading was pretty much covered by limits on placements between banks. Placements are short-term interbank loans that facilitate liquidity. Although interbank placements can be quite large, they were and remain a small part of overall credit exposure and risk. Banks' credit exposure to each other was not significant compared to their credit exposure from commercial lending. By 1987 derivative product volumes had become a very notable new source of credit exposure. Exhibit 10.1 illustrates the growth over the past ten years and how OTC trades have come to predominate.[1]

Until recently, ISDA was perhaps the only source for Global OTC derivative activity data. However, the Bank of International

Exhibit 10.1   Annual National Volume of Derivative Trades

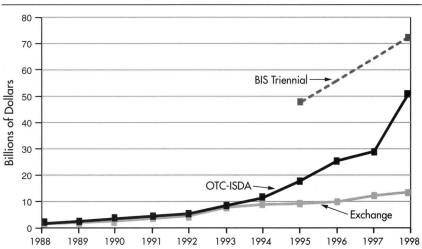

Settlements (BIS) conducted a broader survey of derivative activity in March 1995 and June 1998. BIS's broader studies indicate that OTC derivative market growth may be larger than ISDA found.[2] The two BIS surveys also indicate that growth among reporting dealers has leveled off. The continued growth in OTC trading is being created by other financial institutions, as shown in Exhibit 10.2. The survey notes that "Many of these counterparties have been leveraged funds, which have become major players in the OTC derivatives market."[3] It is quite likely that the torrid growth in OTC activity with this class of counterparties has cooled off after September 1998.

Product diversity over the past decade has also shown tremendous growth. This growth creates an enormous strain on operations. When volumes are doubling every couple of years and a new product is being developed every couple of weeks, the support systems become obsolete as quickly as they can be built. On the operational/administrative side, the personnel are in constant flux, coping with the volume and diversity growth. Trading operations have struggled to keep pace. So how does credit risk, which heretofore was not an important aspect for trading, get considered? Answer: Not very well.

Exhibit 10.2   OTC Market Share Changes 1995 to 1998

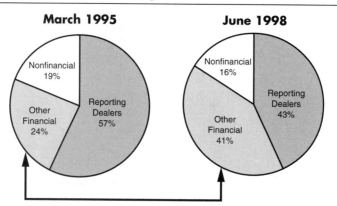

THE VARIABLE EXPOSURE PROBLEM

Credit exposures for these trades have grown at the same rate. A big problem with derivative trades is that their market value varies. This feature makes them wonderful instruments for hedging arbitrage and speculation. However, it generates quite a headache for the people measuring credit exposure. A swap that was originated at the money, may, over its life, come to have significant mark-to-market value, or MTM. Each deal with positive market value contributes to credit exposure. The holder of that positive MTM is counting on the counterparty to deliver that value over the remaining life of the deal.

Credit risk management techniques for these products must accommodate this variable exposure feature. With other credit products like traditional loans, the exposure is stable, so the management techniques focus on portfolio defaults and recoveries. Here in traded products, an extra effort is required to measure the variable exposure. In our look at credit risk for trading, the *exposure* component must be measured accurately first. Then default and recovery considerations can be factored in to get at credit *risk*.

PRE-SETTLEMENT AND SETTLEMENT RISK

Most trading institutions (banks and securities firms) have created vast arrays of credit limits to cover trading activities. They have parsed credit risk into many pieces and typically measure/manage it at a very granular level. They have allocated it along product lines, geography, and even tenor. This is very inefficient for two reasons. It is difficult to reallocate trade limits to match shifting patterns of trade, and measuring credit risk on a disaggregated level fails to capture portfolio effects, which are quite significant among OTC dealers.

 But, as capital markets have globalized, there is a clear trend to measure and manage credit at an aggregated level. At the global level, credit risk for traded products has two components, settlement and pre-settlement risk. Pre-settlement risk is the risk of a counterparty defaulting before a deal has settled, that is, before value exchange has been initiated. Settlement risk is, quite logically, the risk of a counterparty defaulting as a deal is being settled—a counterparty defaults after instructions to transfer value to settle a trade have been initiated.

The rest of this chapter examines trends in settlement and pre-settlement risk management and projects those trends, predicting how scarce credit resources will be allocated at financial firms in the future.

Settlement Risk

On June 26, 1974, a small bank in Germany, Bankhaus ID Herstatt KGaA, which had about $60 million in FX trades settling that day, went bankrupt and closed down. A number of banks had issued payment to Herstatt to settle their FX trades. They did not receive the corresponding currency payments from Herstatt. These failed receipts caused a liquidity squeeze in the markets, and many banks delayed payment on subsequent transactions. Several days of increasing payment disruption followed. Before payment gridlock set in, regulators stepped in and refereed (perhaps strong-armed) an agreement to keep subsequent settlements moving. This incident served as a wake-up call to the industry and its regulators. Bank Herstatt's legacy, aside from a spate of court actions that helped clarify settlement law, has been to give its name to this settlement risk.

Gross Value Exchange   The heart of the settlement risk problem lies in foreign exchange markets where gross value is exchanged and the settlement process is not coordinated. This creates settlement exposures, which are a multiple of the net value being exchanged. In FX trading, a specified amount of one currency is delivered in exchange for a specified amount of another currency. Although the full amount of each currency gets exchanged, and hence is at risk in settlement, the difference in value being exchanged is typically quite small. FX settlement, however, because it occurs on a gross basis, amplifies the exposure.

The settlement conventions for many other OTC products reduce the exposure by settling on a net value basis. For example, on a simple swap, the fixed and floating payment amounts are netted and only the difference between the two is transferred. The netting may even cover broader sets of deals. For example, commodity dealers typically net the settlement of all trades in a given metal. One wire transfer payment (net) gets sent to settle hundreds of trades.

Uncoordinated Exchange Process   The uncoordinated aspect of FX settlements also contributes to exposure by increasing the time period of settlement exposure. Each counterparty delivers the funds to the other at some point during the settlement day. When the trades span hemispheres and many time zones as these trades frequently do, the delivery of one currency can be hours ahead of the receipt of the other currency.

Other trade settlement processes where gross values are exchanged have coordinated the exchange of value to minimize this risk. Securities trades are typically settled through clearing houses, which hold delivery until payment is received. These delivery-versus-payment (DVP) systems reduce settlement exposure to almost nil. Residual settlement exposure remains from the clearing houses' operations and the level of capital they carry to absorb losses from mistakes.

Until recently, foreign exchange trades have had no mechanisms to net or coordinate their settlement process. This is probably because FX trading originated among the global banks. When the trading activity is predominated by the largest, most creditworthy banks (despite Herstatt), there isn't a perceived need to protect settlements against default.

A Growing Problem   So what has happened in the twenty-five years since Herstatt rang the alarm? FX daily settlement volumes have soared over 1,000 fold.[4] An average of $2.3 trillion (all denominations) is transferred each day to settle foreign exchange trades.[5] Numbers that large are hard to grasp, so think of the annual U.S. GDP coursing through global payment systems every three or four days from FX trading. Regulators, including the Federal Reserve Bank, other central banks, and global banks like BIS, have studied the problem and conducted surveys to better understand it and to track trends to manage it. They have uncovered disturbing information. Settlement exposure in FX trades is typically for longer than initially thought.[6] It varies a great deal, depending on currencies traded and bank operations. It typically lasts overnight, and for certain currency pairs, it can span up to five days. This longer-than-expected exposure occurs as much from lags in operations as from time zone differentials.

But the news is not all bad. Many of the payment systems used for settling FX have been revised to mitigate risk. They have accelerated the pace of transfers, set intraday caps on account balances, extended hours of operation to overlap with other payment systems overseas, and moved to real time gross settlement (RTGS). Documentation standards have been introduced and adapted. Also, experiments with netting and coordinating settlements have been initiated. Early initiatives to settle on a bilateral and multilateral basis have provided valuable experience for the most recent and most ambitious initiative to resolve this problem, continuous linked settlement (CLS).[7] The CLS solution is not the only way to solve the problem. One set of banks proposed contracts for differences (CFDs).[8] The CFD alternative may prevail if the ambitious CLS initiative falters.

Continuous Linked Settlement

The CLS initiative germinated in 1995 when a group of major FX trading banks called the G20 formulated this private sector initiative. The CLS bank serves as a special bank clearinghouse whose sole purpose is to settle FX trades. Each participant has a single account at the bank. The account contains various currency sub-accounts. Each FX trade will continue to be settled on a gross basis, but the payment of each leg will occur simultaneously, on a payment-versus-payment (PVP) basis. Like delivery versus payment (DVP), PVP will reduce settlement exposure to almost nil. In addition, while the trades will settle on a gross basis, each participant will pay and receive funds on a net basis. This means that each participating bank only pays in the currencies it owes on a net basis. After settlement, the bank will receive payments in each currency in which it has a net credit balance. This will reduce the liquidity requirements of each participant.

This daily settlement process will start at the same time all across the globe, which is late afternoon in the Far East, around midday in Europe, and quite early morning in the western hemisphere.

Simulations of the process have shown that a very large proportion of all payments can be settled when all participants ante up part of their net payments. The coordinated settlement process allows the trades to clear and settle quickly. Some trades, which would yield account balances that exceed risk limits, are delayed until conditions change sufficiently to clear them. Certain large trades wait until new payments are made or net account balances from other trade settlements become large enough for them to clear. It is anticipated that the whole process can be completed in a two- or three-hour window.[9]

The number and variety of obstacles to creating this process is enormous. There are significant operational, process, and control issues when tens of millions of trades across many currencies totaling more than $3 billion are involved. There are legal and regulatory considerations with every participating country, currency, and central bank. There are very significant technical challenges, including secure, reliable communications around the globe, and very significant processing requirements in terms of speed, volume, accountability, and reliability. This is not a process that can skip a day due to technical problems.

The benefits in risk reduction and increased liquidity are quite enormous, too. Over forty major FX banks have agreed to participate, giving CLS the critical mass to be successful, provided all the other challenges are met. Although the exact currencies that will be included in this process have not yet been determined, CLS will certainly cover all the major ones. The concept stages and specification stages have largely been completed. Design and build stages are underway with a view toward implementation sometime in the year 2000. That date will probably slip, but the tangible progress that CLS has made over the past year or two probably exceeds all progress made in the intervening years since Bankhaus Herstatt forced awareness of the problem onto the banking community.

Pre-Settlement Exposure

When derivative instruments were first developed, pre-settlement risk was typically estimated using a percentage of notional for each year of the deal. There are some banks, particularly in Europe, that continue this practice. However, most banks have evolved to the mark-to-market plus add-on (MTM+) methodology.

Mark-to-Market Plus Add-On

In MTM+, each deal is marked to market (or modeled in thin markets). Then an add-on representing the worst possible change in value is calculated. This add-on calculation is based on three deal parameters: remaining tenor, notional amount, and volatility of the underlying factors (interest rate, exchange rate, index rate, stock quote, etc.). Each bank typically has a proprietary methodology for calculating the add-on. Virtually all use past market prices to calculate future possible value changes to a predetermined level of confidence. For example, there is only a 2.5 percent chance that the deal market value will exceed this worst-case number. MTM+ captures, deal by deal, the potential worst-case change in exposure over its remaining term. The exposure for each deal is described by a rectangle, with height equal to worst-case exposure and width equal to tenor. These rectangles of pre-settlement exposure are then stacked to provide a profile of the worst-case exposure for the portfolio of deals. Exhibit 10.3 provides an illustration of this method.

Exhibit 10.3   Portfolio Exposure Using MTM+

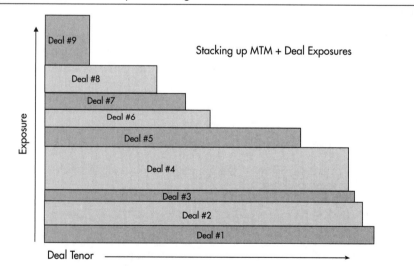

This practice has the following advantages:

▪ *Operationally easy.* This method is easy to install. Both the calculation routines and the methods of aggregation fit into existing operations. Global bank credit reporting mechanisms are geared to measure credit exposure deal by deal and then sum them across locations. With the development of MTM+, a new ruler was installed in the existing operational and reporting framework. Certainly there are complications. Exotic deals, structured deals, and linked groups of deals typically require special MTM+ calculations and special handling. Also, MTM+ exposure is more volatile than traditional credit exposure and needs to be calculated/reported more frequently. But MTM+ fits into the existing operations and reporting structures reasonably well.

▪ *Better than notional.* MTM+ was a large improvement on the prior percent-of-notional method, because many factors that contribute to exposure (current market value, market rate sensitivities, and deal tenor) are incorporated. In addition, this method is conceptually straightforward. Traders can describe it and justify the basis for it, while credit officers can understand it and critically assess it. MTM+ bridges the communication and cultural chasm between trading and credit that exists in many banks.

▪ *Same control parameters.* MTM+, like all prior credit controls, is highly divisible along all the parameters that credit has typically wanted: product, counterparty, geography, and tenor. The MTM+ method allows credit to continue with very finite controls, whether they are appropriate or not.

MTM+ has disadvantages as well:

▪ *Wrong—except at one point.* Each deal's worst-case exposure hits a peak somewhere in its life. Long-term FX deals typically peak at maturity, while swaps peak partway to maturity. The MTM+ method doesn't consider exposure variations within the deal lifecycle. It plunks down a rectangle of exposure sufficiently high to clear the peak exposure and forces that exposure onto the whole life of the deal, regardless of how the exposure may fluctuate. One way to fly a helicopter coast to coast is to fly the whole way at an altitude sufficient to clear the highest peak. This is not very efficient. Even worse, in some cases, MTM+ is adjusted to cover the average exposure rather than the peak. This adjustment makes it less wrong most of the time. However, using our helicopter analogy, when it is wrong, the outcome is not just a loss of efficiency. Exhibits 10.4 and 10.5 illustrate how the MTM+ method overstates exposure for two typical three-year trades, an FX forward and a fixed/floating interest rate swap, with semi-annual payments.

▪ *No offsets or netting.* MTM+ also overstates exposure because it fails to consider portfolio effects. The worst-possible exposure for a portfolio of deals is usually less than the sum of worst cases (deal by deal). Long and short positions in highly correlated currencies provide significant natural exposure offsets. A bank that is long Euros and short Swiss Francs to the same counterparty is generating significantly less pre-settlement

Exhibit 10.4 FX Forward: MTM+ Exposure versus Worst-Case Exposure

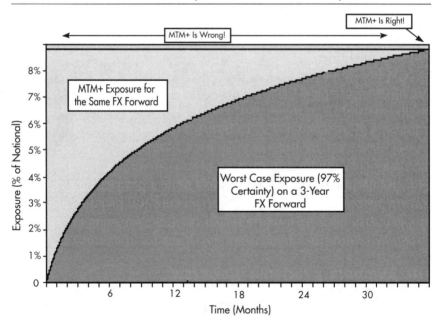

Exhibit 10.5   Interest Rate Swap: MTM+ versus Worst-Case Exposure

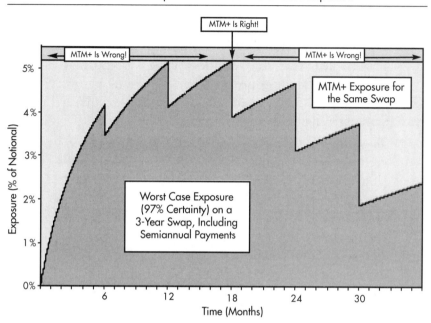

exposure than the MTM+ method calculates. These ameliorating credit offsets can exist among all deals in a portfolio.

Similarly, MTM+ overstates exposure because it fails to consider netting agreements. The net market value of all trades between major dealers is usually a small fraction of gross exposures in each direction, that is, the sum of all trades with positive market value and the sum of all trades with negative market value. Closeout netting takes advantage of this feature to reduce pre-settlement exposure. The netting agreement allows each counterparty to close out its trades on a net value basis. If a closeout netting agreement is triggered, usually from a default, the counterparty pairs close out their book of mutual trades based on the net market value of all trades between them. The deals that have positive market value for one counterparty (they contain pre-settlement exposure for that counterparty) are offset by the deals that have negative value.

∎ *Overstates capital.* Money center banks are developing and using capital return models to measure performance across business lines. The methods for allocating capital under these models are increasingly adjusted for the risks each business is taking. Using MTM+ results in a significant overstatement of the trading portfolio's credit exposure. The trading business gets socked with an over-allocation of capital to cover this credit risk. Trading profit, when measured against this inflated capital requirement, yields a deflated return and understates trading performance.

- *Too granular.* This method blurs the distinction between credit exposure management and other risks, such as operational and product. MTM+ can be selective deal by deal, product by product, and location by location. This specificity tempts credit officers to over-manage. It distracts them from their primary responsibility, which is to define the institution's maximum exposure appetite by tenor. Recently, the director of credit at a large bank noted that he had effectively shut down all trading in the Paris treasury because the employees didn't know what they were doing there. His concern and willingness to fix a problem are admirable. However, credit limits are not the right tool for correcting the perceived deficiency, whatever it was.

- *Air in the measure.* Many banks tacitly accept that MTM+ overstates exposure. They subsequently allow for the limits to grow way past the institution's real credit risk appetite. The head of risk management for trading at another bank recently observed that everyone is aware of the air in the limits. He was comfortable approving exposures that were much greater than the bank's appetite because, total utilization at any one time was only about half. This risk manager's tolerance for approximations was surprising. Credit officers know that as an institution approaches insolvency, it draws fully on all available lines. Yes, there is air in the measure, but that air goes out at just the wrong time—when the bubble bursts.

- *Administrative overhead.* MTM+ has resulted in significant extra administrative overhead. Treasuries frequently have to reallocate credit limits to match shifting trading patterns. Many global banks have created a trading credit administration group whose major role is monitoring utilization and reallocating limits.

■ *Activities constrained.* The growth in FX and derivatives trading has bumped into credit constraints. Banks are quite uncomfortable with pre-settlement exposures to other banks that start to equal their core capital. Further growth in trading activity is largely constrained by pre-settlement risk as it is currently measured. Many initiatives are being taken to ameliorate the problem. The growth of margin agreements has capped pre-settlement risk theoretically. It has introduced a host of other issues: liquidity requirements, collateral hypothecation, and collateral rehypothecation, and so on. A more accurate measurement technique is clearly needed for the liquidity providers in these markets.

MONTE CARLO SIMULATION

 Global banks are migrating to Monte Carlo simulation methods that project the worst-case exposure at the portfolio level, including enforceable closeout netting agreements. They are achieving very significant benefits from this move. This trend appears more fully developed in North American-based banks, but is clearly afoot everywhere. Briefly, this involves the following:

1. Capture all deals in a single global portfolio by relationship.

2. Group the deals into nettable portfolios within the relationship portfolios.

3. Simulate a large number of possible future market scenarios. For example, starting with current prices and using the past correlation between those prices, project a number of possible paths the market could take. Each path is an equally likely and internally consistent (arbitrage free) projection of market prices at specific times, for example, one day, one week, one month in the future.

4. Determine the value of each deal in your portfolio along every projected pathway.

5. Aggregate those deal valuations, using netting, and so on into portfolio valuations for each counterparty at each time point in each path. With 5,000 pathways, you obtain a distribution of 5,000 possible portfolio values for each relationship, at each future time point in the projection.

6. Rank those portfolio valuations/exposures and select the one that matches the confidence level you wish. If you want 99 percent confidence, use the fiftieth worst case out of 5,000 at each future time point.

This brief description greatly simplifies what actually occurs, but is sufficient for seeing the benefits and operational implications. The mathematicians can provide many more quantitative details of how the process works.

Monte Carlo Advantages

Just like MTM+ there are advantages and disadvantages to Monte Carlo simulations:

- *More accurate exposure.* Exposure profiles generated from Monte Carlo simulations reflect the natural offsets and allowable netting within the portfolio. This method also provides exposure through time starting with current MTM. Each subsequent move in portfolio exposure depends on whether the factors pulling it down (deal amortization and deal maturation) outweigh factors forcing it up (market price moves and volatility changes). In short, this method has none of the MTM+ inaccuracies. Whereas MTM+ methodology overstates the actual exposure, simulation models may slightly understate it because they typically assume normal market returns.

- *Lower exposure for bank counterparties.* Reductions in measured exposure vary with each relationship's portfolio and the related legal agreement's netting. The biggest reductions occur between money center banks, securities firms, and other market dealers who have large trading volume and a diverse book.

For those portfolios, the typical reduction in exposure is 50 percent to 60 percent. Frequently, 80 percent reductions have been achieved. Exhibit 10.6 illustrates this difference between MTM+ and Monte Carlo simulation exposure profiles. Monte Carlo simulations wash away the sediment of MTM+ methodology to reveal the contours of the relationship's underlying non-offsetable, non-nettable exposure.

There is a caveat. Exposure reductions for corporate relationships are much smaller, and in some cases, are negligible. This is because trades with corporate relationships are typically all one direction, say, dollars for DM, or fixed for floating. Their portfolios contain few to no offsetting trades.

▪ *Reduced capital requirements, better performance.* The method for allocating economic capital to measure performance varies from bank to bank. Many don't do it at all. Some use the aggregated trading portfolio to determine the level of capital required for credit while others use a measure of the credit exposure in each relationship profile. When banks convert to measuring credit exposure with Monte Carlo simulations, they have significantly increased the trading line's measured performance (return on risk capital) by reducing the capital required for credit risk. These banks are also well positioned

Exhibit 10.6 MTM+ versus Monte Carlo Simulation Portfolio

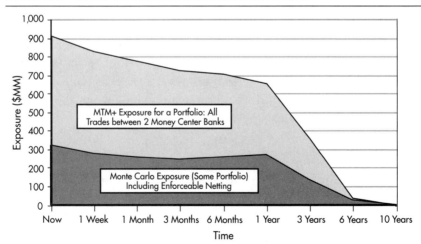

to reduce their regulatory capital requirements for credit when the regulators finally allow it.

■ *Operational simplification.* The need for allocations and reallocations disappears when transactions are globally pooled and exposure/availability is determined at only a global level. All trading locations share equally in the availability on a first-come first-served basis. Also, limit compliance monitoring is greatly simplified. When current credit availability is delivered directly to the traders in the front office, trades that cause a limit excess can be identified as they happen.

■ *Optimization.* When the marginal impact (change in exposure) of a prospective deal is delivered to the traders' desks, along with the risk-based cost of that exposure, activities are optimized. This process provides the mechanism for incorporating credit cost into trading activity. A price for incremental pre-settlement exposure by counterparty tenor can be established and built into traders' P/L. The invisible hand that Adam Smith first described would then direct incremental deal flow to the highest margin products. This "what-if" capability, delivered to the desks along with other analytical tools, has been implemented at one firm and is being built at several others.

This process also provides insights that can improve or optimize trading relationships. One global bank recently showed a trading partner how a handful of derivative trades, all emanating from a minor unit within the trading partner's organization, were using a huge proportion of the available pre-settlement line, crowding out more profitable trading. Both sides in the trading relationship gained when the trading partner reversed those trades.

■ *Better control/better MIS.* Numerous risk management benefits occur when a global Monte Carlo simulation process is in place. Data repositories for transactions, customer information, valuation libraries, market price histories, and analytical routines can all be constructively tapped to better understand the financial risks of the organization. However, these are secondary considerations to the primary benefits—more trading and optimized trading.

Monte Carlo Disadvantages

There are also disadvantages and risks in using Monte Carlo simulation. They are:

- *Global process/higher standards.* Monte Carlo simulations have enormous data requirements, all on a centralized basis. The major sets of data include transaction, customer, market, and model. Global financial firms are not typically able to provide these data sets as required. Obtaining timely, accurate transaction data is the biggest challenge because so many sources must be tapped. *Each trading location or group has to provide complete and accurate transaction data on a timely and consistent basis.* Sources for all other data sets are typically built centrally. Most global banking operations are not well equipped to provide deal details in a standardized format with the degree of reliability required.

    The level of data accuracy, reliability, and timeliness needed to support a local process is lower than that for a global process. There are numerous situations in which data problems are accommodated within the local processes, typically through manual adjustments. However, most chronic problems cannot easily be accommodated in a standard global process. For example, it may take several days to correctly capture a complex, multilegged derivative trade in the local systems. A local process that calculates local usage against a local limit can adapt to this shortcoming much more easily than a global process.

    The output works on a different operational paradigm as well. Credit availability, which equals the global limit minus calculated exposure for each tenor, must be delivered promptly to all traders globally. Mechanisms to capture incremental trades and promptly reflect them in the global utilization must also be built. This is considerably different from the local or regional operations that are in place today.

▪ *Lack of product allocation mechanism.* The MTM+ methodology allows product managers to use credit limits to steer trading to their higher margin products. This ability to allocate credit by product disappears when you move to Monte Carlo simulations. Trading management must develop other more appropriate mechanisms to direct trading activity within their product line.

▪ *Very difficult model.* While the MTM+ methodology has model risk in it, Monte Carlo models have considerably more. They typically assume that the historic price relationships, that is, correlations, will remain static through the forecast years. The models also frequently assume a normal distribution of market returns, which is known to be untrue, particularly over longer time horizons. With Monte Carlo simulation, model risk is significant and requires ongoing consideration. Time will provide data that can validate or disprove the model's validity. Doubtless, enhancements and improved models will be developed and implemented.

▪ *Project failure.* Globalizing any process contains significant risk of failure from the scope of such an enterprise. How do you achieve harmony and uniformity across the many locations? Creating a global Monte Carlo simulation compounds that risk with elevated data quality requirements.

Despite these risks, many global institutions are undertaking to capture and manage their credit exposure for trading on a global level using Monte Carlo simulations. It is a difficult and challenging process. However, it is especially difficult and challenging because of cultural and political obstacles. In the past, trading activities at financial firms have thrived when managed on a decentralized basis. Local office heads, when given the authority, could quickly adapt their activities to the local market conditions and opportunities. This grew a strong decentralized and independent culture, which pervades trading management. A strong set of incentives—both carrots and sticks—are required to achieve cooperation and harmony across these regional fiefdoms.

CREDIT RISK VERSUS EXPOSURE

As noted earlier, the first thing to capture in trading is the exposure that can move. Capturing pre-settlement exposure at the global portfolio level provides significant insights and benefits. However, close on the heels of exposure should be default considerations. One dollar of incremental exposure to a given counterparty may be less desirable than ten dollars of incremental risk to another. The probabilities of default drive this consideration.

It is vital to determine credit risk so that incremental trading can be guided appropriately. There are a host of new tools for measuring default probabilities and default correlations. Although these tools and techniques are very applicable to derivative portfolios, they have had the largest impact on traditional lending. They are discussed in the next chapter on credit risk management for lending. These new default models are the key for pricing/valuing incremental credit exposure regardless of its source (loans or trades).

CREDIT LIMIT PROBLEMS

Currently, credit risk for trading is almost universally controlled through limits against measures of exposure. This is similar to a command economy, which sets quotas. An outcome in command economies is low-quality products that fail to meet market needs. Similarly, using limits for trading takes away the incentive to find the appropriate product mix. Traders can use scarce credit resources on low-margin products as easily as on high-margin products. Not charging for credit leads to indiscriminate usage. There is nothing to stop the huge volumes of low margin trades.

In addition, not charging for credit creates arbitrage opportunities within the firm. Traders can, with minimal effort, convert market risk to credit risk. There are situations where they can reduce charges for market risk by converting it to credit risk. This incremental credit risk is a cost to the firm, but not directly to them. Not charging appropriately for credit risk creates incentives for traders that are not consistent with the firm's objectives.

There are operational considerations regarding limits as well. The limit monitoring/enforcement process at most firms is creaky and operationally onerous. Typically, the report of credit limit excesses is produced overnight in each local back office. An administrator goes through this report to identify/explain the incorrect entries, usually over half the entries. There are numerous sources for the erroneous entries—different naming conventions between front and back office, limit reallocations that aren't reflected in the back office systems, expired limits, and so on. Then, toward the end of the trading day, traders are asked to recall and explain apparent trading excesses that occurred the prior day. A day is a huge time frame to traders. They generally prefer to focus on current market conditions and are reasonably loath to recall and explain circumstances that occurred twenty-four hours ago.

CHARGING FOR CREDIT

The solution to this problem is to drive the cost for credit down to a more granular level. There are several real cases where credit charges, based on marginal impact to the global portfolio, are driven to the desk level. This creates opportunities for win-win situations. In some cases, a firm can reduce both market risk and credit risk by laying off market risk with the right counterparty.

Although the process to charge for credit exposure can be implemented relatively easily, providing the requisite analytical tools is much more difficult. Traders need to see the credit cost of a deal before they do it. They need to be able to find the low-cost counterparty for laying off the risk of a pending deal. They need to know which trades will add to a counterparty's pre-settlement exposure and which will reduce it. Also, the lawyers and credit departments need to be able to examine a global portfolio under various netting and margin/collateral schemes to see what agreements should be negotiated with each counterparty and where to deploy their negotiating resources. All these analytical insights, based on the marginal impact of credit risk on the global counterparty portfolio, have to be delivered in a timely way to all desktops. That is a very tall order.

Exhibit 10.7   Conceptual Framework for Incorporating Credit Risk in Trading Activities

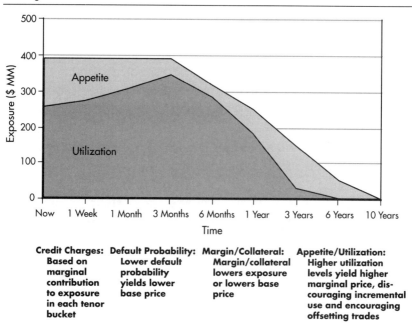

Credit Charges:	Default Probability:	Margin/Collateral:	Appetite/Utilization:
Based on marginal contribution to exposure in each tenor bucket	Lower default probability yields lower base price	Margin/collateral lowers exposure or lowers base price	Higher utilization levels yield higher marginal price, discouraging incremental use and encouraging offsetting trades

Exhibit 10.7 illustrates the conceptual framework for pricing credit exposure for trading process.

The framework needs to incorporate default probability, deal tenor, netting, collateral, and the contribution of specific deals/subportfolios to exposure. The scheme depicted charges for the marginal contribution of each deal or portfolio of deals to the overall credit exposure within various tenor buckets. The marginal contribution includes consideration for netting and offsets. The basic charge incorporates default probability and considerations for credit portfolio concentrations. As credit exposure approaches the firm's overall appetite, charges go up, discriminating toward the higher margin products. Collateral agreements can either cap the potential exposure or lower the base price.

This framework is conceptual, but many firms are moving closer to it. The first Monte Carlo systems that were developed and implemented did not contemplate this requirement. Five years ago when they were created, it was considered a coup just to run a simulation in less than twenty-four hours. Computing speeds have accelerated considerably since then. More recent initiatives start to deliver the analytical capabilities needed to move to this scheme. At several firms, the new credit exposure profile from every significant trade is calculated before the deal is concluded. At one firm, a prospective deal is tested against all liquidity providers, noting the counterparties where pre-settlement exposure increases the smallest amount. For some deals with certain counterparties, exposure can even drop, due to offsets/netting. Finally, one financial service firm charges for credit risk while also maintaining credit limits. Desks incur a cost (on their P&L) for credit exposure based on their portfolio's marginal contribution to the overall credit exposure. The charges are levied within tenor buckets and are based on current credit market prices (credit spreads) for each counterparty. Credit limits for trading have become a secondary concern at this firm.

It is curious that charges for credit risk occur in all markets except the internal ones inside banks and securities firms. This shortcoming is understandable, considering the explosive growth of OTC derivatives and the complexity of these products whose exposure varies. However, this deficiency has lead to very inefficient use of scarce credit resources, significant trader arbitrage, and high operational overhead. The firms that are correcting this deficiency will perform better. Appropriate credit charges coupled with analytical tools can eliminate the inefficiencies and arbitrage within the firm. They align trader's incentives with the firm's overall objectives. When an efficient internal credit market is put in place, trading based on optimized incentives occurs, unfettered by limits.

SYSTEMIC CONCERNS

We now have many examples of rogue traders using derivative trades to rack up huge losses or even bankrupt major institutions. These fiascoes have certainly given derivatives a bad name. But in all the cases, culpability rests more with management than it does with demon derivatives. Recurrences can be stopped cold with effective management control. Each new debacle provides more guidance on what not to do and what management should do. Let's step back from the power that derivatives give to individuals, for we will certainly learn to manage that through time, and try to examine the benefits and risks they bestow on markets and on the dealers in those markets.

Derivatives have forced more efficiency and liquidity in markets. They allow capital users to find the lowest cost of funds through arbitrage. They allow investors to quickly move to the highest perceived returns, risk adjusted. They have bound capital markets more closely together, forcing them to compete. The whole globe has benefited from these market efficiencies. However, we have recently seen the dark side of integrated capital markets. The contagion that started in southeast Asia and rippled around the globe shows how much more closely bound our new markets are. A market problem in one country can cause heretofore unseen consequences in markets a whole hemisphere away. We have not yet fully absorbed this development and its implications.

Finally, derivatives allow market makers to fine tune their market risks and parse it out to each other. With derivatives, banks and securities firms can match their assets and liabilities with much finer precision. They can reduce various market risks. However, on the dark side, each interbank trade becomes a threat of credit exposure to each other. The resulting fabric of commitments among dealers helps reduce the risks at each individual firm, while concomitantly increasing the chance that a single failure could bring them all down. Increased OTC trading has bonded the major traders together in an unprecedented web of credit exposure. The failure of one major player could topple them all. This systemic concern grows sharper with the recent boom in credit derivatives. These products directly circumvent the capital rules established by Basle, and have resulted in higher leverage against credit risks. They also dilute the originating institution's interest (usually a bank) in keeping credit watch over the borrower.[10]

We have seen many studies of systemic risk, particularly of settlement risk. Attempts to consider the interbank pre-settlement risks that have arisen from OTC trades are full of conjecture and not capturing much attention. This systemic risk won't be understood until events focus our attention and help us learn, as Herstatt did for settlement risk.

WRAP-UP

- Credit Risk for trading is starting to be managed along two parameters, settlement and pre-settlement risk.

- Settlement processes are effective in controlling settlement risks in all markets except FX where the ambitious CLS project is underway.

- Most financial service firms are building Monte Carlo-based processes to measure pre-settlement exposure on a global basis capturing the benefits from portfolio offsets and netting.

- Some firms are creating internal markets to manage pre-settlement risk. The market process is much more effective than limits at allocating scarce credit resources and eliminating internal arbitrage.

- Derivative trading has created an unprecedented degree of interdependence among the dealers. This fabric of dependence should be examined by the regulators.

Credit Risk Management for Traditional Lending

11

Traditional commercial lending is undergoing very radical changes. The new perspective that the traders have brought to the table is driving this change. They see a loan as a somewhat liquid asset whose risk/return contribution to the overall portfolio can be measured. This has huge implications that are starting to be felt across the full spectrum of commercial lending.

THE TRADITIONAL CREDIT PROCESS: COMMERCIAL LOANS

Until the early 1970s, the traditional process for originating commercial credit was quite extensive and exhaustive, a natural outcome of buying assets that will remain on the books for years. Units within the bank, typically organized around industry, sometimes with a geographical component, originated and administered loans as part of a broad service menu, building a relationship with each corporation. The other bank services included cash management, treasury, clearing, custody, and other activities that were generally fee-based.

The overall lending process contained several major steps (Exhibit 11.1). The origination step carried through to the signing of a lending agreement. The documentation/disbursement piece picked up from there, ensuring that all the other requisite documentation like articles of incorporation, board authorizations, and so on was perfected prior to any disbursement. Then credit administration continued with the routine loan support functions. Although portfolio management was part of the original process, it has undergone considerable metamorphosis and increased in importance over the past twenty years. Problem loan recognition and workouts cycled

Exhibit 11.1   The Commercial Credit Process in the 1970s

Credit Origination
Marketing: Targets/risk criteria
Structuring
Pricing
Analysis/risk rating
Approval
Syndication

Documentation and Disbursement
Credit Administration
Disbursements and payments
Agency work
Collateral operations
Covenant monitoring
Credit file management
Credit renewals and reviews
Reporting (regulatory and MIS)
Accounting and P&L

Portfolio Management
Appetite by industry/geography
Capture exposure and outstandings by:
    Counterparty and relationship
    Industry
    Geography
    Risk rating

Problem Loan Recognition
Risk rating downgrades
Watch list activities

Loan Workouts
Restructures, charge-offs, etc.
Bankruptcy and litigation
Asset management/liquidation

---

in importance as various economic and industry business cycles occurred.

Credit origination started with the marketing plan where target relationships were identified and tied into risk/revenue profiles drawn up for the lending area. The marketing effort involved ongoing visits from the relationship manager and supporting team members. The client's capital needs were analyzed, and matching loan agreements were structured. The approval process could be quite lengthy, particularly for the largest and longest tenor loans because they required review and approval up through a chain to the most senior credit officers. Throughout this process, the syndication team may have been involved, particularly for the largest loans.

This process even contained a management development/career track within it. Each year, selected set of candidates would go through a credit training program typically in-house and then move to credit analysis positions in various lending areas. Each trainee would gain responsibilities, as merited, moving on to support client visits, deal structuring, and so on. Eventually the program lead to a position in relationship management or credit management. Typically, along the path to those positions, the candidates rotated through assignments in various bank credit areas/operations like, workouts, credit review, cash management, specialized lending, asset-based, or various lending areas (regional or industrial).

COMPETITION AND CHANGE TO THE PROCESS

This expensive and cumbersome process was largely a legacy of the regulated era. Corporations had limited alternative sources for capital. The process achieved its full stature in the era of 3-3-3 banking. Loosely translated, this meant, borrowing funds at 3 percent, creating loans with a 300 basis point spread, and being at the first tee at 3 P.M. That era ended with the breakdown of Bretton Woods agreement and the increased volatility in currency exchange and interest rates that followed. From the 1970s to the early 1990s, market forces wrought changes on the process.

Portfolio Concentrations

The market recession of 1974 and 1975 and the subsequent raft of defaults helped banks realize the importance of portfolio concentrations. While the concept of portfolio concentrations was not new, the ability to monitor them with new flexible computing systems was. They started to build computer systems to capture credit exposures across all operating areas of the bank. Once credit exposure was captured in a central location, banks needed the ability to examine it flexibly along many parameters. What interested the credit managers most was to see their exposures selected along any of the following characteristics:

- Risk rating, both internal and external
- Degree of commitment
- Facility structure
- Outstanding balances
- Tenor
- Industry codes
- Geographical codes, including country and cross-border exposures
- Lending area within the bank's organization.

Banks had to overcome many significant challenges to gather this information. Typically they needed to:

1. Develop and deploy standard identifiers (counterparty, credit facility, etc.) across the bank.
2. Capture the credit facilities that had been approved, in other words, the commitments.
3. Capture the outstandings under each of those facilities on a regular basis.

Each of these tasks was a major initiative itself and each contained a unique set of challenges. It was a major challenge to retrofit counterparty identifiers especially with systems that did not accept them easily. Alternatives, like mapping each system's nonstandard identifier to a standard code, created another set of challenges and risks. Using mapping schemes added another link in an already questionable chain of conversions. Similar data integrity and process problems had to be overcome for the other two tasks as well. For example, the issue of whether outstanding balances reported to the credit exposure system should be reconciled to the general ledger entries was sure to attract strong proponents on both sides.

Overall, commercial lending data on commitments and exposure was reasonably static and quite tractable to the best technology of the time, relational databases. Through the 1980s, many banks captured it and built the ability to examine it constructively and flexibly. Efforts to track migrations in risk ratings, defaults, and recoveries were less of a priority and more of a challenge. Robust data sets for these aspects of credit risk are not very common, although some banks have them.

With the new information systems, the ability to see and manage portfolio concentrations improved. This engendered many new credit limits: limits by industry, geography, industry at risk, cross-border, and so on. With these new capabilities, the portfolio management aspect of commercial lending became a great deal more important and visible. Although the systems helped managers see concentrations of exposures, credit risk measurement at a portfolio level (exposure married with default and loss given default) was still almost purely an exercise in judgment. The managers still had to determine the prudent levels of exposure in each industry, geography, and so on, based almost solely on their experience and wisdom.

Disintermediation

The fixed-income chapter (Chapter 7) noted the shrinking market share of bank loans. In the 1970s, bank customers started increasing their use of capital/debt markets. The investment community grew more interested in buying debt directly from selected corporations. Both investors and corporations could enhance their returns by removing the banks as intermediaries. Removing the banks from the middle frequently removed a significant cost that was not providing commensurate value. The first customers to go straight to the markets were, quite logically, the largest, best known, and most creditworthy. They gained the biggest reduction in funding costs by leaving.

This disintermediation led to tremendous risk and price pressures on banks. The overall risk profile of their loan assets migrated up, as their best customers left them, and the least creditworthy customers remained. At the same time, the loan margins shrank from the competitive pressures. Banks were in the awkward position of having higher credit risk coupled with lower profit margins. They had to take significant steps to price their loans more closely according to their inherent risks. At the same time, they had to respond to price pressures by driving the costs to administer loans down. They have cut costs considerably since the 1970s. However, loan costs remain significant. Banks continue working to improve pricing and to cut costs.

Secondary Loan Markets

Starting in the early 1980s, banks started building and expanding their loan distribution networks to other banks. Using a distribution network, money center banks could sell pieces of their loan commitments as they made them. By selling down these assets, they could make a small spread, move the assets off their books, reduce the regulatory capital required, and enhance their return ratios. The purchasers, usually middle-market and smaller banks, were able to add high-quality loan assets to their books at a very low origination cost. This secondary market for loans grew quite rapidly through the 1980s and 1990s.

In 1985, a company called Loan Pricing Corporation[1] (LPC) started gathering the prices various loans were fetching in the nascent secondary market and publishing them monthly. These *Gold Sheets* quickly became a standard reference for the market. As the market developed, LPC expanded its position as the information provider. It augmented its loan prices with data on risk, default rates, loan structures, and other information relevant to debt trading. It moved to electronic media for capturing and distributing its information. It has even developed analytical routines that help examine the risk/return inherent in various loans. This source of price and risk information contributed to transparency and increased liquidity in this growing market.

Risk-Based Capital and Arbitrage

In July 1988, a committee of central bankers from the OECD, under the auspices of the Bank of International Settlements, agreed on a common framework for calculating levels of bank capital. This committee also established minimum levels of capital required for international banks. This framework created broad classes of assets and required specified minimum levels of capital required for each group. This was the regulatory response to the erosion in capital levels at banks around the globe that occurred in the wake of deregulation. The participating countries accepted this accord and agreed to apply it universally no later than 1992.

The original objectives, to strengthen the safety and stability of the international banking system and to diminish a source of competitive inequality among international banks,[2] were well served. Using this standard, the banks in all participating countries showed significant improvement in their capital levels from 1989 to 1992.[3] It engendered serious managerial focus on capital adequacy, altered the lending practices at many banks, and created a bit of a scramble to build the systems and processes to calculate/report capital adequacy. It also helped level the competitive field by inhibiting banks from achieving extraordinary shareholder returns through leverage, which produced lower capital and higher risk.

However, over the longer term, the accord has become an albatross.[4] The capital requirements are uniformly applied to broad sets of assets and do not reflect the large range of real risk within each group. For example, all private sector debt is weighted at 100 percent, which requires a capitalization level of 8 percent. The range of real risks, as reflected in market prices is huge for private sector debt. The markets tell us a loan to General Electric should require considerably less than 8 percent capital reserve, while a loan to a local Tokyo construction company, a depressed sector at this time, should require considerably more than 8 percent. We see similar distortions in other asset groups, with zero capital being required for OECD government debt, whether it is the United States, the United Kingdom, or Turkey. The accord has other deficiencies that have an economic impact.[5] The impact is frequently contrary to the two goals of the accord. They may distort credit market prices, inflating rates for customers with low credit risk and encourage banks to hold riskier credit portfolios. They discourage optimal hedging of credit risk by failing to fully recognize offsetting exposures. Finally, banks, with these capital reserve requirements are competitively handicapped vis-à-vis other financial service organizations. These deficiencies and their impact have led to serious discussions to modify the accord.

In the meantime, risk capital arbitrage is the only viable alternative. In the past few years, banks are increasingly able and willing to finesse these rules through arbitrage. Credit derivatives and securitization provide two new ways to move loan assets off banks' corporate loan books, greatly reducing the regulatory capital requirements. Business news journals record almost weekly how major global banks are issuing Collateralized Loan Obligations (CLOs) and Credit Linked Notes (CLNs). Some banks intend to securitize 20, 30, even 50 percent of their loan portfolio. The Bank of International Settlements (BIS) has calculated that about 25 percent of the loan assets at the largest U.S. banks have moved off the balance sheets.[6] There are other economic drivers for banks to securitize their loans, but the risk-based capital requirements they face are certainly adding to the impetus.

This puts bank regulators in a very awkward position. They tacitly acknowledge that their capital controls are obsolete and can be circumvented, yet given the global market perturbations in 1998, they have hesitated to endorse revisions that rely on models that are not accurate.[7] The 1988 accord has become, at the very best, an encumbrance on the marketplace, diverting resources and attention from the real credit risks and the real value/prices. A harsher view is that it distorts current markets, creating overcharges for the best credits and undercharges for the worst. The regulatory rules may be encouraging the banks to increase their risk and increase credit leverage.

In June 1999, BIS issued a discussion draft for revising the accord. The new guidelines will address the most glaring problems with the current measures of adequacy.[8] Also, the proposed revisions go beyond purely mechanical measures of capital adequacy. The revised accord would include reliance on supervisory oversight and market discipline as well as capital adequacy. There is no date for when this accord will be finalized and when it will become effective. The current stage of consideration will end in March 2000 with comments being submitted to BIS. The current glacial pace is consistent with these sorts of initiatives. That pace puts the revised accord at least three years away from implementation.

SUMMARY OF CHANGES TO THE PROCESS

Exhibit 11.2 summarizes the changes to the process that have occurred since the 1970s, along with the forces that wrought those changes. In short, the forces for change to traditional commercial lending have come from increased competition, price transparency,

Exhibit 11.2   Evolution of the Credit Process

Credit Origination	Force Causing Change
Credit Origination Marketing: Targets/risk criteria Structuring Pricing Analysis/risk rating Approval Syndication	**Force Causing Change** Resulting changes
Documentation and Disbursement **Credit Administration** Disbursements and payments Agency work Collateral operations Covenant monitoring Credit file management Credit renewals and reviews Reporting (regulatory and MIS) Accounting and P&L	**Portfolio Concentrations** More accurate and timely measures of portfolio concentrations More active portfolio exposure management
Portfolio Management Appetite by industry/geography Capture exposure and outstandings by: 　Counterparty and relationship 　Industry 　Geography 　Risk rating	**Disintermediation** Narrower credit spreads Riskier portfolios Leaner process Examination of where value is added
Problem Loan Recognition Risk rating downgrades Watch list activities	**Secondary Markets** Asset sales networks Price transparency Loan market liquidity
Loan Workouts Restructures, charge-offs, etc. Bankruptcy and litigation Asset management/liquidation	**Risk Based Capital** Risk-capital arbitrage through asset sales and securitization

plus liquidity, and efficiency in debt/loan markets. This has led to an ever-increasing pressure to price loans according to their inherent credit risk. The U.S. markets appear to have led this change. Within the debt markets, the proportion that is issued directly into capital markets as bonds is higher in the United States. Put most succinctly, corporate debt has a smaller market share of U.S. capital markets and bank lending has a smaller market share of the debt markets. The banks have been disintermediated out of their market share as competitive pressures from viable substitutes continue to mount.

And it is just beginning. The forces and the resulting changes to commercial lending were already quite apparent when, in the early to mid 1990s, new models for credit risk accelerated them even more.

THE PRIOR MODELS FOR CREDIT RISK

We have already noted that default is the key to credit risk; it is the Rubicon—there is no going back. It is the watershed of debt value. At default, the value of a firm's debt typically drops precipitously to a fairly low percentage of par. How far it drops depends a great deal on the structure of the debt, its collateral, and seniority, that is, where it ranks within the capital structure of the firm. So how does the industry determine the odds of default, this vitally important possibility?

In the past, rating schemes, both internal and external, were the major method for grading credit risk. Internal rating schemes vary with each organization that has created one, but their purpose shapes their form. For example, when used to identify deteriorating credits, they tend to have fewer grades. However, if used to measure profitability or to set pricing, they tend to have more grades.[9] External rating schemes differ slightly from the internal measures, because they cover publicly issued debt and seek to determine ability to repay in stress situations. Internal ratings typically use normal, unstressed, situations to examine repayment capabilities. In all cases, the process for grading credit risk is qualitative and somewhat subjective.

This rating process is frequently criticized as a lagging rather than a leading indicator. The contention is that it doesn't provide any information that the market hasn't already provided. Indeed, studies have shown that changes in risk grade contain very little new information. The studies show that market prices for debt (the spread) reflect changes in credit risk well before the rating grade is changed. When a grade is changed upward, the credit spread has already narrowed, and conversely, when a downgrade occurs, the spread has already widened. These changes frequently occur even before any public announcement that the grade is being reviewed.

Another lagging indicator frequently used for assessing credit risk are the firm's financial statements. Many banks time their annual reviews of specific industries, such as, banking, insurance, automotive, and so on, to occur shortly after the annual results for that industry are posted. Their intention is to utilize the most current performance results in their considerations. These review sessions also cover the relationship managers' talks with company management and their view of the firm's prospects. There is active consideration of the prospects. However, the data being examined is from past performance. Using call reports, accounting statements, and risk ratings to determine creditworthiness has been likened to using a rearview mirror to drive a car. Let's see if the markets might provide a more forward-looking view.

THE NEW MODELS FOR CREDIT RISK

The new models for credit risk bring quantitative rigor to heretofore qualitative and descriptive gauges of credit risk. These models predict default probability of specific debtors and across portfolios of debtors. Since actual defaults and other credit events are so rare, a richer source for credit information had to be found. The models infer credit risk from market data: equity prices, credit spreads, macro-economic variables, and balance sheet data. As a group, these models indicate that a great deal of useful credit information can be gleaned from these market data sources.

Each of the models quantifies one or more of the factors that we know, intuitively, has an impact on defaults or credit risk. For example, one model projects the migration of credit risk ratings over time to yield measures of credit risk. Another quantifies the relative contribution that various macro-economic factors have on default rates. In a separate vein of development, a recently developed model/system seeks to relate loan structure elements in the specific loan agreement to loan value. More models will certainly be developed along with expansions and improvements to this existing set. This active academic research is closely linked to developments in the markets. As this is being written, highly regarded contributors to risk theory like Robert Jarrow, David Lando, Stuart Turnbull, Robert Geske, and Jerome Bok are researching and proposing additional credit models.

Case Study: KMV

KMV is a small closely held firm, which has largely precipitated the recent credit risk movement. The initials KMV stand for the firm's founders, Stephen Kealhofer, John McQuown, and Oldrich Vasicek who have been working on quantifying commercial credit risk longer than most people in the field. Their model is notable in its simplicity. The complexity and challenge occurs in converting the concept into a practical application. Essentially, they use option-pricing techniques, along with equity prices and balance sheet information to predict the default probability of individual firms. Then they examine how those default probabilities correlate in a portfolio to determine the risk/return contribution of each asset in the portfolio. Their default prediction application is built on the foundation laid by Black, Scholes, and Merton and their portfolio management application is premised on Markowitz's portfolio optimization work. This case shows how the theories that were developed and utilized for managing market risk have been adapted for credit risk. We will look at the default predictor after a brief look at credit law.

Credit: Law and Incentives

In 1897, the British system of jurisprudence in a precedent setting ruling, *Salomon v. Saloman & Co.*, released an individual from his closely held company's debts. The concept of limited liability for companies had been hotly debated before this case. The debate raged for a considerable time after it and even flickers to this day in economic policy articles.[10] Before this case, the distinction between the obligations of a business entity and the obligations of its owners were not clearly drawn. This case established a legal precedent for the put option imbedded in debt. It has since been widely, almost globally, replicated in many legal systems.

Fischer Black and Myron Scholes' seminal publication in 1973 containing the formula for valuing options noted its applicability to corporate liabilities.[11] Robert Merton enhanced this application of option theory by showing how it converts into the interest rates that corporations pay for debt.[12] Equity holders have an implicit call on firm value, which has been sold to them by the debtors—the debtors are short a put. The strike price on both these options is the firm's debt. The equity holders can claim all market value in excess of the firm's obligations, or debt. However, if the firm's market value falls below its obligations, the equity holders can put the firm's value to the lenders/debt holders in lieu of repayment. Exhibit 11.3 shows these related claims on the firm's value.

Exhibit 11.3   Equity and Debt Holders' Claims on the Firm's Value

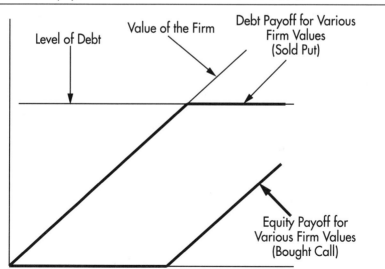

Let's examine how a loss in the firm's value affects the value, not the payoff, that equity and debt holders have. We will start with a firm that is deeply solvent, with value of $10 million and debt of $1 million and move gradually to a deeply insolvent firm. Suppose the firm lost $1 million in value from the $10 million starting point. The equity holders lose virtually all of that $1 million, because the firm is still very deeply solvent. The losses in firm value will continue to hit only the equity holders' value until the firm's overall value gets closer to its $1 million debt level. At some point, say a loss from $4 million to $3 million, the loss in value is not borne exclusively by the equity holders. Some portion of that loss in value starts to hit the debt holders' value, because the certainty for repayment has been materially diminished. A loss from $3 million down to $2 million significantly increases the chance of repayment trouble. As a result, we see a greater proportion of the loss accruing to the debtors, and less hitting the equity holders. When the firm's value approaches its debt, the proportion of loss sharing is equal. When the firm value equals its debt, $1 million, a loss in value is shared equally between the debt and equity holders. All subsequent losses in firm value will hit the debt holders harder than the equity holders. As the firm becomes extremely insolvent (usually default has occurred by this point), the equity holders see very little change in value for changes in the firm's value, as their call for any residual value is so far out of the money (Exhibit 11.4). The debt option and equity option values are a mirror image of each other.

A clash between lender and borrower incentives develops within firms, especially as a firm approaches insolvency. When owners' equity shrinks, their potential for further loss becomes limited, since they can put those losses to their debtors. They can become bigger risk takers. Suppose a business owner with $1 million in equity comes across the following business possibility: With no initial investment, he can buy a 50 percent chance for a $5 million gain coupled with a 50 percent chance for a $5 million loss. Prudent investors would not risk their money on such a dicey proposition. However, with the put option, this owner's return profile is a 50 percent chance of $1 million loss and a 50 percent chance of $5 million gain. In this example, the lender would bear the brunt of this new risk. In

Exhibit 11.4   Debt Put and Equity Call Options: Reciprocal Values

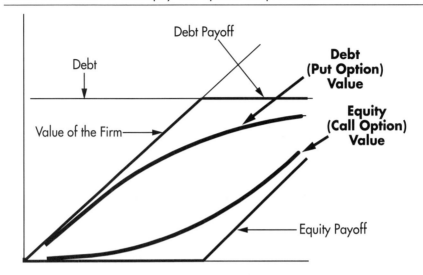

terms of Exhibit 11.4, equity holders have an incentive to increase the volatility of their returns. That incentive grows larger as their equity shrinks. By increasing volatility, they flatten both the option curves, increasing the value of their position at the expense of the debtors.

This example illustrates the inherent conflicts of interest in lending markets and explains why lenders wish to extract promises and covenants from the borrower regarding prudent use of the funds. Lenders need to combat the built-in economic incentive for the borrowers to take imprudent risks with their money. Creditors seek ways to reduce the option value that they have provided to the equity holders. They try to constrain volatility with covenants, they try to accelerate maturity with cross-default clauses, and they frequently try to force liquidation to recover residual value as promptly as possible. In terms of Exhibit 11.4, they are trying to push the curved lines of *option value* out toward the *payoff lines*.

This agency problem helps explain why S&Ls, which were known to be in trouble by the mid-1980s, ran up additional billions in losses. Legislators and regulators allowed many S&Ls with little or no equity (even negative equity in many cases) to remain in business. Lawmakers' ability to ignore basic economic principals achieved legendary proportions when they let these entities continue in business, allowing them to invest in a broader set of products (read riskier) to earn their way out of trouble. The lawmakers opened up a free casino for the S&L owners. With little to none of their own money at stake, the owners were allowed to chase almost every high-risk, big payoff scheme that showed up. Research indicates this negligence added $150 billion to the bailout tab.[13]

The example also shows how leverage is very important to credit decisions. The stellar returns that Long Term Capital Management LLP (LTCM) achieved in 1996 and 1997 were at least partially attributable to leverage. Reports indicate that LTCM carried $25 of debt for every dollar of equity. With that leverage, it only needed to return 1.15 percent above its funding costs on its total assets to achieve a return of 30 percent on the equity. In 1997, when it returned 40 percent to its equity holders, if it was still leveraged at 25 to 1, it achieved the stellar return on all assets of 1.6 percent. The other edge of the leverage sword came into play in 1998. Long Term Capital's thin cushion of equity was quickly used up in the market perturbations that followed Russia's default on sovereign debt. The institutions that provided all that leverage to LTC, through debt, suffered significant losses.

KMV's Default Model

 KMV's default prediction model is premised on these mirror options. The value the equity holders hold is the firm's total market value minus its debt. Exhibit 11.5 illustrates this premise graphically. The value of the put option that the equity move depends on:

1. Strike price, in this case, the outstanding debt
2. Value of the underlying, in this case, the value of the firm
3. Volatility of the underlying, in this case, the volatility of the firm's value
4. Time to option expiry, in this case, tenor of the debt.

Exhibit 11.5   Determining Default Probability Using Option Valuation

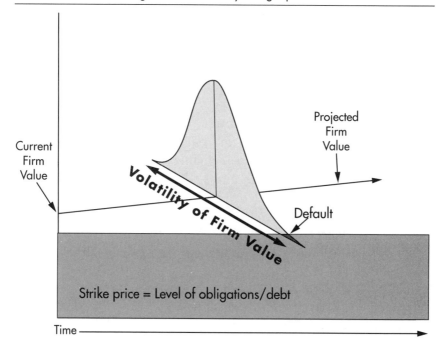

Note that a shorter period or multiple periods can be used by adjustments to the option valuation model. The EDF™'s (Estimated Default Frequency) that KMV calculates are calibrated to one year.

The strike price equals the firm's debt, which can range from the current liabilities to the sum of all borrowings. Current liabilities and how those liabilities will change in the immediate future have the biggest impact on solvency. The impact of aggregate debt levels is captured in firm value and volatility of that value, discussed next.

The greatest unknown in this picture is the value of the firm and the volatility of that value. These two numbers are very difficult to determine precisely. KMV has kept a black box, marked proprietary, around the exact details of how they make these estimates. However, they do indicate they use balance sheet information and derive the capital structure of the firm, for example, leverage, and so on. They include a series of boundary conditions, like industry parameters, in their calculations. Equity market price data plays a major role, as they provide the best estimate for the value of the equity holder's call option. They also use an option-pricing model.

KMV's estimate of a firm's predicted value, and the volatility of that value converts into a mathematical "distance to default." For example, a firm with a predicted market value of eight million dollars, a standard deviation of value of two million, and debt of four million, is two standard deviations away from default. KMV's final step is to convert this distance to default into a probability of default. For the conversion, they use a database that captures all firms' performance over the past twenty-five years, including defaults. From this database, it is possible to select all firms whose distance to default was two standard deviations and determine what percentage defaulted one year later. That percentage becomes the scale for the one-year EDF for this firm.

Of course, the devil is in the details. Estimating of the value of the firm, both current and projected, and the volatility of that value is not a simple calculation. The next step, applying the scale to convert distance to default into probability of default, is also complex. Although some critics have called this scaling step a fudge factor, they do not dispute the validity of the results.

Years to Develop   KMV's initiative and the effort described has spanned decades and several organizational iterations. They have focused on converting this model into a practical application. Two of the founders, McQuown and Vasicek, worked on the problem while at Wells Bank in the late 1970s. In 1983, the three founders created Diversified Corporate Loans. Its purpose was to use quantitative models to purchase a properly diversified portfolio of loans, achieving higher returns with a more efficient portfolio. Although this venture was not a commercial success, they established the foundation for success. In 1989, they formed KMV and used the model purchased from their prior venture as the basis for building their default predictor application. They started providing EDFs for firms in 1991.

KMV actually has two default predictor models, one for public firms and one for private firms. More information is available for public firms, and it typically is available sooner. With less complete information for private firms, the private model uses more proxy information to estimate values and volatilities.

Validated Results KMV's EDFs have been scrutinized for their validity. Ross Miller, president of Miller Risk Advisors, examined the predictive power of EDFs vis-à-vis standard S&P ratings.[14] He selected all firms that had the same rating, and then ranked them within that rating by the EDF that KMV provided. He then tracked which firms defaulted over the next 12 months, 13 to 24 months, and 24 to 36 months. Within each set of firms that had exactly the same S&P rating, he sorted by EDF. He created a kind of Bingo card for each group of rated firms. If EDFs are better default predictors, we would expect the defaulting firms to concentrate in the lower strata of each bingo card. If not, the defaults should be more evenly scattered throughout each standard rating. Miller's results are shown in Exhibit 11.6. KMV's EDFs for all eighty-seven companies

Exhibit 11.6 Companies Rated B- by S&P in Order of EDF Rating

0.02	0.04	0.13	0.15	0.16	0.16	0.26	0.26
0.28	0.28	0.30	0.30	0.43	0.48	0.51	0.51
0.56	0.63	0.65	0.68	0.68	0.71	0.74	0.75
0.75	0.76	0.79	0.80	0.86	0.87	0.88	0.88
0.90	0.95	0.99	1.00	1.12	1.12	1.17	1.20
1.20	1.22	1.32	1.33	1.35	1.43	1.58	1.72
1.74	1.75	1.87	1.92	1.96	1.99	2.06	2.07
2.16	2.23	2.54	2.64	2.65	2.71	2.80	3.01
3.03	3.06	3.22	3.31	3.32	3.32	3.49	3.63
3.69	3.81	3.91	4.02	4.12	4.13	4.97	5.75
6.95	7.09	7.76	7.88	8.75	10.42	17.02	

Defaults for S&P B- Companies at the end of 1989 ordered by EDF

Key

- ■ Defaulted within 1 year
- ■ Defaulted between 1 & 2 years
- ▨ Defaulted between 2 & 3 years
- □ Did not default in 3 years

that were rated B– by S&P at the end of 1989, ranged from .02 percent to 17.02 percent. Within one year, four had defaulted, noted with the darkest shading. Eight more defaulted within two years, noted with lighter shading. In the third year, one more defaulted shown in the lightest shade. Miller also tested the predictive power of EDFs using a statistical method called Kolmogorov-Smirnov. It corroborated these results.

Use in the Marketplace   Default is a key driver of loan value. Accurate, timely, and finely graded probabilities of default help loan portfolio managers know the value of their loans. EDFs quickly became the common reference point in secondary markets for loans.

With credit risk becoming more liquid, the game becomes a bit like musical chairs; don't be caught standing when the music stops. The default predictor model temporarily provides creditors an opportunity to sit down—sell ahead of others because they know the music is about to stop. There are plenty of anecdotal stories to support this. But selling loans at par, just before they tank, is a surefire way to destroy relationships and kill liquidity in the credit markets. The advantage is only temporary because everyone else will obtain the product and have the same foresight.

In the long run, to be viable, the secondary loan markets must provide more economic value than facilitating the movement of a hot potato, potentially bad credit. Diversification is the only way to relieve credit risk in a way that provides economic benefits to all participants. Much like fertilizer, too much credit risk to a given company, industrial sector, or economic region can be poison. The way to obtain benefits is to spread it around. Because banks have traditionally served specific commercial markets, they have tended to originate and hold credit portfolios full of toxic concentrations. One U.S. money center bank may develop strong relationships and knowledge of the communications industry, while another may have strength in real estate, and so on. Similarly, a bank in the United States will have U.S.-based loans, while a bank in Germany will have concentrations in German loans. Although these relationships are valuable for originating credit, they create sub-optimal levels of credit concentration within each bank. KMV devised a measure of credit portfolio diversification that helps identify these toxic concentrations of credit.

KMV's Portfolio Model

We noted earlier that defaults are too rare to measure directly, so a proxy to actual observations had to be found. When we move to portfolio considerations, we need to reliably capture the correlation of defaults, which is an expansion of the default problem. Another proxy, for how default events are linked together, is necessary.

KMV's process of deriving default probabilities from equity price creates a very useful set of data, estimates of the firm's value, which can be used for portfolio analysis. These values and how they correlate, go up and down in synchrony, are the key that KMV uses to move from default predictions for each individual credit to predictions of default across the whole portfolio. This allows each credit asset to be measured in terms of its risk/reward contribution to the portfolio that is held, and that has very significant implications. Many banks have created a credit portfolio management process based on the portfolio measures of risk and return that KMV's model provides. A case study of one is provided later in this chapter.

CreditMetrics Model

 In late 1997 or early 1998, J.P. Morgan, in collaboration with others, issued CreditMetrics™. This and all other risk products were subsequently spun off into a risk services subsidiary, The RiskMetrics Group.[15] CreditMetrics was a logical extension of its very successful launch of RiskMetrics in 1994. CreditMetrics calculates a Credit VaR, just as RiskMetrics obtained a market VaR. Similar techniques, like measures of value, volatility, and correlation, are used in both methodologies. However, that is where the similarity ends. Credit VaR is calculated only at a portfolio level, and the model components that drive credit VaR have to do with exposure, defaults, and loss-given default, such as recoveries.

At a high level, the methodology obtains three major inputs before running a simulation to create a distribution of credit returns for the portfolio. The three inputs, which require calculations and models themselves, are the exposure profile of each asset, the volatility of value caused by credit events, and the correlations for credit events. As noted earlier, the exposure profile is relatively static, except when the portfolio contains derivatives whose value moves with market changes. The volatility input/calculation is where a lot of the action is. Its central driver is credit ratings. Essentially, rating transition matrices drive a calculation of the volatility of value due to credit quality changes. The correlations input is also full of action. It captures how default and other credit events, such as a downgrade, correlate within the portfolio. These correlations are derived from the industry and country weightings that the user assigns to each obligor. The model then uses these inputs in a simulation that creates a distribution of possible returns.

More importantly, the simulation also produces numerous statistics about marginal risk. The marginal statistics help managers understand each asset's contribution to portfolio risk/return. It also lets managers examine the portfolio along many parameters. This helps identify concentration risk, determine economic capital/reserves, adjust portfolios to enhance risk/return, and perform sensitivity analysis. Extensions of the methodology are even helping to price credit derivatives.

CreditRisk+

Shortly after Credit Metrics appeared early in 1997, Credit Suisse First Boston introduced CreditRisk+™. It is a simpler model, with default rates being a direct input, rather than a modeled process, dependent on several inputs. The segment model for determining the correlation of defaults is simpler, too.[16] It is generally easier to implement than the other models.

McKinsey's PortfolioView Model

Meanwhile in 1998, Tom Wilson at McKinsey and Company issued the PortfolioView™ model, which his team had been developing. The key aspect of this model is that it considers how macro-economic factors affect credit defaults and migrations. It can also fold in country and political risk as a shaper of credit events.[17]

Summary of the Portfolio Models

It is tempting to compare and evaluate each methodology, describing its strengths, weaknesses, and general applicability to various asset and product classes. However, there are many representatives from each supplier who will provide that information just for the cost of a phone call.

 Let's focus on what these models have in common and their impact on the traditional credit process. Exhibit 11.7 shows how they all use market data to discern credit portfolio risk. Each emphasizes one of several factors that we know contributes to credit risk. KMV uses equity prices to model firm value, volatility, and credit risk. McKinsey's works the other end of the spectrum, using macro-economic scenarios to estimate credit risk. Each provides valuable new insights about the credit risk in our portfolios.

Together, they provide risk measures, which create a powerful impetus for holders of portfolios with credit risk to manage them much more actively. This in turn provides a powerful impetus for more liquidity in credit markets. These tools are reshaping how

Exhibit 11.7   Comparison of the Credit Models

Credit Model	Method for Default Prediction	Method for Default Correlation
KMV's models	Use financial and equity data in option valuation model Analytical process	Derived from equity, firm value and default probability correlations factor model
CreditMetrics	Use historical transition matrix ratings or other input	Derived from equity correlations within country and industry
CreditRisk +	Use historical default rates. Input	Derived from segment analysis
Portfolio view	Use a simulation of macro-economic factors	Derived from default migration probabilities factor model

credit is originated, priced, structured, and distributed to the ultimate holders/investors.

Loan Structure and Value

KPMG has approached credit from the perspective of loan value at origination. It models the risk-adjusted profitability of each transaction, rather then the portfolio approaches just discussed.[18] KPMG's main premise is that understanding loan value at the beginning affects profitability more directly than achieving a diversified portfolio. The key to managing value creation in lending is to institute a disciplined, rigorous approach to transaction valuation that explicitly considers the embedded options and loan structures (seniority, security, guarantees, prepayment, etc.) inside each agreement. This quantitative process can replace the current practice, which tends to be ad hoc, inconsistent across the various lending areas, and quite malleable to market pressures, meaning that loans are priced at whatever the market will bear.

The loan analysis system (LAS) determines loan value using decision tree analysis, a standard derivative valuation technique. Its major output is the net present value of the loan, risk adjusted for loan structure, multiyear credit risk and benchmarked to the market. However, it has numerous other outputs and can be used to experiment with structural and price elements to see their impact on value. It takes as input details about the loan structure: fees; the counterparty utilization levels; default transition matrix; default rates; recovery rates; cost of data, loan, and administration; market data market prices; and interest rates. Given all these inputs, LAS models the state-contingent cashflows of each loan by analyzing specific time nodes in the decision tree. The factors affecting these cashflows include risk rating migrations, default probability, and interest rate fluctuations. Embedded options are exercised as appropriate by lenders and borrowers at each time node in the tree. It then summarizes the resulting cash flows to get the Loan NPV and other relevant statistics like implied duration and market-based capital requirements.

Models like KPMG's when combined with the increased liquidity and product alternatives in credit markets, such as credit derivatives, will help market participants understand the components of a loan's price and judge its relative value. Their understanding is deeper when they can analyze the credit risk premium (the risk-neutral default probabilities through time) and see how that premium along with the liquidity risk premium contribute to a loan's price.

CASE STUDY: BANK OF MONTREAL

Although better than its peer group, Bank of Montreal suffered significant credit losses through the 1980s. Losses in real estate marked the beginning of the decade, followed by energy and less developed country (LDC) losses in the middle years, capped with even larger real estate losses toward the end. Significant capital had been invested with either zero or negative return, and the bank's equity had not gained value. The U.S. market had seen a decline in equity value for such names as Citibank and Bank of America and the demise of Continental Illinois, among others. Against this backdrop, Bank of Montreal (BMO) decided to make a fundamental change in its corporate banking business and credit risk process with large corporate and government borrowers.

The Philosophy

This change was predicated on the following beliefs regarding credit risk management:

1. Effective management is not possible without measurement. Measuring default risk requires more science than art. A more quantitative and consistent process is required.
2. The nascent loan syndication/loan sales market will grow exponentially, leading to greater liquidity in credit assets.
3. Separating the risk decisions, which include credit evaluation, from the reward decisions, which include relationships

management and sales, is fundamentally incorrect. It leads to inconsistent and inappropriate decisions.

4. Excessive losses arise from inadequate diversification, not from an inadequate credit-decision process.

5. The key role of management is to measure and control undiversifiable risk.

6. The markets and eventually the rating agencies will reward banks that demonstrate an ability to manage portfolio loss volatility through time.

Senior management's conviction was strong enough to sponsor and launch a risky and controversial loan portfolio management initiative.

Challenges and Solutions

This initiative faced three major hurdles: entrenched beliefs, entrenched processes, and lack of an appropriate information infrastructure. These challenges, which are very typical for this sort of initiative, are described briefly, along with how they were overcome.

Entrenched Beliefs and Processes   In starting on this initiative, these beliefs were far from universal. Measurement techniques were a source of great discomfort for nonmathematical analysts, whose defense was generally that credit risk evaluation is an art, not a science. The traditional approach was guarded by an intricate infrastructure of credit policies and procedures that had been developed through the generations and handed down for safekeeping. Many of these policies had moved from rules of thumb to dogma. As with most banks, no attempt was made to measure risk correlation, but rather, control was exercised through industry limits and default was seen as a failure in credit evaluation rather than an event in the normal course of a risk-taking business. Nor was there a general view that loan distribution and syndication were positive events. Maintaining market share was a focus, and there was great concern over the impact on long-standing relationships.

The new group also faced an entrenched process. The credit risk group was comfortable with its role and responsibility as independent and sole arbiter of credit risk in the bank. Credit alone determined the level of risk, assigned risk ratings, advised on deal structure/size, and set limits. They were not sanguine about sharing some or part of their responsibilities, especially with a new unproven group that appeared quite naive about commercial credit. The relationship side was equally wedded to their established process. They were concerned that new measures of concentration would disrupt their ability to maintain and develop their relationships.

The key prerequisite to overcoming these challenges was clear support from top management. At BMO, the new senior executives openly supported the creation of a Loan Portfolio Management Group that was not only mandated but also empowered to implement tools for risk/reward measurement, tools for default risk evaluation, and tools to measure diversification/concentration risk.

Two additional keys to resolving the impasse were communication and collaboration. Loan management put on seminars where the logic of these new tools won converts and overcame resistance. The group also worked with the credit and relationship groups to collaboratively develop the revised roles and responsibilities. These initiatives helped overcome the resistance to change and, over time, a great deal of support became evident.

Data Problems The final major problem was data, especially data on commercial loan transactions. This problem is not unique to BMO. A large corporate loan portfolio is unlike any normal receivable ledger. A highly customized loan agreement underlies each debt. Each agreement defines pricing, maturity, currency, covenants, and more. Most of the debts are on a contingent basis, where the borrower has rights to draw. Each borrower typically has multiple agreements to serve various capital needs, such as a term loan for project finance and a revolver for working capital. This makes record keeping very complex, and banks, as early adopters of computers, are often saddled with old, outmoded mainframe systems for their critical applications and data. Moreover, these systems are geared to statutory and regulatory processes rather than management reporting. With acute data and information deficits, BMO was not in a unique situation.

Significant resources were required to build the systems infrastructure that the group needed. One of the biggest challenges was to capture some 3,000 unique loan agreements in all their glorious detail, including all the embedded options, covenants, and pricing features. Significant effort was also required to capture facilities, commitments, and outstanding balances. In short, Loan Management required an enormous and continuing effort to obtain a complete, accurate, and timely loan information base to support its analytical process.

The Result

At BMO, the Loan Management unit evolved separately from the loan origination process. In effect, loan portfolio management became an investment operation, buying credit risk sourced by originators (relationship managers) and buying other credit risk to diversify the portfolio. The group adopted the KMV technology at an early stage. KMV proved its value when it prompted the sale at close to par of three loan positions with high EDFs that subsequently defaulted. BMO also became a leader in the development of markets for credit derivatives. The group sees them as a vastly promising tool for both hedging and diversification, without adding contingent funding risk.

After getting firmly established at the portfolio management end, the group integrated its methods into the whole credit process. It provided its analytical and pricing tools to the credit originators, approvers, and distributors allowing them to structure and price new credit that moves smoothly through distribution to secondary buyers and leaves the optimum hold levels for the bank's portfolio. In sum, loan management became the mainstream. Many process improvements continue. Assets that would help diversify the portfolio are going to be passed along to the originators as good targets, where very competitive pricing will be available. News wire and Internet feeds from equity analysts, filtered for the names in the portfolio and prospect list, are being developed. BMO has found that equity analysts are an important source of information. They often lead in discerning credit events.

Relationship Concerns The effect on bank clients has been a cause for concern. Many strong and lasting relationships can be threatened by this change. The bank's largest and most enduring clients are often buyers of multiple bank products. Decisions are rarely black and white, and skilled client management remains a key to success.

In many ways, applying modern portfolio theory to a large pool of corporate credit risk is still unproven. If the beliefs at BMO are correct, banks that have applied portfolio diversification policies in a meaningful way will show substantially less volatility in a troubled market. In theory, well-diversified loan portfolios will suffer much smaller losses in an economic downturn. However, it will be hard to prove. A single large corporate default, which can occur almost at random, could nullify this bank as an example. This new "loan portfolio management theory" requires at least one trip through a major downturn at several institutions before compelling data on its efficacy will be available.

Portfolio Management The market's response is clear. In 1997 and 1998, Bank of Montreal completed two debt issues, CBOs, in which investors bought notes in a pool based, in large part, on BMO's proven ability in managing debt portfolios. In 1998, Bank of Montreal's CLO pool was among the best received of all such issues. The Portfolio Management Group believes the market recognizes their advances.

Internally BMO has instilled the mantra of diversification and the discipline of central portfolio management. Externally they have contributed to numerous conferences, magazines, and seminars communicating their experience. Altruism is not at work here, just enlightened self-interest. BMO believes that more banks practicing active portfolio management will bring more liquidity to the markets. More market liquidity allows BMO to manage its loan portfolio more actively and efficiently.

BMO Summary

In sum, the world of bank loans has changed; the change is substantial and still growing. Banks are no longer the storehouse of debt, but the originators and managers of debt. In this world, investors become the focus, and the distinctions between market and credit risk become smaller. This change enhances all parties involved. The banks and their stockholders benefit from reduced earnings volatility. Borrowers benefit from the lowest possible funding costs. Meanwhile, investors are given another asset class to add, judiciously, to their diversified portfolios. This change is occurring, in historical terms, amazingly quickly.

CREDIT MARKET TRENDS

The Bank of Montreal example provides a clear view of how credit markets and the traditional credit processes within originating institutions are changing. The use of quantitative models to predict default probability and diversify a credit portfolio is quite new and revolutionary. It is another piece of the emerging GRM process. It has been embraced with varying degrees of enthusiasm at each bank. Some banks have undertaken to securitize vast portions of their portfolio. The primary motive for this extensive move may be to finesse regulatory capital requirements with portfolio efficiency a secondary objective. Others are entering the fray a little more slowly. All are at least examining how portfolio management might impact their returns and most are developing the ability to adjust their holdings.

Infrastructure Challenges

Many firms are unable to manage loan portfolios globally because they don't have the data. The loan process is quite decentralized in many firms. Each region has the detailed loan information (seniority, security, options, MAC clauses, etc.) that must be aggregated to support a global loan portfolio management process. Many firms are constructing this infrastructure now.

More Liquidity in Credit Markets

Credit risk is starting to look a lot like any other risk in the marketplace. Vast reservoirs of concentrated credit risk are flowing into these markets with surprising rapidity.

Product breadth is expanding, and the investor base for these products is growing. Market mechanisms to publish prices, match buyers and sellers, and settle are starting to develop. Standardization is underway, from establishing definitions of credit events to standardizing the products offered. Securities firms have also entered the fray. The markets that trade credit risk will undoubtedly develop further. The Internet will certainly assist in bringing liquidity to this market. By the time this book is published, some entity will probably be providing a place in cyberspace to post bids and offers for credit risk on various names. Mutant Technologies, formed in 1999, is one example.

There are caveats, because credit is different from other risks. Credit swaps and options will probably remain more complex and less liquid than other swaps and options. They will be the first to freeze in times of market stress. All these credit market developments are largely premised on the compelling but unproven assumption that diversification of credit risk can be measured and that it does provide benefits.

Revised Credit Origination Process

The practice of buying and holding loans to maturity is gone forever. It creates concentrations of risk that cost more than the benefits it buys—improved relationships, ancillary fee-based business, and so on. Origination of all credit risk, including leases, letters of credit, and guarantees, in addition to loans, will become much more closely linked to market prices and portfolio management considerations. As with public issues of equity or debt, the loan originators will poll the price/appetite levels in the markets with both the internal credit portfolio manager and external asset sales group to determine how much debt to originate and how to set up the structure and price.

Distribution capability may become as important or even supersede traditional relationship management, as the key for winning new loan origination business.

The market niche that commercial lending fills will become more clearly defined, if any niche is left at all. The whole credit process must become more streamlined and efficient. The originators will excise various steps in the process that do not add value. Candidates include in-house qualitative analysis and internal credit ratings, especially for counterparties on which extensive market information is available.

The investment community will become much smarter buyers of credit risk. Methods to value credit risk will become more standardized, and prices will fall into line. In the meantime, valuations can be pretty wild and woolly. I heard of a recent deal in which one firm was seeking to sell its exposure to a low-rated, high-default probability name. Most of the credit dealers in the community would not take the exposure without charging about what the owner thought it was worth. However, one dealer accepted the risk for approximately 25 percent of what all the others would have charged. That range of values among the dealers will not remain in the market for very long.

WRAP-UP

- Quantitative models to predict default probability and correlations of default have had a profound effect on traditional commercial lending.
- Markets to securitize and to swap credit exposure have developed very rapidly.
- Loan portfolio management capabilities, based on these new models and markets, are being developed at all major banks.
- The traditional credit process is rapidly shifting. Banks are becoming credit intermediaries and much smaller credit investors.

RISK IN PORTFOLIOS

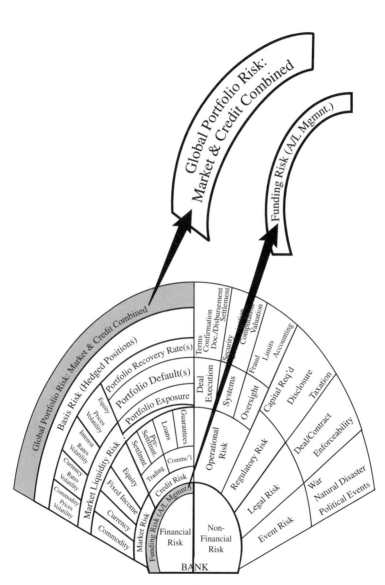

The Portfolio Risk Spectrum

This section broadens previous discussions of risk in portfolios to consider all the risks across all the markets. It traces the development path of tools to measure risk at a portfolio level and projects how they will expand to become the basis for GRM, including the Asset/Liability management function. The path begins back in the evolution of tools to measure portfolio market risk, some of which we've already seen applied to credit. It then examines the ways in which simulation models are being extended to more fully capture the dynamics of risk. These global risk models are adding very useful insights and aiding business decisions across a very broad range of levels within a firm, from the most granular (whether to buy/sell a specific MBS) up to strategic levels (where to build refineries around the globe or how much of a life insurance portfolio to hold versus re-selling to re-insurers).

Market Risk in Portfolios

12

W hen you group a set of similar trades together, the aggregate market risk is almost inevitably less then the sum of market risks added up deal by deal. It is easiest to see this with the longs and shorts for the same item because they cancel each other out. For example, suppose you are long 10,000 Euros in 5 weeks and short 8,000 Euros in 4.5 weeks. Your net market exposure is long 2,000 Euros for 4.5 weeks and long 10,000 Euros between 4.5 weeks and 5 weeks. This is considerably less than the risk in the two separate positions. When you look at the offsets in a portfolio of 100 or 200 Euro positions, say, equally balanced between longs and shorts, we can see a net Euro position through time that is much closer to 0. We can net out the positions, because the correlation is 1.

Portfolios get reductions in aggregate exposure from correlated positions as well. In the example above the correlation was 1, a Euro position correlates perfectly with another Euro position. When positions are highly correlated, say a long Euro and short Swiss Franc position, we get almost, but not complete offsets. Even positions that are only slightly correlated can contribute to this portfolio effect. *Correlation is the glue that allows us to aggregate returns on individual assets into a return for the portfolio.*

PORTFOLIO RISK MEASURES: THEIR EVOLUTION

The Traditional Measures: Duration, Greeks, and B.P. Shifts

Prior to the 1980s, most major dealers worked on a less centralized basis and were not as concerned about risks on an aggregated basis.

They focused on the risks at the desk and other lower levels of aggregation. For interest rate instruments, they looked at gaps between long and shorts and differences between fixed and floating obligations. They calculated the value changes that would occur with a basis point shift in yield, the 01 reports. They also looked at duration. For option portfolios, they looked at the Greeks (see Chapter 7).

As option and swap markets boomed in the 1980s, the shortcomings of these measures became more acute. Market intermediaries moved from trading specific positions to trading the risk elements. For example, options traders are either going long or shorting the Greeks. They describe their position as long or short volatility in various markets. They focus on the most efficient ways to reduce their gamma risk and they wonder whether their delta hedge strategy is sufficient when prices move rapidly.

Also, as markets became global, financial firms needed to measure the overall market risk they were taking across all markets and all instruments. None of the existing metrics could do this. The Value at Risk (VaR) measure was developed to fill this need. The most public example of this development was J.P. Morgan's widely publicized 4:15 report, so named because at 4:15 P.M. every day, the chairman received an aggregate measure of the firm's market risk based on positions at the close of the prior business day, quite timely for that era. This risk number was premised primarily on VaR methodologies, although measures of loss from stress were used for some positions.

Value at Risk—VaR

Two events in the middle 1990s helped catapult VaR models into almost universal use. First, in October 1994, J.P. Morgan launched a standard VaR framework called RiskMetrics. It described in detail a standard VaR methodology and published market data sets to be used for VaR calculations. This provided a standard benchmark for risk professionals to use. It also provided credibility to the VaR methodology. RiskMetrics has expanded and improved through several versions since it was introduced.

Second, in January 1996 the Basle Committee on Banking Supervision finalized a set of standards for determining capital adequacy covering market risk. This proposal broke new ground by allowing banks to use internal VaR models to determine the market risks, subject to a stringent set of characteristics. The new accord went into effect in January 1998 and provided a strong incentive, in the form of lower capital requirements, for banks to develop internal VaR modeling capability.

As a result, VaR has become the standard risk measurement tool, used almost universally. It is based on quantitative forecasting models and starts with a fairly straightforward definition. VaR is defined as the worst-case loss that could occur for a given portfolio subject to

1. A specified set of risks and
2. A given level of confidence
3. Over a given time horizon.

VaR has flexibility. It can be applied to single positions through the full portfolio of assets at a firm. It can measure just a single risk (price risk, basis risk, etc.) or higher risk aggregates (overall market risk and overall credit risk). Most importantly, it provides a measure of risk that cuts across all markets. Let's illustrate the general concept.

Level of Confidence For any portfolio, we obtain a forecast of possible future values that could occur over the given time horizon. The various prediction methods and the time horizons will be covered later. Given this distribution, we can determine the worst-case loss at various levels of confidence. Exhibit 12.1 shows the 40 to 1 loss $X and 100 to 1 loss $Y. This means that 99 percent of the time we shouldn't lose more than $Y, and we should expect to lose $X or less 97.5 percent of the time.

If statistics are used to create this forecast using a normal distribution with an average return and standard deviation (sigma), the two losses can be easily described as a multiple of the sigma. The 1 in 40 loss converts to approximately 2 standard deviations and the 1 in 100 loss converts to approximately 3 standard deviations. On the other hand, if the forecast is obtained using a discrete set of

Exhibit 12.1   Value at Risk (VaR) Illustration

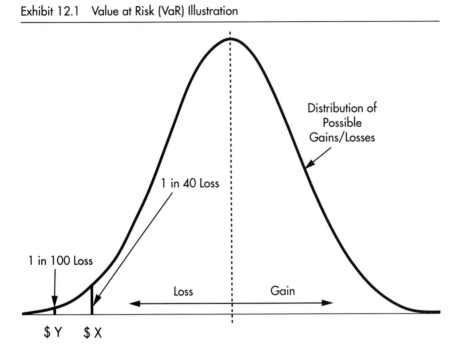

scenarios, such as actual market moves from past history, we would convert our confidence level into a specific observed loss. For example, with a forecast containing 400 future values, the 1 in 40 loss would correspond to the tenth-worst observed loss, and the 1 in a 100 loss would correspond to the fourth-worst observed loss.

Backtesting and Confidence   A nice feature of the VaR calculation is that it can be verified and recalibrated if necessary. VaR experts routinely perform these calibrations by using one set of historic market data to derive their models and then applying another set of price histories to confirm its accuracy. This is called *backtesting*.

A look at how backtesting works reveals a key feature of VaR models. Suppose you picked a lower confidence interval, say 1 in 10. You expect to observe a loss greater then your VaR about 10 percent of the time. With about two months of actual data, say, forty actual samples, you can expect a loss greater than your VaR about 4 times. With a sample that size, you can confirm whether the model is accurate or needs to be recalibrated. In statistics, sampling theory is well developed and allows the quant. jocks to confidently validate VaR, given these inputs. With a higher confidence interval, say 1 in 40 and the sample size, our expectations for observing a VaR excess drop to 1. Validating that VaR is more tenuous, unless we go for more than 40 observations. With a very high confidence interval, say 1 in 1,000, the validation and calibration breaks down. There are not enough observations to confirm a one in a thousand event. A sample with 1,000 daily observations covers years and exogenous factors could influence the results. The VaR model can be calibrated and is most accurate for the more frequently occurring loss amounts. We cannot have confidence in VaR for the rarest events and corresponding largest losses. *VaR is not designed for measuring risk out in the tail.*

Time Horizon   In VaR models for market risk, the market liquidity for the instruments in the portfolio drives the time horizon selected. For instruments in deep and liquid markets, say, government bonds, NYSE, and Nasdaq stocks, and highly rated short-term commercial paper, the time interval is quite short, typically one day. Traders are usually able to liquidate these instruments in that time frame. For less liquid instruments, say, high yield bonds or commercial mortgage backed securities, the holding period is longer, frequently a week or a month. When VaR models are used to calculate credit exposure, the time interval becomes multiple time periods that cover the life of the whole portfolio. It frequently spans years. We covered this manifestation of VaR in the credit section.

FORECASTING FOR VaR

Now let's get to how future portfolio values are generated. There are three major VaR methodologies: parametric, historic simulation, and Monte Carlo simulation. Each is described next, along with its strengths and weaknesses. Each method uses past market history in a slightly different way to create a forecast. Conventional wisdom on which forecasting technique is best has shifted from parametric to Monte Carlo.

Parametric VaR Models

Parametric VaR models capture past market moves in parameters—volatility and correlation of value—for a wide variety of standard instruments/tenors. These parameters become a framework for the projection of risk. Picture a grid on which each vertex is a value point for the standard instruments. Some of these vertices capture value of a major index at points through time. For example, the U.S. government bond could have vertices (zero-coupon rates) for 2, 4, 7, 10, 15, 20, and 30 years. Each of the points has a value and volatility associated with it. Each point is connected to all the others by correlation.

Positions or portfolios whose risk is being measured are mapped into this matrix. For example, the principal repayment of U.S. government bond with a 25-year maturity would be split and mapped to the 20- and 30-year vertices. The split would not necessarily be equal. The semi-annual interest payments would be mapped as appropriate to the points noted above. When all positions in the portfolio are mapped to the vertices in the model, the most recent volatility and correlation is applied to the values at each point to obtain a distribution of future values.

RiskMetrics RiskMetrics is the most commonly used parametric VaR model. RiskMetrics Group provides a detailed description of its specific methodology and updates volatility and correlation data sets daily. These data sets are publicly available, posted on a Web site each day, and provide the latest calculated volatility for a number of instruments in various markets: FX Rates, money market rates, government bond 0 rates, various commodities, and so on. The Risk-Metrics Group, now spun off from J.P. Morgan, provides an extensive description of how these data are gathered and calculated.[1] For example, the volatility is calculated using an exponential weighting scheme in which the most recent price changes are weighted more heavily. They also describe exactly how they overcome numerous statistical issues, like price gaps that occur when a given market is closed for a holiday or how they adjust for market timing differences, such as Tokyo and London closing prices differing from New York market-close price.

Parametric VaR Strengths/Weaknesses   As VaR models go, parametric VaR is quite easy computationally. It is also quite easy to implement, as RiskMetrics provides a transparent and widely accepted standard. Many software vendors have developed packages that easily convert positions, calculate the VaR, and combine it with fairly sophisticated analytical reports. Parametric VaR was the first widely used method, and remains in place at many locations.

It does have weaknesses. It assumes normal distributions that typically underestimate the risks in the tails. Another problem is that it doesn't capture the risk from convexity. In terms of the Greeks, parametric VaR captures delta risk quite well, but not gamma, theta, or vega. This makes it particularly inaccurate for portfolios with options or imbedded options in them. A recent extension of the parametric model has been devised which does capture certain types of gamma or nonlinear risk. This newer model is more complex and still only an approximate solution.

Historic Simulation VaR

Historic simulation VaR models don't use statistical techniques to generate the forecast. Past market price moves are applied directly to the current portfolio to calculate a set of possible future portfolio values. In a nutshell, you run your daily P/L process over and over again, using the history of past daily market price moves. You've calculated the value of your portfolio as of close of business. You've got the positions, the valuation models, and all the closing market prices required for valuation. If you've got a history of these closing market prices, you're all set to make your forecast. You simply apply each daily price move directly to your current portfolio and record how much the value changes. One year's history will give you more than 200 possible future portfolio values. You can even apply weights to the most recent price moves to count recent history more heavily, but that would introduce statistics. Once you've got the forecast, you can determine VaR by ranking the value changes by size and picking the one that corresponds to your confidence level. For example, with a forecast of 200 and a 97.5 percent confidence level, we would use the fifth-worst return as our VaR.

Historic Simulation VaR Strengths/Weaknesses   This method has an elegant simplicity about it. It covers all market risks, because it uses actual market results. It does not convert them into a model, which is then used generate the forecast. So, unlike parametric VaR, it captures gamma and all the other Greeks. It is also reasonably easy to implement, albeit harder than implementing parametric VaR.

The historic VaR method also has shortcomings. Whatever market trends are in the history you use are built into the VaR you calculate. Some risk professionals see this as a problem. Also, it is harder to extract the risk factors (risks to a specific currency or interest rate) with this methodology. It can be done—it is just more difficult than with other VaR methods with those factors built into the forecast model. Finally, historic VaR doesn't work when longer intervals are required. If we wanted the one-week VaR, two years of market history would yield only about a hundred forecasts, just barely enough. Note, overlapping the sample periods would lead to invalid results, since they are no longer independent observations. If we tried for the ten-day holding period that BIS requires for regulatory capital, we'd need three years of history to get sixty observations. This is not acceptable.

One final note is that historic simulation VaR requires more administration. No standard data sets are available. The institutions that use it must maintain a very robust database of market price history. When they switch valuation models, they've got to be sure they have a valid market-time series for the new valuation model.

Monte Carlo Simulation VaR

The Monte Carlo model is easy conceptually but most challenging to implement. This forecast method is based on simulating a series future market conditions—creating scenarios and then valuing the portfolio in each of those scenarios. It is a stripped-down version of the credit Monte Carlo simulation model described in Chapter 10. It projects scenarios over a much shorter time, one day or ten days, and doesn't include the netting considerations required for credit. It is the most computationally intense VaR method; frankly, it is a statistician's dream. It was first implemented for portfolios with a lot of embedded options like MBS and option portfolios.

Monte Carlo Simulation requires a very complex set of algorithms and lots of data processing power. Also, the results are frequently hard to track back through the processing. It is, however a model that measures gamma risk/convexity. This is critical for portfolios with options or embedded options. It also provides an employment guarantee for the mathematicians and technical staff who run them.

The Move to Monte Carlo Simulation   VaR has been in fairly broad use at U.S. banks and securities firms for more than five years now. Over that time many firms have progressed from parametric VaR methods toward Monte Carlo simulation. This evolution is consistent with market and technical trends. The product mix in the markets has shifted to more instruments with embedded options. Monte Carlo VaR is best at capturing the resulting gamma risk. On the technical side, continued jumps in computing speeds have reduced run times for Monte and are making it more practical.

VaR Summary

VaR has many strengths that have lead to its rapid expansion. As we have seen above, it is particularly useful for comparing risks across various markets and portfolios. It allows us to compare on a consistent basis the market risks that various traders incur: fixed-income, currency, commodity, equity, and so on. It also allows for the decomposition of those risks into smaller components. It can be extended to credit risks as well.

The feature of quantifying relative risk across various markets opens the door for risk-adjusted measures of performance. No longer do we have to look only at the return a trader, desk, or business line achieved—we can look at that return in the context of how much capital was required to cover at least market risk, providing a fairer measure of performance. Finally, for market risk applications the accuracy of the model can be constantly tested and recalibrated as needed.

VaR also has weaknesses. First, VaR is just one number and market risk has many dimensions. To describe your risk using it alone, without supplementary information, is like painting with one color and one brush. You simply cannot depict the full texture and range of your market risks with VaR alone. Also, VaR doesn't work well in certain markets and for certain extreme events. VaR is generally most reliable in deep liquid markets where stress and other events occur less frequently. However, VaR is not accurate when markets make extreme moves. For example, VaR models would not have provided an accurate picture of the equity market losses that occurred on October 19, 1987.

VaR's predictive power and utility in emerging markets and markets with low liquidity is much poorer. In these markets, stress and other events influence the markets as much as historic price behavior. So VaR, which makes predictions based exclusively on past market behavior, is not the best choice.

In short, VaR models do not provide an accurate measure of the losses that occur in extreme events. This weakness is clear from the backtesting/calibration discussion. The extreme losses farther out in the tail are not captured in these models that frequently assume normal distribution of returns. Stress and scenario testing are currently the best way to understand the potential for extreme losses. They are a natural complement to VaR analysis.

STRESS TESTING

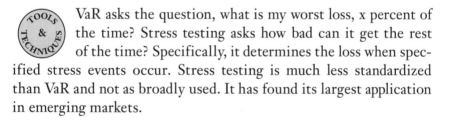 VaR asks the question, what is my worst loss, x percent of the time? Stress testing asks how bad can it get the rest of the time? Specifically, it determines the loss when specified stress events occur. Stress testing is much less standardized than VaR and not as broadly used. It has found its largest application in emerging markets.

Stress Scenarios

To examine losses from stress, we have to specify stressed market scenarios. These scenarios come from three sources. First, there are simple shocks. These are a series of standard and straightforward price moves that are applied to portfolios. For example, all yield curves might get four simple stresses: a parallel shift up, parallel shift down, a steeper curve (short end drops and long end rises), and a flattening/inversion. For a credit risk shock, we might double all credit spreads or we could specify a 50 percent jump in default rates. Past market stress events provide a second source of market scenarios. The stock market moves in October for selected years—the Mexican Peso crisis of 1995, the ERM or pound peg crisis, and recent global contagion in 1998—can be used as sources for stress scenarios. Our third source comes from management, which can provide a set of likely stress events based on their experience and judgment.

Each source provides insight into where the portfolio is vulnerable to large losses, but each also has problems. Arbitrage issues hit the simple stress and management prediction scenarios hardest. Past market stress situations are suspect because, like lightning, stressed markets don't hit the same way twice.

Arbitrage Issues

It is difficult to create stress scenarios that are arbitrage-free. A radical change in one or more sets of market prices ripples out through the market fabrics to create large changes everywhere. Model makers are challenged to create all the market price changes in a stress scenario while concurrently maintaining an arbitrage-free equilibrium. For example, the simple interest rate shock of a parallel shift upward implies the related currency will become stronger across the boards. How much of that strength will hit the spot rate versus forward rates? Even more difficult, how will expectations about volatility shift for both interest and currency rates? These expectations are reflected in the option prices, so they must be determined if an arbitrage-free equilibrium is to be maintained.

The arbitrage issue looms largest for the scenarios incorporating management predictions. The simple shock scenarios dimension the risk to specific market drivers. They are designed and used to measure value change from specific rate changes. They are not typically used to measure risk across the whole market fabric. Similarly, the stress scenarios from history may contain windows for arbitrage, but they reflect real market conditions. In any case, the arbitrage opportunities are quite rare in the stressed markets because bid/ask spreads become very large, if there are any bids at all. When managers provide predictions, their forecast covers specific parts of various markets, leaving many other market price changes "blank." They typically want to see the full impact of their predictions on the portfolio, including the ripples across all of the market fabric. So, assumptions about how to fill in the blanks have to be made.

Stress Measurement

The stress scenarios need to be applied to the whole portfolio. This is difficult when the aggregate portfolio is not captured in a single data warehouse, as is frequently the case. Many institutions, particularly banks, run their stress testing against a decentralized portfolio. They transmit each scenario or have a standard set of scenarios, which are applied to the various portfolios. Resulting value changes are then aggregated.

Uses of Stress

Stress measures are used most extensively in emerging markets. Returns in these markets have not behaved the same way the returns in OECD markets have. The standard risk measurement tools, many of which assume a normal distribution of returns, have not worked here. Frequently, the worst loss from a series of simple shocks to an EM portfolio is called VaR and aggregated into global VaR reports. This practice justifiably bothers risk professionals, as it dilutes VaR's meaning—accuracy and potency. It does, however, highlight the key challenge for broader use of stress testing.

Stress testing helps dimension the risk in extreme market events, but it doesn't provide any insight into the likelihood of these losses. It identifies vulnerabilities to specific market factors and even provides a relative measure of the potential losses. It will become a much more valuable tool when ways to reliably predict the probability of these events are developed. Eventually stress testing will become a tool for quantifying losses based on management's educated guesses about large market moves and the likelihood of those moves. This will be much easier when the transaction book is in a consolidated data warehouse and when arbitrage-free methods are developed to fill in the blanks, that is, to extend specific predicted price changes out across all market prices.

THE LESSONS OF 1998

The year 1998 was very interesting for risk management professionals. Financial markets behaved quite differently from all predictions. For the first time, global contagion swept from non-OECD markets across to OECD markets. Perhaps most alarming was the liquidity freezes that hit some of the deepest and most reliable markets. Before 1998, few market professionals believed a freeze in the LIBOR swap market and off-the-run U.S. bonds was anything but an extremely remote possibility. Those beliefs have been revised.

The connections across financial markets have grown much stronger over the past twenty years. This has forced greater efficiency into all those markets. It has also bound them more tightly together in terms of performance and risk. 1998 showed that geographical dispersion no longer guarantees diversity in your portfolio. The correlations across markets have become stronger and, in times of stress, can move toward unity.

One conclusion from 1998 is that stress testing is important, too. It complements VaR. VaR alone has proven insufficient, especially in the extreme markets. It is not designed to be a reliable measure of extreme market losses. Although stress testing is not as quantitatively rigorous, it helps gauge risks from extraordinary conditions.

WRAP-UP

- Portfolio measures of risk have emerged in the 1990s supported by developments in models, computing power, and communications.
- A little push from regulatory agencies has extended the use of VaR.
- In 1998, the limitations of VaR methods became very apparent, prompting new searches for tools to measure risk from extreme market moves and illiquid markets.

Simulation **13**

Monte Carlo simulation and other open-form techniques will become the basis for measuring risk in large portfolios. In the past, the goal was to obtain closed-form solutions, equations that pre-ordained the answer once the variables were filled in. Open-form techniques, which have only become feasible with the advent of computers, do not produce a single predetermined result. They generate a whole distribution of possible outcomes, each of which has allowed the variables to migrate within predefined limits. Open-form techniques are a better choice where there are many variables that influence the outcome and when those variables can shift through time.

These techniques have already become the basis for most GRM activities. We've already described why Monte Carlo is the de facto choice for measuring market risk in portfolios with embedded options and for measuring pre-settlement credit risk. In the banking and securities world, the Monte Carlo models are filled with distillations of past market history.[1] Using Monte Carlo this way provides an objective forecast of future market conditions and an objective measure of risk. Monte Carlo simulation allows for subjective issues, such as management beliefs or concerns, to be incorporated in the forecast. Scanning the ways in which Monte Carlo is being applied in other industries will illustrate how flexible and potentially useful it is.

One software vendor has built a product that incorporates portfolio strategies with adjustments that would occur in response to various market conditions that are modeled.[2] The resulting risk measures include consideration for how a portfolio holding will be adjusted in response to various market conditions. For example, when the simulation forecasts a scenario with hard economic conditions, the lender will tighten its credit underwriting standards, raising the overall credit quality of its retail loans. When the economy is booming, the lender may lower his credit standards and increase his loan book. The key point here is that Monte can dynamically model these portfolio adjustments that are likely to occur along each projection into the future. Other portfolio models assume a static portfolio.

Asset/liability risk in banks used to be measured with durations, basis point shifts, and the Greeks. The growth in derivative instruments has introduced a great deal more gamma risk into both sides of the balance sheet. There has been a significant move to measure the asset/liability risk with Monte Carlo simulations and other simulations that capture the gamma risk.

These models also expand the traditional role of asset/liability management upward toward balance sheet structuring. In the past, A/L largely worked at a granular level, adjusting mismatches in duration and fixed/floating rates. A/L management is becoming much more closely linked with the other risk management functions (market and credit). For example, using Monte Carlo, risk teams can model securitizations, and other broad financial engineering techniques, which strengthen the balance sheet.

Insurance companies have been making use of these new techniques, too. They have created Dynamic Financial Analysis (DFA), really another form of Monte Carlo simulation. It aids decisions like pricing, re-insurance, securitization, asset allocation, and more by showing their impact on cash flow, surplus, statutory financials, GAAP financials, and capital ratios. DFA differs from the financial applications described so far, because it accommodates both hard and soft inputs for projecting the scenarios. It can use management's opinions as well as market history for creating forecasts.[3] These opinions are gathered in the form of a range of possible values and associated likelihoods. There are vendor packages that support this form of analysis.[4] The developers of stress scenarios might use some of the pages from this script. Just like other financial institutions, insurance companies are moving to incorporate the new quantitative models to support decisions at all levels of their organization.[5]

Some large firms are even starting to use forms of Monte for decision support—resource allocation, planning growth, and so on. Simulation captures the dynamics and provides management with a clearer view of the impact of their decisions.

Getting back to a more parochial, financial service view, Monte is the only model available for linking market, credit, and operational risk. Major market perturbations beget credit problems. Market and credit risks are not independent. Operational breakdowns and losses are also much more likely in times of market stress. Monte is flexible enough to start to capture these dependencies and reflect them in the results.

CASE STUDY: GLOBAL OIL CO.

This case illustrates the compelling benefits from measuring and managing risks at the portfolio level. Specifically, it shows how this company is centralizing its measurement and management of certain specific financial risks in response to the developments in markets, technology, and models. It also looks at the impact of those trends on the management of its core business activities.

Operations

Global Oil Co. is among the largest oil companies in the world. It is in the top ten along many measures: reserves, transport, processing, retail, chemicals, and so on. It operates in over 100 countries, employs over 100,000 people, and deploys over $50 billion in capital. It is a fully integrated company moving oil and gas products from underground through refining and processing on to final consumers, both commercial and retail. It has associated business activities in gas and power, and chemicals.

Organization

Global Oil Co. has a complex corporate structure, created in response to international tax codes. Its structure reflects a decentralized history and culture. It has hundreds of operating companies under its major lines of business.

Risks

Global Oil Co. faces very diverse and significant risks. To accurately depict them, we would have to expand the nonfinancial side of our risk spectrum. Operational, technical, political, and environmental risks are all major concerns for a multinational integrated oil company. Global Oil Co. takes significant project risk when large chunks of capital, high technology, esoteric engineering, key project management skills, and much more must be orchestrated constructively to achieve success. We would also need to expand the event, political, and legal sectors of the spectrum to reflect the risks incurred when doing business globally.

One major risk is inherent in its core business of moving petroleum products out of the ground through pipes, and via tankers, refineries and pumps to consumers. The market price available at any one of the many links in the chain could drop below the costs, creating a loss. Indeed, the whole value-added chain can be squeezed, as was the case through early 1999. From 1997 through to early 1999 world oil production exceeded demand, depressing retail prices and squeezing profitability at all the oil majors. Because this company is fully integrated, that is, it is in the full value chain from reserves to consumption, it is insulated from losses that might occur at isolated points in the chain. However, it was not immune to the industrywide squeeze. Major oil companies' returns can also suffer when the smooth flow of product through its significant infrastructure of capital-intensive assets is disrupted.

There are significant financial risks that arise from any major oil company's operations as well. It raises billions in capital to finance projects, creating interest rate risks to manage. It deals in over 100 currencies, creating currency transaction volume and breadth as large as that of a major bank. Its hundreds of operating companies need to fund their daily activities and manage their cash. It also must insure against the significant environmental hazards inherent in its operations and manage significant investment risks in various pension funds.

Amid this cornucopia of potential risk management stories, we will focus on the company's financial risks and core business risks. In both areas, incentives to go global with risk management, despite a tradition/culture for decentralization, have been compelling.

Decentralized Treasuries

In the past, each local operating company managed its financial risks from operations at the local level. Consistent with its decentralized culture, Global Oil Co.'s financial risk management was delegated to each business. Each operating unit had a treasury to handle cash management, FX exposures, and short-term borrowing needs for its operations. This typically meant that each operating group was responsible for projecting its cash needs, determining the risks, and hedging them. Central management provided very clear and conservative guidelines on what risks the local treasuries could hedge and what instruments they could hedge them with, but left each business free to work within those guidelines.

Not all decisions were delegated. Large projects involving major capital expenditures have always been reviewed and approved in a central forum with capital provided by Group Holding Companies, if appropriate. However, each operating unit managed its own cash and currency positions through local third-party borrowing/deposits and local FX trading.

The FX risks varied with the operations of each business. Typically, the exploration side has expenses in local currencies and revenues from oil sales in U.S. dollars, while the process and retail end have expenses in U.S. dollars (crude and finished product purchases, and revenues in local currencies). With many businesses using local hedges to balance their chronically short or chronically long USD positions, there was a significant opportunity in pooling FX exposures to a global portfolio.

Similar opportunities existed in the cash management as well. First, Global Oil Co. was engaging in much more activity than needed on a pooled basis. Loans in one operating unit, which could be offset by deposits in another operating unit were both being handled by local banks. Similarly, long USD positions in one unit were not pooled with short USD positions in another. Both were being hedged in the FX market. Second, the local businesses could not obtain the best market prices for their activities. Both their trade volumes and their credit ratings were lower than the parent company. Global Oil Co. was not leveraging its considerable bargaining power in the markets. For FX, centralized trading would yield volume discounts. For cash management, the parent company's triple-A rating could fetch better loan rates than the lower rated operating subsidiaries. Third, not all businesses were measuring their risks and hedging them optimally. Risk management practices, systems, and sophistication varied.

The parent company knew of these inefficiencies and wanted to resolve them. However, there were obstacles. There was a wide divergence of systems and processes across the operating units. IT integration would be difficult. There were capital barriers and withholding tax issues as well. There is always organizational resistance to this sort of change. Over the past ten years, several of these obstacles have shrunk or even disappeared. IT integration is much easier today, as it has become an established business practice. Barriers to capital flows and tax issues have lessened greatly as well. Also, costs for the special risk management skills and systems have escalated, creating a cost savings incentive for a single trading center. With these developments, the business case for central management of cash/borrowing and FX became conclusive.

Central Treasury

About two years ago, a new central treasury group was formed with a mandate to provide financial risk management services to the operating units at price levels that reflect the efficiencies gained from going global. The initiative had two phases. Phase one centralized the cash management and short-term borrowing activities, whereas phase two will do the same for currency risk measurement and management activities.

At this writing, phase one has been implemented in more than thirty countries, covering more than half of its cash-management activities. This new treasury group has effectively become an internal bank for the businesses. Approximately $12 billion of local debt and temporary cash surpluses are being intermediated through this internal bank. The local bank spreads on both sides has been kept in house and the central treasury's net borrowing is much lower, and at lower rates. The extra costs of this new group for special risk management resources and systems is more than offset by savings in the many local treasuries who no longer have to support local cash management.

Phase two promises similar benefits by extending central treasury service for FX risk. It is already underway, expanding from a core capability established with the euro conversion. Significant benefits from volume discounts and reduced overall hedging volumes have already been realized.

There was some resistance to moving toward centralization. This challenge was overcome gradually through communication of the business rationales, demonstration of results, and realignment of targets. The most compelling argument came with demonstrated value. When the central treasury group offered transactions at rates as good as or better than local banks, the business case was too convincing to ignore.

Oil Risk Management

Global Oil Co.'s risks in its core business are similar to the risks examined in the Enron case with a few extra factors that greatly increase the complexity and on a scale that dwarfs Enron's gas risks. Although natural gas undergoes very little processing between well head and delivery, oil goes through quite a number of processing steps as it is transformed from crude oil into a wide variety of finished products, such as, fuel oil, jet fuel, chemicals, and plastics. The transport links in the oil chain are also more varied. There are pipelines from well heads to ports, then tankers from ports to refineries, then more tankers or pipelines for moving refined product(s) to storage points, and, finally, many forms of distribution to retail and industrial consumers. The processing and transportation logistics in this chain create a much more complicated set of risks to manage and requires the close integration of market risk and operational risk. Global Oil Co.'s daily delivery of energy is more than 100 times greater than Enron's.

Every day Global Oil Co. moves over 5 million barrels of oil through the chain from crude oil to finished petroleum products. To support this core business, Global Oil Co. has built an oil trading center using the external markets to manage its portfolio of exposures from this flow of oil. The trading company is responsible for managing all of the risks related to the movement, whether the oil has been sourced from their own reserves or externally. Their mandate is to maximize the overall benefit from moving this oil through the chain, which contains many market interfaces. Very few of the hydrocarbon molecules make it all the way through in Global Oil Co.'s hands. The aggregate traded physical volume is quite a bit larger than the company's base business volume. Measurement and risk management of the traded business occurs on a portfolio basis.

Global Oil Co. pools its oil flow to ensure optimal execution of the numerous operational options inherent in its activities. In addition to oil assets, Global Oil Co. has many other assets, including refineries, tanker fleets, storage facilities, and pipelines, whose utilization needs to be maximized. The trading company uses external markets to achieve that optimization. For example, decisions about which ships to load with what product, how full to fill them, and where to dispatch them are made by balancing Global Oil Co.'s needs against the current markets. Suppose a shipload of oil from the Middle East is scheduled for delivery to the eastern United States in three months. Market and operational conditions may occur to cause the trading company to redeploy that delivery to the Far East, and replace the U.S. delivery from the market. In this context, oil market prices are just one of many factors, mostly operational, that drive the trading and the operational decisions. Within this broad spectrum of operational risks, the trading group measures and manages oil price risk along three dimensions: outright price risk, exposure to the main marker price differentials, and backwardation risk. *Backwardation* occurs when the spot price rises above the forward price. Similar to an inverted yield curve, it is triggered by high demand or tight supplies. Backwardation occurs much more frequently than yield curve inversions. However, price risk is clearly just one of the many considerations that drive the trading company's decisions.

The price hedging opportunities vary along the value chain as well. Crude oil is a relatively homogenous product moving through deep and standardized channels around the globe. The oil markets, with just three primary product indexes, West Texas Intermediate, Brent, and Dubai, provide standard markers which correlate quite closely to Global Oil Co.'s physical price exposure. At this front end of the chain, Global Oil Co. can obtain substantial price insurance, low basis risk, from a liquid market. At the product end of the chain, flow is spread across a diverse set of finished products to a diverse set of customers. Finished products have a much wider range of quality. Consequently, the markets for finished petroleum products provide hedges with more basis risk in them. Global Oil Co. is quite active in these markets, but its risk management challenge is a little more complex here.

While Global Oil Co. has managed its oil product flow on a centralized basis for decades, it has never done it as well as it does today. The trading companies' sophistication and ability to coordinate activities have never been higher. Advances in computing, communications, and operational/risk models have provided substantially enhanced capabilities, even though they are only partially incorporated. Market risk measures like VaR have been incorporated and are used extensively. More interesting is the extension of the models to cover their core business risks. Simulation models are now also being introduced to help configure the operations.

This case illustrates the compelling economic arguments for managing risk at a portfolio level. Effective tools and techniques for measuring and managing global risk portfolios are now available, and they provide large tangible benefits in terms of lowered costs and greater efficiencies. These arguments are overwhelming for all firms that are major global intermediaries in any market.

WRAP-UP

- Monte Carlo simulation and other open-form techniques will become the basis for measuring risk in large portfolios.
- These techniques can incorporate the dynamics through time into the measures of risk.
- Advances in computing speed make it feasible to apply this form of analysis to a much broader set of business problems.

DEVELOPING A GLOBAL RISK MANAGEMENT PROCESS

Risk Management: The Vision and the Reality 14

There have been tremendous changes in financial markets these past twenty years. The fabric of market risk is much more precisely measured and priced. This precision harmonized with the evolution of derivative products. Together they facilitated the parsing and repackaging of market risks into securities that more closely match investor/end-user appetites. Derivatives have greatly facilitated hedging, forced greater market efficiency through arbitrage, and probably enhanced market liquidity. We have seen technology rapidly force greater standardization and efficiency into all the markets. The sophisticated models that were developed to cover market risk are being adapted to measure credit risk in creative and exciting ways.

Most important for risk managers, an internally consistent set of tools for measuring all financial risks has emerged. This tool set is applicable across all the financial risks in the most liquid markets. While the applicability of these models is not universal, the core risks at most global financial institutions can now be measured with enough accuracy to provide management improvements.

What does this mean for global financial institutions? Risk has become the new management imperative in finance. Risk is on the cusp of becoming the new currency within financial institutions. It is now possible to estimate the marginal impact of every major deal on the overall risk profile of the firm. Market risk and credit risk can be quantified and considered against the return a deal provides. Each deal's contribution to shareholder value or its risk-adjusted return on capital can be determined. These measures create a framework for harmonizing activity at financial firms. A direct connection between the firm's appetite for risk, defined by senior management and the deals that are executed at the most granular levels can now be created in the form of risk-adjusted pricing. Eventually, all deals will be charged for the incremental risks they create for the firm, market, credit, and operational risk components. The price will be scaled to the firm's appetite for that incremental risk, and trading will gravitate to the most appropriate products.

The first two sections of this book described the development of financial risk measures that can be used to create this pricing framework now. This is beginning to occur in the form of capital allocations for risk. Indeed, The Chase Manhattan Corp. has begun using such a framework called Shareholder Value Added (SVA). Many other financial institutions are developing enterprise wide risk-management frameworks. The stated objective for many of these initiatives is improved control. That objective can and should be revised to include aligning incentives.

These frameworks include the third set of risks, operational risks, and they can be incorporated as well. However, they use a different set of measures, which are currently a bit rudimentary. There is a tremendous effort underway to better quantify operational risks, and those measures will become more robust.

Let's describe the GRM vision for financial risk a little more specifically and then look at the significant infrastructure and process changes that are required to support it. There are compelling reasons for creating the infrastructure, even if it never achieves the risk-management nirvana described. Finally, before we get too excited about the possibilities, we'll look at the major impediments that must be overcome to achieve this vision. They are not small.

THE VISION FOR RISK MANAGEMENT: GO GLOBAL

The Global Risk Management Process

Global risk management is:

1. The consistent, accurate, and timely measurement of all risks in the firm

2. The process by which those aggregate risks are attributed to deals, portfolios, and various business lines, and how charges for them are levied

3. The process by which groups within the firm are allowed to use/consume incremental risk and absorb charges for it

When implemented effectively, GRM becomes the internal framework for ensuring that scarce resources within the firm, primarily capital, are channeled into their most productive use. It is not centralized management of all risks. It is centralized measurement of risks integrated with a transparent and equitable process for incurring incremental risk. It gets to the heart of how financial service firms make money: they must intermediate financial risks more efficiently than the external markets. GRM can enhance the collaboration among all groups that create risk while simultaneously clarifying and enforcing senior management's risk appetite for various risks. We will look at the three steps specifically.

Consistent Measurement Current convention breaks all risks into three subsets: market risk, credit risk, and operational risk. We've looked at market and credit risk extensively, how they differ, what they share, and the emergence of a consistent set of financial risk measures that cover both. A combination of VaR-based and stress-based models is currently the most complete way to quantify these financial risks. Operational risk measures are available, too. The standards and models for risk measurement in all these areas are sure to evolve, so the process must have "plug-n'-play" compatibility for model improvements.

The risk measures must be consistent with outside markets to prevent arbitrage. For example, the securities firm that charges capital for credit risk all the way down to the desk level bases its charges on the market spreads for each name (the spread above the risk-free rate that each name has in debt markets). Based on the spreads, they calculate a term structure for credit risk. This creates fluctuations in credit charges, which are not popular. When market credit spreads widened sharply in late 1998 and the resulting charges hit the desks, the words *not popular* understate the traders' reaction. However, since charges are based on market rates, arbitrage opportunities are eliminated, and arguments against it are stifled by market reality. This method is not without controversy—opponents say the spread contains a liquidity premium, or that it is too volatile. But it has worked. Traders are much more careful with credit risk now that they are charged for it even if the charges aren't perfect.

We compare this situation to that at another major institution where charges for credit risk are not levied down to trading businesses. Because this institution does charge for market risk, internal arbitrage occurs. Recently, the trading group entered into a deal that created tens of millions of dollars of incremental credit exposure, enough to require approval for a big limit increase with that counterparty. The deal significantly reduced their market risk. The group effectively converted market risk into credit risk. They were being charged capital for the market risk and the credit risk was free, at least for them. The aggregate change in risk to the institution is not known and probably was not optimized with this trade. This arbitrage opportunity, from market to credit risk, is available in many trading organizations. *It will not end until credit risk management moves from the back office where it has been relegated and is fully incorporated into traders' dealing activities and incentives.*

Allocation The allocation of overall risk should be based on the marginal contribution each sub-portfolio makes to the aggregate levels of risk. A dealer/desk or business line whose set of deals actually reduces overall risk should get a credit instead of a charge. This is the only way to motivate the business to price the risk-reducing deals appropriately. The challenge of building an infrastructure to support this level of risk allocation is substantial. Also, the challenge of how to determine the marginal contribution of each portfolio and each risk is substantial.

There are several ways in which risk can be measured and charges in the form of capital allocated.[1] The methodology debate rages and will continue for a long time. One method measures earnings at risk, whereas another is based on measures of asset volatility. The simplest approaches examine the risk/return profile of each deal, without attempting to see its marginal impact on aggregate risk. No models currently treat market and credit risk as dependent variables, which is generally acknowledged to be the case.

None of these methods is *the* right one, rather they all are. Even the crudest and simplest allocation methods are providing better guidance for incremental trading than the "limit" process which is currently in place almost everywhere.

Incremental Dealing Most institutions control incremental trading through risk limits. They provide room for more dealing in products, business lines, and specific deals that are perceived to provide the highest risk/return ratio. This limit process has been in place for a long time. However, limits are a tool for control, not efficiency. Centrally planned economies achieved remarkable control with their production quotas. They also achieved monumental inefficiencies. Limits within financial houses create similar inefficiencies and abuses. A senior credit officer once commented to me, "I've lowered limits to the trade group in Paris. Their operation stinks. They don't know what they are doing there." His power to set granular limits took him well beyond his job of defining the overall credit appetite for given counterparties. Granular limits also constrain the movement of credit availability to match shifting patterns of trade.

With the advent of global risk management, a more efficient and effective alternative is available. Control and efficiency can be achieved with an internal market for risk. The control occurs through a sliding price scale for the risks being incurred. As a given level of risk approaches the firm's appetite, the price for more of that risk goes up. Incremental use will occur only if the deal's return justifies it. Similarly, the internal market can provide an incentive to reduce the risk with a credit based on the same sliding price scale. Deals that offset and reduce specific risks should be priced lower. The efficiency is achieved through the free internal market. Incremental dealing will flow to those products and services that create the largest risk-adjusted returns. There are strong links between this internal market and external markets. As noted above, the internal market pricing must prevent arbitrage by closely matching what dealers can obtain in external markets.

A key concept here is how this link between internal and external markets will reinforce the firm's natural strengths. The firm's margins are greatest where it is most efficient vis-à-vis external markets. The firm will automatically grow where it has a franchise, that is, where the firm is a more efficient intermediary than the markets. When the firm establishes an internal market that accurately reflects its risks/costs (not easy), it builds dynamic response and opportunism into its process.

The challenges to achieving this transition are very large. The path for something of this scope is full of compromises, stopgap measures, and temporary solutions that are dictated by reality. However, the trend is compelling and significant.

The Global Risk Management Infrastructure

To support the three steps in GRM, a global infrastructure needs to be built. GRM is at the nexus of high technology, mathematically intense quantitative models, and complex operations and processes. Building the operations and process takes a very long time. Exhibit 14.1 shows the major components of the GRM Infrastructure.

Risk engines perform the calculations that measure risk. They include a wide range of algorithms and programs. Valuation models are at the simpler end of the gamut and simulation models are at the other end. All these engines need to be easily invoked and run promptly for trading portfolios, and perhaps less rapidly for credit portfolios.

Data sets contain the prodigious amounts of information required to support the risk engine processing. Major data sets for input include: transactions/deals, current market prices, various model support data (price histories, variance and correlation tables, etc.), and major outputs (exposure calculations and other risk information). Another major data set that supports risk processing from start to finish is the static information. This is a bit of a misnomer, really, since much of this data can be quite dynamic. Static information includes data about customers (keys, hierarchies, contractual arrangements), risk appetite/limits, product tables, and internal organizational frameworks (booking entities, account charts).

Exhibit 14.1   The Global Risk Management Infrastructure

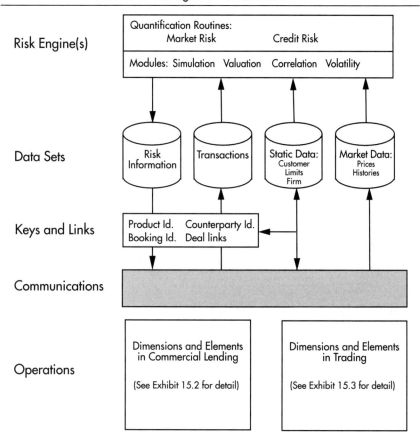

The data keys provide the vital linkage across sets of data that is necessary for a global process. Standards for global identifiers (counterparty IDs, booking IDs, product codes) need to be established and followed by all participants. Any break in these key links jeopardizes the global process.

Fast, reliable communications are a key element to the global process. These links effectively bring all trading or business locations into one virtual space, enabling a global process. The global process can get hit quite hard by breakdowns or degradation of service.

The last element is operations, both the nitty-gritty daily activities in every business line and the operations and controls over the

GRM process. The global operation must work in close coordination with operations in each location.

Global risk management can provide a lasting competitive advantage, but it takes a considerable investment of both money and time to get there. Fortunately, there are other very significant reasons for building the pieces. Certain parts of the process, notably in credit risk management, provide immediate and significant benefits. They can be cost-justified on a stand-alone basis, without consideration for how they contribute to GRM.

Market Risk Is Now Global

We know how markets have globalized. The risks have globalized, too. Since 1994, we have experienced a series of ever-more serious examples of global market contagion. The Tequila effect that we saw from Mexico's Peso devaluation in late 1994 was the first sign of global risk in the markets. It disrupted a whole continent. All of Latin America experienced problems precipitated by Mexico's actions. Our next talisman came in 1997 with the devaluation of a minor currency in Thailand. This seemingly minor event affected a whole hemisphere. It created an economic tsunami that rushed over all the Asian Tiger markets, including the powerhouse economies of Korea and Japan. These perturbations caused concern in the United States and Europe and influenced certain market sectors there as well. Our most recent contagion in the second half of 1998 was truly global in its impact. Russia's failure to service its debt and the subsequent divergence of spreads across all markets around the globe was unprecedented. The ensuing liquidity problems and losses in major markets created a bewildering phenomenon for most financial firms and risk managers.

This last contagion appears to have had two major results. The risk-management models have been found wanting, yet the importance of the risk-management function appears to have risen at many firms.[2] VaR risk models have lost credibility and many assumptions about liquidity in certain deep markets have also been knocked over. The mathematicians are back at their drawing boards, sifting through more models, seeking better predictions.

They will doubtless find improvements. Models to get at the risk out in the tails, where VaR was never very good, are being examined. Models to capture liquidity freezes are also being researched.

Given the failures, the increased importance of risk management at firms appears a bit odd. However, firms have recognized that their market risk processes, which have been largely regional or local, need to be globalized. Timely, accurate information about all positions is a prerequisite for effective management in this new global marketplace. You can't run flexible "what if" stress tests or determine global VaR accurately without a central transaction file. When the next contagion hits, the winners will be the ones who have correctly measured the stress on their whole portfolio and adjusted their holdings to achieve some immunization.

Having the global transaction pool available also provides significant opportunities to control exposures as the next market crisis unfolds. Many firms today cannot coordinate their activities in stressed markets because they don't have the requisite information at hand. It can take twenty-four hours or more to gather all their relevant positions and exposure. Early in 1998 I was describing to a colleague, perhaps a bit too enthusiastically, the risk management process that a firm had recently built. It contained a near real-time repository of all OTC activity. I noted how useful it would be if another crisis hit. He wryly noted that the company would have a ringside seat to its own demise. When the market troubles did hit later in 1998, the firm benefited greatly from knowing its exact positions. That knowledge enabled managers to reduce specific exposures, focus on key settlements, and ameliorate losses. My colleague's firm, which had prescient management but did not have timely knowledge of all their positions, did not fair as well.

Credit Risk Always Was Global

The arcs prevail in credit risk. We cannot measure credit exposure and credit risk until we aggregate the information on a global level. In capital markets we do not know what the settlement exposure will be at various points in the future until we capture all the trades and their settlement mechanisms globally. We cannot measure the pre-settlement exposure with another trading counterparty until we run all the trades, netting agreements, and margin/collateral agreements through models that project those exposures. Only after obtaining the exposures can we consider defaults and recoveries, which will get us to credit risk in capital markets. On the traditional lending side, we do not know the exposures until we gather them globally for each counterparty. More importantly, we cannot see the toxic concentrations in our credit books until we apply models of default and default correlation to the global portfolio.

What is exciting about credit risk is the number of new opportunities to measure and manage it more effectively. Trading groups can do more trading under lower credit limits when they measure their risk on a global portfolio basis that includes exposure reductions from portfolio offsets and netting agreements. Also, by going global, they can move beyond limits. As noted, charges for credit risk based on marginal contributions to the global portfolio can be calculated and applied. Trading will gravitate to the trades with highest return risk-adjusted. Along the same vein, commercial lenders can now uncover and sell down concentrations of credit risk that their origination process creates. New loan origination can be guided and priced based on internal and external credit markets—the credit portfolio managers define internal hold levels and prices and the syndication/asset sales/credit derivatives groups define external credit market conditions.

Technology Now Enables GRM

The RM infrastructure described above was not feasible five years ago. Developments in computing speed, data storage and access, communications costs, and the risk models have moved this global risk management infrastructure from impossible to imperative. Let's look at the process infrastructure to see how these developments make them feasible.

GRM's voracious appetite for data is enabled by the steep drops in storage costs coupled with the increased speed in access. The really big data sets, including market prices and histories, including risk simulation runs, can all be stored at costs that are a fraction of what they were ten years ago and retrieved at speeds several orders of magnitude faster. The data keys and links are enabled by software that assures that changes to keys will ripple around the globe and that adjustments are being made where needed. Faster computing speeds make many risk models, primarily simulations, feasible. With computing speeds of just five years ago, many of these runs would take weeks instead of hours. Communications improvements, both higher speeds and lower costs, have also enabled a global approach. The flow of information from locations around the globe to the data warehouses, the delivery of risk analytics and information back to those locations, and the communications for monitoring and controlling these flows would not be possible without the fast and cheap networks of today. Distance is no longer a factor when communication occurs via satellites.

Risk Management's Evolving Role

Risk management's earliest role was to insure the institution knew and controlled the risks it was taking. It was essentially a control function. There were significant challenges in establishing control as the markets globalized, trade volumes burgeoned, and new products flourished. Amidst all this growth, risk management examined the dark side by asking the question, how much can we lose? Given this role, it sometimes developed adversarial relationships with the trading groups.

But risk management's role has been expanding. It started to provide risk-adjusted returns and other measures of trading efficiency.[3] Its performance measurement role has expanded at some firms to help allocate capital on a risk-adjusted basis. It is also starting to influence compensation and bonuses, the real meat of the matter. But risk management's ultimate holy grail is optimization. Knowing and controlling the risks is a first step in a long, challenging path to optimal behavior of all decision makers in the firm and to maximized shareholder value.

THE REALITY AT GLOBAL FINANCIAL INSTITUTIONS

There are significant impediments to moving toward this vision. The common belief is that the risk models and the technology present hurdles to getting there. This is perhaps the natural result of having the mathematicians or computer personnel run the projects. They focus on the problems they are trained to solve. Also, these were the first and the major hurdles that had to be overcome. With advances in technology and standardization of the metrics, those are much smaller. The biggest impediments now, are in the organization, motivation, and operating infrastructures of these firms. Here is the set of big impediments that block the path to GRM.

Spaghetti Bowl of Systems and Processes

Fifteen years ago, the chief credit officer at the bank where I worked caused a big problem by asking a simple question. He wanted to know his credit exposure in Brazil. So he asked three different groups, the Brazil country head, the global credit exposure team, and the country exposure group. He probably wasn't surprised that the answers were not identical. He was however disappointed by the range of answers. A flurry of memos and mad scramble ensued, first to clarify his definition of credit exposure and then to sort through the transactions that this group or that team had missed or double-counted. It turned out that the actual credit exposure was slightly higher than the highest answer he received—no one group had captured all of it. I wonder, fifteen years later, and ironically, with Brazil making headlines again, what we might learn by repeating this exercise.

All global financial service firms have within them a mélange of systems and processes that contain tremendous data redundancies and significant data problems. Disparate functions like back office processing, financial control, and regulatory reporting have led to disparate systems. Each specialized system contains the data that it needs to perform its function. The charts that show data flows among these systems start to look like a bowl of pasta. Unfortunately, this leads to tremendous duplication of data, and inevitable disparities. Also, the responsibility for data ownership has been lost in this explosion of systems. A constant stream of new systems initiatives, along with the occasional firm merger, have contributed to this potpourri. Reengineering opportunities and initiatives abound.

Unfortunately, the markets and the technologies have grown and evolved so rapidly that the requirements and the capabilities shift before any reengineering cycle can be completed.

This quagmire of data seriously confounds the task of extracting reliable information for risk management. My personal experience is that professional risk managers spend at least 80 percent of their time with data problems. Descriptions of a regional market risk-management process as it moves around the globe corroborate this observation.[4] The data problem becomes more acute when you move to a global risk-management process, because a flaw anywhere affects the whole process and can be much harder to trace.

Perhaps some of the latest technical developments will help rationalize this mess. Solutions like middleware may facilitate the smooth accurate transmission of data between all the systems that need it and eliminate data redundancies and problems. The advent of straight-through-processing, through which deals get confirmed, booked, accounted for, and settled without ever being subjected to human intervention may also help clear up the problems. However, I am not holding my breath.

Regional Fiefdoms

Most large financial institutions expanded globally through decentralized management. They found the most effective way to grow was to put their best people in a new office and give them wide latitude. Each regional manager could quickly adapt to local market conditions and promptly move to a profitable footing by deploying resources on the most fertile local opportunities.

This pattern has created a powerful set of regional managers who will not voluntarily enlist in the infringement of their authority. GRM is a real dilution of their power. The head office will have a clearer view of the risks that each manager is taking, and the potential rewards being achieved. With GRM, decision making will become more transparent and collaborative through the central office. Regional managers will lose autonomy.

They have many ways they can resist this change, aside from overt refusal to participate. More subtle and effective forms of resistance are available. Questions of resources and priorities can frequently bury a risk initiative. "Do you want me to be ready for Y2K or have this risk project completed?" is one of the most frequent questions that arises. The euro conversion got top billing before that, and another important initiative may arise by January 2000. There are legitimate questions that senior management must address. Will they provide funds for needed resources? Does this risk initiative have higher priority than the new trading system, and so on? Other more insidious forms of resistance are also possible. Machiavelli, move over! A regional manager just might consciously select a software package or build a local process that he/she knows is incompatible with the global process. He or she may also provide the least competent local resources to support the global initiative.

Merger Hangover

An urge to merge has been popular among the large financial institutions recently. A scan of the top fifty banks and the top twenty-five securities firms, by asset size, shows about half of them have undergone a merger in the past ten years. Although these mergers seem to be completed relatively quickly from an outsider's perspective, it takes much longer to align the internal operating processes. I've seen a trading operation with three different back-office operations. Two mergers had not yet been integrated. One of the mergers was five years old. This situation is not uncommon, and it contributes to the spaghetti bowl and data problems noted previously.

High Failure Rates

No one talks about it, yet financial professionals know that strategically driven initiatives to globalize any part of the trading or credit processes fail at alarmingly high rates. The only relevant study I've found determined that 92 percent of all large IT projects fail to deliver full functionality, on schedule, in budget.[5] I suspect that the financial service sector achieves a higher failure rate. More specific research and objective information on failed initiatives could provide a valuable opportunity for all of us to learn and improve. Again, I am not holding my breath. Financial institutions are quite sensitive about discussing their multimillion-dollar, multiyear strategic initiatives and perhaps even more sensitive to the extent any of those initiatives aren't becoming real.

Absent studies, we have to rely on our experience. Here are my vignettes and war stories. I have consulted in over a dozen banks and securities firms over the past fifteen years. I have heard about several dozen others through benchmark surveys, sales calls, etc. I don't know of any projects that delivered all functions originally specified, on the original schedule, at the original cost. If we use the *original project plan* as our gauge to success, every project I have worked on has failed. I'm eager to provide all the equivocations, for example, in this case I salvaged a project already in deep trouble, and on that project we trimmed non-essential functions to deliver the vital capabilities on time, etc. The truth is that the design and plan phases chronically underestimate the challenges these projects must overcome.

I take comfort from my colleagues' experiences. Usually by the second beer, they divulge at least one project horror at their institution. None has been able to claim a success measured to the original plan. At conferences where I speak, I have started asking two questions. How many of you know of a recent project at your institution to go global with some aspect of risk management? Did any of those projects succeed (deliver the functions promised, on schedule, and within budget)? At over five conferences in the past year, all hands rose for the first question and no hands remained up for the second.

During breaks I solicited the participants for why the initiatives didn't work. The overwhelming response was problems with the data. Some knocks on technology occurred. Interestingly, the quantitative models that frequently capture a large share of project effort and budget simply aren't a cause for failure. In working on these projects, I see major process problems as the primary reason for the unenviable record of achievement.

So, armed with the knowledge that we have a strategic imperative to go global while facing very big challenges, let's look at the development model before getting down to what works and what doesn't.

Wrap-Up

- Risk is on the cusp of becoming the new currency within global financial institutions. To survive they must value and allocate risks more efficiently than external markets.
- The impediments to this transformation are operational and organizational, not technical.

The Global Risk Management Development Model

15

Risk Management is situated between senior management and the operating infrastructure. A colleague describes this as being squeezed in a vice, caught between senior management's wishes and the reality of operations. I prefer to view it as a vital connection between strategic imperatives and daily practice. Let's look at the three pieces (Exhibit 15.1).

Exhibit 15.1   Risk Management: Development Model

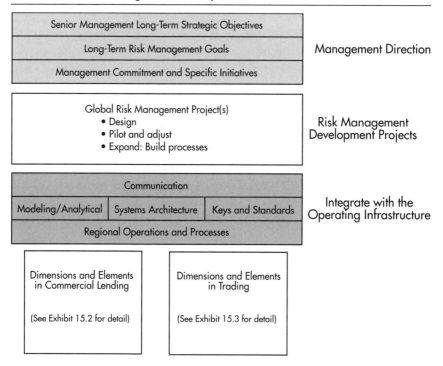

Senior Management Long-Term Strategic Objectives	
Long-Term Risk Management Goals	Management Direction
Management Commitment and Specific Initiatives	

Global Risk Management Project(s)
• Design
• Pilot and adjust
• Expand: Build processes

Risk Management Development Projects

Communication

| Modeling/Analytical | Systems Architecture | Keys and Standards |

Regional Operations and Processes

Integrate with the Operating Infrastructure

Dimensions and Elements in Commercial Lending

(See Exhibit 15.2 for detail)

Dimensions and Elements in Trading

(See Exhibit 15.3 for detail)

MANAGEMENT DIRECTION

Senior management provides overall direction, based on strategic considerations. After examining the firm's strengths and weaknesses and its position in the markets, they determine long-term objectives and specific goals to meet those objectives. With the rapid market changes, strategic planning has become more important for financial firms. Both the functions that financial service firms provide and how they provide them are changing. Financial service firms have traditionally facilitated the efficient allocation of capital by pooling it and then assisting in its movement across geographical boundaries and across time.[1] With the development of derivatives, their role in pooling and allocating risk, as well as capital, has become equally important.[2] Risk managers can help senior management understand these functional shifts, particularly the emergence of markets for risk. They also can convey the strategic importance for internal risk management, illustrating how it can align motivations, creating more optimal behavior and enhancing shareholder value. It is much more than a tool for control.

After establishing what business activities the firm will conduct, management must define how the resulting financial exposures will be measured and managed. The first mandate is for control—to manage volatility, market risks, and to comply with regulatory disclosures, and so on. The second mandate would be to align incentives by measuring performance, assist in incentive compensation decisions, allocate risk capital, determine shareholder value added, etc.

RISK MANAGEMENT DEVELOPMENT PROJECTS

The risk group helps organize and focus strategic directions into achievable projects. The members must collaborate actively with the businesses to insure project feasibility. The artful aspect of risk management is how well it integrates with the existing business infrastructure. It must be independent but not adversarial. Most importantly, the projects have to link key objectives with daily activities. Each project's objectives, design, and schedule should reflect this linkage.

INTEGRATING WITH THE OPERATING INFRASTRUCTURE

Now for the devil, which is in the operational details. Global risk projects have intense data, communication, and processing requirements. They are dependent on various business lines for many sets of the data. They are also dependent on the business lines to help them capture all the important nuance and variation that exist across markets so the global risk measures are right. Finally, they have to work with each business to ensure risk information is delivered and used effectively.

Exhibits 15.2 and 15.3 show the similar dimensions and varying elements between operations for commercial lending and trading. The specific activities in lending are quite different from those of trading. However, the dimensions in their operations are almost identical. Note that lending organizes around industries as well as geographies, while trading typically goes only by location.

Building an effective risk process on top of these operations requires a clear knowledge of where the foundation is weak and where it is solid. This knowledge provides a general framework for describing

Exhibit 15.2   Dimensions and Elements in Commercial Lending

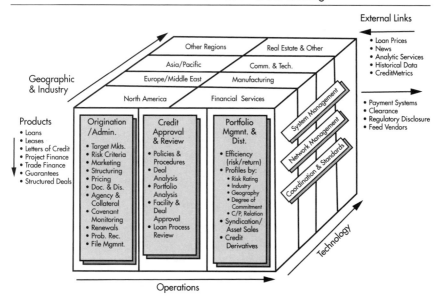

Exhibit 15.3 Dimensions and Elements in Trading

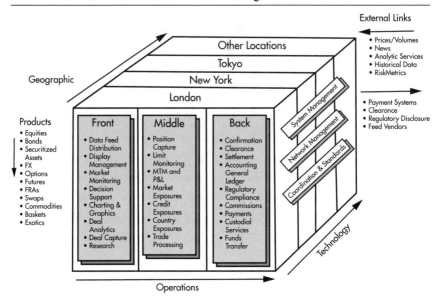

and understanding all the operational variances. The risk team and project group have to develop a detailed operational understanding of each location and each line of business. Knowing details about products, operations, technology, and external links in each location brings the team close to the requisite level of understanding.

WRAP-UP

- Effective risk management processes provide a vital connection between strategic imperatives and daily practice.

- To be effective, risk management processes need to understand and incorporate variations inherent in many markets around the globe.

Developing GRM: What Works, What Doesn't 16

I love it when Jean Luc Picard says, "Make it so." His words trigger frenzied but wonderfully coordinated activities. Within minutes those charged with "making it so," through adroit and sometimes creative work at their highly engineered control stations, deliver full functionality, on budget, and always just in time. If only it could be that easy with any aspect of risk management. Here are guidelines on how to "make it so" in our world.

THE CHASE EXAMPLE

The story at Chase Manhattan Corporation is still unfolding. Here is what had happened through 1999. In early 1998, Chase Manhattan Bank completed building a global risk management process that is closer to the global risk model than that at any other institution I know. It includes market, credit, and operational risk measures across all activities. The measures of credit and market risk lead to allocations of capital and charges for the use of that capital that are applied to every business. The charge for holding this allocated capital is set quite high initially at 13 percent. This rate helps to ensure that any new business transaction will be profitable.[1] Both the market and credit risk components use VaR-like models and stress models to assess the risk.[2] In market risk, the stress scenarios have been adjusted to match world developments and management's concerns (scenarios they think are most likely to occur). The original set of five scenarios were largely based on prior market moves in stressful times: the October 1987 equity crash, the November 1994 peso devaluation, and so on. Recently, another four scenarios were added, which are largely based on management judgment on how currencies, interest rates, and other variables will move.

In credit risk, capital allocations cover deployed assets and contingent exposures like stand-by letters of credit. The capital required for loans varies with risk ratings that are determined by a group entirely independent from the transaction sponsors. Chase also examines portfolio concentrations and puts its credit portfolios under stress. Credit risk for trading is supported by a database of all OTC transactions globally. This transaction warehouse also supports regulatory reporting.

Has Chase benefited by adopting this process? Its relatively steady earnings through 1998 have been at least partially attributed to their risk-management process.[3] Most other major banks suffered through significant losses in 1998. Some have attributed Chase's performance to good luck. They point out that Chase does not have a significant equity business where the largest losses occurred. However, Chase's stock outperformed all peers by rising 30 percent in 1998. Most others were flat to down. Also, the new process has significantly modified behavior. In the six months following its implementation, asset growth, which had been chugging along at 16 percent annually, was zero, while revenue growth continued growing at its prior pace.[4] Early in 1999 one of the architect's of this new process, Chase's CFO, Dina Dublon, noted that managers are much more stingy with their capital.[5]

Chase is perhaps unique in how extensively it has gone with global risk management and pricing. Its measures of risk and subsequent pricing are not complex and may not be the most accurate or discriminating schemes available. Arbitrage opportunities probably exist within it. However crude it may be, it has established a foundation upon which all deals are measured and has had a very big impact on behavior. It can and will become more sophisticated and discriminating over time.

Pieces of a GRM process are being put in place at many other firms. We noted earlier how a major securities firm applies charges for credit risk to its trading businesses. Bankers Trust, before it was absorbed by Deutsche Bank, had designed and was implementing an integrated, firm-wide portfolio approach to risk measurement. This approach was going to capture the relationship between market conditions and credit risk, with default probabilities going up or down in different market conditions. Projects like these are under consideration almost universally.

FEATURES OF SUCCESS

Senior management involvement is a prerequisite for success. No global initiative can overcome the major impediments noted above without direct sponsorship from senior management. The regional managers will respond to only those carrots and sticks provided by their managers. The challenge of converting regional fiefdoms into a globally integrated firm can only be achieved with direct involvement at the top.

Chase Manhattan Corp. has top sponsorship for its ongoing initiative. Thomas G. Labrecque, president and CEO, recently characterized himself as someone leading an institution that depends, for its success or failure, on how well it manages risk.[6] Marc Shapiro, the vice chairman of finance and risk management, provided almost daily oversight of the numerous projects that make up their global risk-management initiative. They went beyond sponsorship; they were actively involved in the design and construction of their global risk process. They owned it.

The only successful global projects that occurred without explicit senior management ownership worked because benefits accrued directly to the sponsors, the trading business. Several capital markets groups at banks have installed global portfolio measures of their pre-settlement exposure. The reductions from portfolio offsets and netting freed up credit lines, allowing them to conduct a lot more trading, and in one case reduced allocated capital for credit risk (economic, not regulatory), improving measured performance.

Focused Scope/Cross-Functional Involvement

The whole GRM process will take time to build. Firms can best focus on those parts of the process that provide an immediate payoff. Typically, I've seen the market risk piece tackled first then credit risk later. However, at many firms, credit risk initiatives tend to provide the largest benefits.

Highly touted market and credit risk integration hasn't happened yet except in a few vendor solutions. Most institutions that have built their market and credit risk processes in-house have kept them separate. The urgency to go global appears to preclude merging them anytime soon. Once they have both evolved to global operations, the opportunities for synergy (a single transaction warehouse, standard library of valuation models, single set of market history to serve both) are significant and may prevail. Also, the dependencies between market and credit risk cannot be captured in risk calculations until these processes are integrated. Vendors who largely started with systems to support market risk are currently extending their systems' functions to provide credit risk as well. The synergies are built into their system architectures.

Successful projects have fostered global cross-functional involvement. Global projects like this don't fit well in the typical financial firm's organizational and operational structures, which are largely matrices of geography and product. A uniform standard of activity has to be built across the products and geographies and across the institution's operations. Cross-functional teams with active representation from the dealers, the various systems, and the administrative operational support need to be enlisted and actively engaged throughout the project. This cooperation addresses the needs and problems of each area while building a valuable structure for bottom-up rather than top-down decision making. This eases and speeds implementation.

Evolution or Big Bang?

The first globalization initiatives to meet success were those that evolved slowly. They started as pilot projects that adjusted to problems through several iterations before gradually expanding to global coverage. The more revolutionary approaches, trying to implement in a big bang, failed. These initiatives are more likely to fail because they try to do too much at once. However, recently some big-bang projects have succeeded. Evolution is the lower risk way to go, but there are circumstances in which big bang can work.

You must use evolution when the infrastructure isn't there. To be successful, the global process must mesh with the existing processes and systems in every location, not just extract data from them. Such integration takes time, especially if you have to adapt to processes, systems, and operations that are different in each location. In these cases, successful initiatives start with selected locations (say London and New York, where the benefits can be measured and extrapolated), a selected product set, and selected relationships. Expansion to more locations, products, and relationships occurs after the benefits are made tangible and initial process flaws are found and corrected. Time is required to tune the process. It is also needed to build and expand the experience and knowledge base. This evolutionary approach is slower, more economical, and less risky than big-bang approaches.

Big bang has worked where the infrastructure is strong. I know of two big-bang approaches that worked. In both cases, the firms had standard hardware/software in place at all locations; a resilient, reliable, and responsive communications network; and an operations support process that was already coordinating their activities globally. In both cases, the global process developed in iterations. A pilot process was built and tested in major dealing centers. After corrections and adjustments, the process was extended in test mode to all locations, where it ran on a parallel basis for several months. The big-bang conversions occurred over weekends, mid-month to avoid interference with month-end activities. This big bang approach is considerably faster than the ponderous product-by-product, location-by-location pace. It is, however, quite risky.

Process Controls

GRM, to work properly, needs data from a large number of disparate sources. All the data needs to be consistent, timely, and accurate. Each source for data is a source for potential errors. The more global you are, the more vulnerable you are. You have more sources for error and more of your operation is affected by any error. For example, when you are calculating pre-settlement exposure for a global portfolio, you are vulnerable to every transaction system in every location. When one fails—or worse, supplies incorrect data—your risk calculations, resulting exposures, and calculated availability used around the globe can be wrong.

I recently helped a major bank implement global credit risk process for trading. The system, at its core, was a masterful blend of technology and risk metrics in Monte Carlo simulation. It could run hundreds of thousands of transactions, through tens of thousands of market paths it had created, value every deal at every time node, and determine the worst-case portfolio exposure in run times that measured in minutes. Unfortunately, the process around it was completely automatic and devoid of quality checks. The system ran continuously, around the clock, taking the latest transaction and market information and starting a new run as soon as it finished the last one. The new exposure profiles and resulting availability under limits were delivered to traders around the globe without human intervention. When bad data came in, incorrect information was automatically delivered to the traders. This problem, which was annoying for FX products, became quite acute when we expanded product coverage to derivatives.

The most common response to the data problems is to screen for them and fix them. This is what most market risk managers spend 25 percent to 30 percent of their working time doing.[7] Correcting the data ensures the results of what the risk group must deliver. Unfortunately, it also removes the pressure for finding and fixing data problems at their source. Many data problems recur at very high rates. What can we do to reduce this recidivism?

Data Rx

There are several possible prescriptions for the malady of data problems. One alternative, which a firm uses, is to *not change* the data. The risk management group logs all possible errors and requests explanation from the source. To ensure prompt consideration, the operating area that sources problem data is assessed charges, scaled to the magnitude and frequency of problems. These charges hit the business P&L. This becomes one of the many ways operational risk can be measured and used to optimize performance.

This institution also insists that all transactions transmitted to the risk area from each business tie to general ledger totals every day.

This demand creates a significant reconciliation effort as back-to-back trades and other internal transfers must be backed out. It causes even more trouble when a G/L posting is wrong. A single summary adjustment can be made on the G/L. However, to correct the error at the deal level, which risk requires, a complete revaluation must be done. However, this institution requires it. It provides confidence that the numbers going to regulators and into risk reporting are vetted. It also ensures that the originators own the data they source.

The key here is to create effective ways to solve data problems at their source. The systems people at firms do a fine job defining the data they expect in a feed, but not as well at defining quality measures that insure the feed is valid. Quality standards that address both data accuracy and data timeliness need to be built into the sources for these feeds. Managers of the source processes must be told about the mistakes and be expected to fix them. Charging for mistakes can help.

Another tactic for ensuring data Rx, is to weave the global data into the daily processes and activities. When data is used at granular levels, mistakes are noticed and corrected.

Data Integrity

Just as real estate markets are based on location, location, and location the mantra for GRM should be data integrity, data integrity, and data integrity. This is not the sexy, glamorous part of going global, but it is the critical foundation and should dominate management's attention until it is clearly resolved. It also takes longer to achieve than any other part of going global. *Achieving the standardized, uniform practices around the globe that contribute to data integrity is a challenging management exercise.* A vital part of the equation is each organization's culture for team building, consensus building, plus leadership and project management; but those aspects can only be discussed on a case-by-case basis. Let's look at the process mechanics that contribute to data integrity. To go global an organization must have standards for describing its transactions and its global keys.

Each transaction in your global portfolio needs a uniform identifier of global keys for the customer, the product, and your own organizational entity that entered into the trade. Here is a brief discussion about each.

Customer Keys   Many global financial firms have the greatest difficulty with defining and disseminating customer keys for use in bank operations. There are substantial issues on how to categorize customers and place them into relationship hierarchies. Those issues frequently confound the more straightforward exercise of defining a key identifier for each customer and legal counterparty and getting that key accurately entered for each deal.

Consistent and controlled application of customer identifiers for each transaction is a critical prerequisite for global credit risk management. Both netting and overall measures of relationship exposure are dependent on this identifier. Typically, a lot of work on this process is required. The few firms that have successfully implemented global customer keys will achieve extraordinary returns in the future. They are positioned to improve upon firms' heretofore abysmal ability to determine which relationships and which products are most profitable. Global customer identifiers are critical to more than managing credit risk for trading.

Another technique to overcome the diversity of counterparty identifiers is to map them. Each regional transaction system keeps its set of counterparty identifiers. When that system's transactions are fed to the global process its identifiers are mapped to the corresponding standard global identifiers. This approach diffuses responsibility for getting the counterparty right and it adds another link in an already long set of system links that typically make up transaction data feeds. However, this mapping technique is in place and works at several major global institutions.

Product/Deal Keys   Most banks and securities firms have less difficulty with their product and deal keys, which are more consistent, but may contain regional and local variations. These keys are important because they frequently drive the specific transaction details that are transmitted. The record for a forward FX trade is quite different from the record for an amortizing swap.

Organization Again, most global banks know which legal entity from their side (branch, trading subsidiary, etc.) is the counterparty to each transaction. This information needs to be captured for G/L, tax, and netting purposes. Also, global banks include other organizational identifiers (desks, profit centers, geographical regions, etc.) to enrich MIS reporting.

Standardized Transactions Many global firms have made good progress at defining standards for describing their trading transactions. They've frequently defined a generic file format to capture all traded transactions. Care needs to be taken to ensure that generic format is populated the same way across all regions and systems. Also, care needs to be taken to ensure that this generic form captures all relevant data, like early termination clauses, linked deals, reset dates, and so on. Another big challenge is capturing complex derivative deals. These deals are frequently so complex that various legs need to be entered into different transaction systems. It can take several days for these deals to get into the various systems and to be correctly linked. Transaction data problems also arise around deal events, such as, rate resets, early termination dates, swaption expirations, and so on.

With the advent of e-commerce, a standard eXtensible Markup Language (XML) is being established to describe all transactions in a standard format. This standard, aimed at facilitating communication between counterparties, will also help with communication within each counterparty.

Global banks have not put too much effort into standardizing and capturing their loan agreements on systems. Each loan contains specific features and is unique. However, progress is being made at banks where loan portfolio management has been a priority.

Build Windows, Not Black Boxes

The global risk process cannot become a black box spitting out results that are automatically gospel. Producing results without showing how they were reached is a problem, especially when results don't match expectations. Users must see and understand what the risk calculator is doing. With each run, users need to be able to see shifts in their deal portfolio, including new deals, deals gone, the impact of market shifts, and many other transaction shifts that contribute to the new risk calculations. Also, they need drill-down capability on the other sets of data that contribute to the new exposure like customer data, market price data, and so on. These windows help the user understand how the simulation worked and are vital for credibility and problem diagnostics. These windows also become the basis for the what-if capabilities that need to be at the fingertips of the dealers if they are going to optimize their consumption of risk.

Also, windows into each process step are required for proper quality control. Flexible inquiry into each source of data—particularly transaction and market data, which are most dynamic—should be built. Access to information about normal baseline process, including typical deal volumes, deal rejects, and so on, is also very useful for prompt problem recognition and resolution. The quality control processes noted below will rely heavily on windows into each process step and into the simulation run itself.

PITFALLS TO AVOID

I have seen too many global risk initiatives that were like the movie *Field of Dreams.* The prevalent belief has been, "If you build a data warehouse, they will come populate it." Such projects inevitably have delivered far less than promised, if they delivered anything at all. Even worse, they consumed significant resources and jeopardize the credibility of all such ventures. Each failure discourages senior managers from further investment. Many of these projects don't fall over until the conversion phase, after they have consumed significant resources. Populating the systems with data is hard; keeping them populated with good data is harder. Here are some questions that may help avoid this pitfall.

1. Have the designers and analysts worked with end users, the middle and back-office personnel in each location? Day-to-day users know all the deal idiosyncrasies and current process problems. Project managers and designers need to know these issues and problems and resolve them. Going to just

one location does not work; trade structures vary a great deal in each location, so the problems and issues vary.

2. Have the people responsible for delivering the data been identified? Have they reviewed the plan, including their responsibilities, and accepted it? An astonishing number of projects proceed quite far toward completion without any coordination with the data suppliers.

3. Does the project plan to work with real data before the final phase, when all the software has been built? Every part that is built should be checked with actual data files well before the final conversion and implementation. The sooner real data is used, the sooner the real problems and issues are uncovered.

4. Has data conversion been planned and tested? Normally the conversion process is chronically underplanned and underestimated. Even worse, it typically occurs in high-pressure situations, when the project is late, over budget, and everyone is screaming for tangible results. Consider building data conversion early, so you can work with real data throughout your process.

Just for Senior Management

Fifteen years ago, my employer built a state-of-the-art system to capture and report credit exposure. Our project team did a great job, so we thought. In six months, starting from scratch, we designed, built, and populated a database that captured all credit facilities and outstandings for our $64 billion book. Remember in that era, $64 billion put us in the top five U.S. banks. Our team was pleased to provide any reports senior management or the regulators wanted. Our state-of-the-art SQL gave us very flexible access to our relational database.

We were not pleased when we circulated the detailed reports for each lending area. At aggregate levels, our information was acceptable, but at the granular level it was woefully inaccurate. Our capture of credit facilities did occasionally bear some resemblance to the real approved facilities. Our outstandings were clearly not linking under the appropriate facilities. It took us another year and a half to build accuracy at the granular levels. To get there, we had to extend the system to capture significant aspects of credit exposure that we'd missed in the original design (asset sales, agency work, etc.). We also built system support for various credit processes to assist with incremental approvals, renewals, credit review meetings, watch list reporting, and so on.

Risk management data must be integrated within the fabric of daily operations. Putting the risk information in front of those who know it best provides a reality check on both your data and your models. This compares with a global development project I heard of where, over a year after the official implementation, reports are still circulated on a very narrow basis and data issues abound.

Methodology Battles

Risk professionals are typically quite quantitatively oriented. They generally have advanced degrees, which match their intellects, egos, and pay. These are positive traits when they occasionally have to work with traders. However, when you get several risk professionals in a room and ask them to determine the most appropriate risk methodology among the many that are available, a potentially explosive situation develops. Protracted battles have cropped up over issues that affect the right side of the decimal place. When methodology battles flare up, the first question should be the impact on the calculated risk. Let the battles rage only on those issues that hit the left side of the decimal place, the parts with a first-order effect on the calculation.

Models Über Alles

Also remember, the quantitative models are just a piece of the overall global process. Other assessments can and should contribute to management decisions, especially where credit risk is concerned. Late in 1998, at a credit risk conference in London, the debacle of Long Term Capital Management came up. The attendees were almost exclusively quantitatively oriented risk professionals. They were collectively scratching their heads and wondering where they could obtain credit data on hedge funds, so they could quantify the credit risk. After some discussion, they generally agreed the paucity of data made the problem quite intractable.

A bank credit officer noted that they could ask the hedge fund officers to disclose leverage and other key credit information, such as, general positions, daily income/volatility, and so on. He noted these disclosures would be part of many normal credit processes. Given the risks that hedge funds take and the leverage they typically employ to boost profit, the traditional credit process would include covenants and monitoring/disclosure agreements before any extension of credit. These traditional credit practices really are the most efficient sources for the information with which to appropriately structure credit risk at these institutions. The value of the traditional credit processes are not always understood or fully appreciated by the more quantitatively oriented risk professionals.

New Operating Model

The requisite skills for managing the new global process are different from the skills employed in regional or local risk processes. With the global process, limit allocations and reallocations disappear and compliance monitoring is simplified. However, the new process is more vulnerable to problems, with a single bad data input able to debilitate all trading globally. It is also more time sensitive, with any delay impacting trading somewhere around the globe—the sun never sets on this trading process. The team that supports this process must be very strong in quality monitoring and quick to identify and resolve problems. GRM needs quality support on a twenty-four hours/seven day-week basis.

Create a Global Support Team   A new global team is needed to support this process. They must be available around the clock and around the globe to continuously monitor the quality of the process and correct problems prior to delivering credit availability to traders. This team will help identify and correct chronic problems from the data input side. To do that, the global process needs to be developed.

Build in Quality Monitoring and Contingency Processes No matter how adaptable and robust your new global process is, it will break down from time to time. It contains too many dependencies and too much complexity for it to work perfectly, all the time, right from the start. Major control points to monitor quality and invoke contingency routines need to be built in. Yet, it is difficult to predict ahead of time where to install the bells and whistles and what should trigger them. During your pilot implementation, the following control points will provide valuable information:

▪ Review incoming transactions from various systems before they are accepted. For batch feeds, typically derivative transactions, are transactions counts and contents reasonable when compared with prior feeds? For incremental transactions are the keys and the contents of each deal acceptable? Indeed, are the keys and contents of the batch feed acceptable, too? If data in any feed appears unreasonable, contingency plans to correct it must be invoked and the problem should be noted for follow-up and correction at the source.

▪ Review market price data before it is used in a simulation. Is each price and volatility shift within established parameters and is the set of price/volatility shifts within parameters predicted by the model? Reviewers should be asked to validate each market move that is outside of tolerances. Again, any problems should be noted for follow-up with the source.

▪ Check all output before it is delivered to users. Have shifts that exceed specified tolerances occurred in the last run? Similarly, have any significant shifts in availability under limits occurred in the latest delivery? If so, what caused the shift? Is it due to valid market and trading activities, or is it due to a data or processing problem? If the shift is due to a problem, contingency plans to correct the information must be invoked and the problem should be noted for follow-up and correction.

Starting with these control points on your two most volatile inputs and your primary output, you can launch the pilot process.

Learn from it and adapt the controls as required. Eventually your quality monitoring and contingencies will cluster around your specific recurring problems, the ones that have not been corrected at their sources.

WRAP-UP

- Building an effective global risk management process is extremely difficult. Data problems provide the biggest and most enduring issues.
- Prerequisites for success include:
  —Senior management involvement
  —Focused scope/cross-functional team(s)
  —Process controls and data integrity
- Pitfalls to avoid include:
  —Field of Dreams projects
  —Methodology battles
  —Just for senior management

Conclusion

THE TEN COMMANDMENTS FOR GOING GLOBAL WITH RISK

1. Align with Strategy

Align risk projects with corporate strategy and objectives. The risk-management process must be consistent with senior managers' views and philosophies. The objectives and scope of risk projects, especially global ones, should reflect their priorities.

2. Align with Capabilities

Align risk projects with internal capabilities. Risk management processes cannot function effectively unless they are built upon and consistent with the internal operations of the firm. One bank launched a global risk project but had to delay it until it established a communication network that was fast and reliable. Its communications at the time, telephone lines and modem, couldn't support a global risk process. You cannot build risk processes without the requisite infrastructure.

3. Obtain Sponsorship

Obtain sponsorship from senior management and from the beneficiaries. GRM projects cannot succeed without clear priority from senior management. The various constituencies in global financial institutions have other priorities and other problems. They will not provide the level of cooperation required unless it is directed from their managers. In addition, GRM projects have a much greater chance of success if business lines obtain benefits and sponsor it as well.

4. Go for Tangible Benefits

Go global first with the parts that get you the biggest bang. Currently, credit risks appear to be the most fertile areas for improvement.

Specifically, initiatives to better manage commercial loan portfolios and initiatives to globalize the measurement of pre-settlement exposure appear to provide big benefits.

5. Design Windows, Not Black Boxes

Users must see and understand what the risk calculator is doing. With each run, users need to be able to see shifts in their deal portfolio, including new deals, deals gone, the impact of market shifts, and many other transaction shifts that contribute to the new risk calculations. They need drill-down capability on the other sets of data that contributed to the output. Any invisible pieces—black boxes—inevitably create credibility problems.

6. Open Analysis and Results

The only way you can confirm you are getting risk right is to make the models openly available. The healthy, sometimes heated, debate that occurs in this transparent process ensures that you build a vetted and more appropriate risk process.

7. Create Plug-Compatible Models

Risk models are in a continuous improvement mode. They are evolving almost faster than one can implement them. Processing efficiency is lost by separating the models/engines from the data. That loss is more than offset by the gain in needed flexibility.

8. Plan for Iterations

Whether you go for a big-bang or an evolutionary approach, you can be sure that adjustments to your process will be necessary. Even if you scope, design, and plan a project that builds on existing capabilities, which leads to a project with only minor adjustments, the objectives and scope of these projects can frequently shift. Creating space in your plans for these adjustments and corrections is wise, even if you do not know what they are right now.

9. Start Data Now

Start on your data *now*. Your data is your biggest problem and will take the longest to get right. It will remain your biggest problem long after you have completed all other phases of the project. Gathering and using the data is the only way to identify and fix the problems. It also guides where you build control points to insure process integrity.

10. Start Global Support Team Now

Start on your global support team now, too. The members are the ones who will support the new global operating paradigm, which must run to a much higher standard than local processes—all information must be right or the global process is wrong. They will be empowered if they grow with the process as it is built, not have it dumped on them when it is complete. Also, this team's perspective is invaluable in working through the many process details that are required. They will help ensure that you build a process that works.

FINANCIAL RISK DEFINITIONS

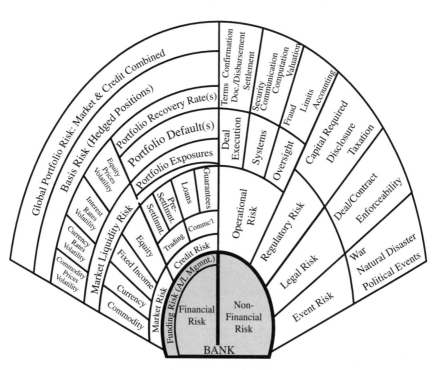

The Spectrum of Risks

Financial Risk: The risk of loss from holding positions that are subject to change in value with changing market conditions. This risk includes all changes in market conditions, such as, prices, volatility, liquidity, and credit risk, the ability and willingness of counterparties to honor their contractual oligations.

Lloyd's of London provided re-insurance without protracted and significant losses for 300 years. The equity holders in this enterprise started to think they were purchasing annuities rather than placing their considerable assets at risk. With a history of profits without significant loss that spans centuries, such a belief is understandable. Lloyd's accumulated $8.6 billion in losses in the three years from 1988 through 1990. The equity holders achieved a better understanding of the financial risk they were incurring.

Asset/Liability Risk: This is the risk that current obligations/liabilities cannot be met with current assets. This is a fundamental risk in all organizations, which must maintain liquidity or they become insolvent. In financial institutions, this risk is quite significant because many liabilities can be accelerated if the market perceives a weakness. Markets and regulators have demanded that financial institutions maintain a high level of capital to protect the fund providers and a high level of reserves to safeguard against "runs."

Market Risk: This is the risk that positions can lose value due to changing market conditions including prices, volatility, and market liquidity. It also includes basis risk for hedge positions. Market risk, along with credit risk are the two major components of financial risk. Market risk, which consists primarily of price risk and volatility risk, occurs within the major market sectors.

Commodity Market Risk: This is the risk of loss from having position(s) in any of the commodity markets. There are certainly a tremendous variety of them, ranging from agricultural markets, which include various grains, meats, produce, and wood products to minerals and metals. More recently, the energy market has undergone an expansion as electricity has deregulated and become a commodity whose price fluctuates.

Currency Market Risk: This is the risk of loss from having positions in any of the currency markets. The risk can be from outright positions. It can also reside on the balance sheet or in the income flows of a company. Many Thai companies were carrying currency risk on their balance sheets with assets in Thai baht and liabilities (loans) in U.S. dollars. In the summer of 1997, they were bankrupted overnight by a 20 percent reduction in their Bhat assets or (depending on how you look at it) a 20 percent inflation of their dollar liabilities. Other firms suffer large fluctuations in income when earnings denominated in foreign currencies must be converted and reported in dollars.

Debt/Fixed-Income Market Risk: This is the risk of loss from holding positions in debt markets. The loss can occur from fluctuations in interest rates and from changes in the perceived ability of the counterparty to repay.

Equity Market Risk: This is the risk of loss from holding positions in the equity markets. This is investor risk and almost everyone is familiar with it. Like the other markets it contains price, volatility, and liquidity components.

Market Liquidity Risk: This is the risk of loss from being unable to buy or sell positions easily, at a low transaction cost. The speed and ease with which a buyer/seller can convert assets into cash and vice versa varies with each class of assets in the market. Gold, for example, is much more liquid than real estate. In addition, liquidity fluctuates over time. During August and September 1998, some of the most liquid markets, such as the U.S. government bond market and the swap markets became considerably less liquid.

In the early 1990s, a steep spike in interest rates caused large losses in many tranches of mortgaged-backed securities (MBS). The market for these instruments froze because no one was interested in bidding for them, even at huge discounts to their remaining fair market value. That liquidity freeze helped keep MBS prices depressed for a long time.

Basis Risk (Hedged Positions): This is the risk of loss from hedging market exposures with instruments whose change in value does not exactly offset value changes in the position being hedged. The mismatch could be in terms of maturity, the underlying instrument (e.g., short a government bond to hedge a long corporate bond position, or some other characteristic). These "small" differences can sometimes cause the combined position to be much more risky than thought.

On May 1, 1997, J.P. Morgan lost $20 to $40 million due to basis risk on one trade. The trader sold a yen/dollar option, and bought the same option from another counterparty. Both the bought and sold options carried the same "knock-out" feature. (The trade is canceled if the dollar/yen exchange rate is greater than 127.3.) This looks like one of those perfect hedges, rumored to occur only in Japanese gardens. The problem was a mismatch in maturity. The sold option expired six hours before the bought option. The exchange rate was below 127.3 yen when the sold leg matured but moved above that barrier by the time the bought leg matured. The hedge, the bought leg, was knocked out by the shift in dollar yen rates, leaving J.P.

Morgan with an unhedged loss. Ironically, if the deals had not contained the "knock-out" feature, Morgan would have made money on the basis risk (timing) it was holding.

Credit Risk: This is the risk of loss from failure of a counterparty to perform as agreed (contracted). With the growth of over-the-counter (OTC) trading activities, credit markets have two distinct areas where credit risk occurs. First is the traditional debt markets, where corporations or governments have issued debt securities or borrowed money. The second is the interbank/financial intermediary markets, where trading activities have produced significant credit exposures between the liquidity providers in these markets.

Trading Credit Risk: This is the risk of loss from the failure of a trading counterparty to perform its trading obligations as agreed. The largest exposures for this risk typically occur between major global trading counterparties (e.g., liquidity providers in several markets). Unlike traditional lending, these exposures change value with changing market conditions (prices, volatility). Note, however, the largest risk of loss is linked but not directly proportional to the largest exposures. Credit risk combines exposure with default and recoveries. Thus a lower exposure can have a higher risk if the default probability is much higher.

Presettlement Risk: This is the risk of loss from failure of a trading counterparty to perform as obligated, but before the trade actually settles. If a counterparty to a deal that matures in six years, defaults after three years, the other counterparty may have to go into the marketplace and "replace" the defaulted deal. This potential replacement cost is based on the market prices and other factors, like applicable netting agreements and collateral, at the time of the default.

Settlement Risk: This is the risk of loss from failure of a trading counterparty to perform as obligated during the settlement process. Most settlement processes for financial transactions have established safeguards to greatly reduce this risk. For example, most equity and debt purchases settle through clearing houses which hold deliver until payment is received (DVP). Other financial products frequently settle on a net difference basis. In most swaps, just the difference between the fixed and floating leg is transmitted. Daily settlement amounts between the biggest traders (liquidity providers), especially when they do not occur on a net basis, are very large. The failure of a major financial institution to honor its side of these trades, could cause significant loss and serious market disruption.

In 1974, a small bank in Germany, Bank Herstatt, which had $60 million in FX trades settling the next day, closed its doors. The three days of increasing payment system gridlock that followed served as a wake-up call to the industry and its regulators.

Commercial Credit Risk: This is the risk of loss from providing credit to corporate counterparties. Extensions of credit can take the form of direct loans and contingencies/guarantees.

Loan Risk: This is the risk of loss from loaning money and having the borrower fail to repay, either due to default or because they are not willing to repay. Most analysis in commercial lending considers how the borrower will repay.

Guarantee Risk: This is the risk of loss from providing guarantees or letters of credit. These are forms of contingent credit exposure (e.g., the exposure is contingent on other events occurring).

Portfolio Exposure: A measure of the possible loss that could occur with each given counterparty and with groups of counterparties, for example, industries, countries, and economic regions. When traditional credit products, such as, loans, leases, letters of credit, and guarantees, are transacted, the exposure is known and static. Capturing credit exposure for the corporate counterparties that typically use these traditional credit products is fairly straightforward and consideration quickly shifts to "default risk" for them.

When the portfolio contains a significant proportion of derivative trades, exposure might undergo large shifts with changes in market conditions. Therefore, measuring portfolio exposure to the dealer/banks where derivative trades predominate, is a much more difficult exercise. Typically, the overall portfolio exposure is much less than the sum deal by deal exposures, due to portfolio effects (natural offsets), close-out netting agreements, and margin/collateral agreements.

Portfolio Defaults: A measure of the rate at which exposures convert into losses due to default. Default consideration occurs on both a granular level, "counterparty by counterparty" and at various portfolio levels. At the granular level, the credit managers rate the counterparty's ability to repay loans. At the portfolio levels, credit managers consider how defaults might correlate (e.g., occur together).

Historically, default analysis has been more qualitative than quantitative. Credit analysis was based on qualitative assessments of the firm's prospects, management, and so on. Recently, quantitative default models, driven by market data have been developed and are rapidly been adapted.

Portfolio Recovery: A measure of how much credit risk is ameliorated by loan recoveries, which reduce the loss when a counterparty defaults. Loans can contain features and structures which create higher recovery rates, significantly reducing credit risk. The two-loan structure considerations that most directly impact recovery rates are seniority (where the loan is situated within the borrowing firm's internal capital structure) and security (what collateral secures the loan).

Global Portfolio Risk: This is the risk of loss from all financial risks, including the combination of credit and market risks. There are fundamental factors, like economic conditions, which create a link between them. Market and credit risks are not independent from each other, yet most financial firms measure and manage them separately.

Risk-management models and technology have recently become sufficiently robust to start to capture this relationship.

Notes

Chapter 1 Global Risk Management's Emergence

1. Frank Fabozzi, *Handbook of Fixed Income Securities*, 5th ed. (1996).

2. Table 1.54: Mortgage Debt Outstanding (as of end of 1998), *Federal Reserve Bulletin* 85, no. 6 (June 1999).

3. C.F. Simans and John D. Benjamin. "Pricing Fixed Rate Mortgages; Some Empirical Evidence," *Journal of Financial Services Research* (1990).

4. Peter L. Bernstein, *Against the Gods, The Remarkable Story of Risk* (New York: John Wiley & Sons, 1996).

5. H. Markowitz, "Portfolio Selection: Efficient Diversification of Investments," *Journal of Finance* 5, no. 31 (1952): 369–382.

6. F. Black and M. Scholes, "The Pricing of Options and Corporate Liabilities," *Journal of Political Economy* 81 (1973): 637–659.

7. Charles Smithson, "Extended Family," *Risk* 10, no. 12 (December 1997): 158–163.

Also, Emanual Derman, "The Future of Modeling," *Risk* 10, no. 12 (December 1997): 164–167.

Chapter 2 The Full Spectrum of Risks

1. "International Conververgence of Capital Measurement and Capital Standards," Basle Committee on Banking Supervision (July 1988). http://www.bis.org

2. William McDonough, "Amending the Accord," *Risk* 11, no. 9 (1998): 46–51.

3. "A New Capital Adequacy Framework," A consultative paper issued by the Basle Committee on Banking Supervision (June 1999). Available: http://www.bis.org

4. Martin Mayer, "The Dangers of Derivatives," *The Wall Street Journal* (May 20, 1999): A20.

5. A. Gooch, L. Klein, M. Grothenhalper, J. Hutchinson, and A. Clark, "A Review of Case Law Affecting Swaps and Related Derivative Instruments." Robert J. Schwartz and Clifford W. Smith, Jr., eds., *Derivatives*

Handbook, Risk Management and Control Chapter 4 (New York: John Wiley & Sons, 1997).

Chapter 3 The Contours of Financial Risk

1. For example, various meat prices are posted at www.urnerbarry.com

Chapter 4 Market Risk: Tools and Uses

1. Elizabeth Ungar, *Swap Literacy, A Comprehensive Guide* (Princeton: Bloomberg, 1996): 13–16.

2. Ibid., 24–30.

3. Charles Smithson, *Managing Financial Risk*, Yearbooks 1996 through 1999 for summaries of each of these losses (New York: Canadian Imperial Bank of Commerce). http://www.schoolfp.cibc.com/home.htm

Chapter 5 Commodity Market Risk Management

1. A real example is: Ford owns a major steel production facility.
Also, "Ford Plans Aluminum Foundry," *Foundry Management and Technology* 125, no. 12 (December 1997): 8.

Also, "Ford Plans to Secure Magnesium Supplies," *Purchasing* 122 (February 13, 1997): 2.

For GM, see "An Ironclad Deal with GM," *Business Week* (March 8, 1999): 36. Big Auto Co. practices forms of this lock-in strategy, too. It is not necessarily one of these firms.

2. "Derivative Practices and Principles, The Group of Thirty," Washington DC, July 1993. *Framework for the Evaluation of Internal Control Systems* Basle Committee on Banking Supervision (Basle, Switzerland, January 1998).

3. "Offshore Texas Gas Shut-In by Tropical Storm," *Gas Daily* (Arlington, VA: Pasha, September 10, 1998): 1.

"Tropical Storm Frances Takes the Market for a Ride," *Gas Daily* (Arlington, VA: Pasha, September 11, 1998): 1.

"Georges Cuts Off Majority of Gulf Production," *Gas Daily* (Arlington, VA: Pasha, September 29, 1998): 1.

4. Estimates provided by Enron Capital and Trading.

5. *Pipeline & Gas Journal* 225, no. 4 (April 1998): 88.

6. *McKinsey Quarterly* no. 2 (1997): 122.

7. *Harvard Business Review* 74, no. 1 (January/February 1996): 136.

Chapter 6   Currency Market Risk Management

1. "Reducing FX Settlement Risk," New York Foreign Exchange Committee (October 1994).

2. Janet Lewis, "The Rise and Fall of Foreign Exchange," *The European*, no. 341 (November 21, 1996): 21.

3. Ibid.

4. "Ties That Bind," *The Economist* 347, no. 8067 (May 9, 1998): Financial Centres, 5.

5. Rita Koselka and Matthew Schifrin, "Brother, Can You Spare an EMU?" *Forbes* 158, no. 15 (December 30, 1996): 120.

6. Laura Kodres, "Foreign Exchange Markets: Structure and Systemic Risk," *Finance and Development* 33, no. 4 (Washington, DC: International Monetary Fund, December 1996): 22.

7. For extensive and insightful analysis, see William H. Buiter, Giancarlo Corsetti, and Paoloa Pesenti, "Financial Markets and European Monetary Cooperation: The Lessons of the 1992–93 Exchange Rate Mechanism Crisis" (Cambridge, MA: MIT Press, 1998).

8. "Chemical Reports Peso Loss," *The Wall Street Journal* (January 4, 1995): A3.

9. Charles Smithson, *Managing Financial Risk*, Yearbook 1999 (New York: Canadian Imperial Bank of Commerce). http://www.schoolfp.cibc.com/home.htm

10. A. Gooch, L. Klein, M. Grothenhalper, J. Hutchinson, and A. Clark, "A Review of Case Law Affecting Swaps and Related Derivative Instruments." Robert J. Schwartz and Clifford W. Smith, Jr., eds., *Derivatives Handbook, Risk Management and Control* Chapter 4 (New York: John Wiley & Sons, 1997).

11. *Risk* 10, no. 12 (February 1997): Editorial Page.

12. Gary Shoup, "The Currency Management Program," *Currency Risk Management: A Handbook for Financial Managers, Brokers and Their Consultants* Chapter 6 (New York: American Management Association, 1998): 121.

Chapter 7   Fixed-Income Market Risk Management

1. "Sumitomo Accuses Two Banks of Fraud," *American Metals Market* 107 (June 4, 1999): 1.

2. Merton H. Miller, "Functional Regulation," Robert J. Schwartz and Clifford W. Smith, Jr., eds., *Derivatives Handbook, Risk Management and Control* Chapter 14 (New York: John Wiley & Sons, 1997): 446–451.

3. David L. Scott, "Brady Bonds," *Wall Street Words: An Essential A to Z Guide for Today's Investor* (Boston: Houghton Mifflin): 40.

4. David Smith, "Techniques for Deriving a Zero Coupon Curve for Pricing Interest Rate Swaps: A Simplified Approach," J.C. Franks and A.S. Wolf, eds., *The Handbook of Interest Rate Risk Management* Chapter 2 (IL: Irwin, Burr Ridge, 1994).

5. Frank Fabozzi, ed., *The Handbook for Mortgage Backed Securities* (Chicago: Probus, 1995).

6. "The Great Price Depression," Frank Fabozzi, ed., *The Handbook for Mortgage Backed Securities* (Chicago: Probus, 1995): 297.

7. Joseph Hu, "Prospects for Recovery," *Mortgage Banking* 56, no. 4 (January 1996): 38.

8. Robert J. Schwartz and Clifford W. Smith, Jr., eds., *Derivatives Handbook, Risk Management and Control* (New York: John Wiley & Sons, 1997): 5.

9. Bond Glitches, "Preversals" *The Wall Street Journal* (November 6, 1998): A2.

10. "Quirk in Yields Is Making Bonds Attractive," *The Wall Street Journal* (February 2, 1999): C1.

11. Elizabeth Ungar, *Swap Literacy, A Comprehensive Guide* Chapter 2 (Princeton: Bloomberg, 1996).

12. "SEC Chairman Voices Criticism of Bond Data," *The Wall Street Journal* (April 26, 1999): C18.

13. "Transparent Reluctance, Pensions and Investments," *The Wall Street Journal* (Editorial) 26, no. 20 (October 5, 1998): 10.

Also, "A Bill to Increase Bond Transparency," *The New York Times* (April 25, 1999): C8.

14. Gregory Zuckerman, "Trading Bonds Online Slowly Catches On," *The Wall Street Journal* (April, 26, 1999): C1 and C18.

15. Charles Jones et al., "Developing and Implementing Risk Management Systems," *Horizon '98* no. 168 (The Barra, Inc. Newsletter, fall 1998).

Chapter 8   Equity Market Risk Management

1. James K. Glassman and Kevin A. Harsett, "Are Stocks Overvalued? Not a Chance," *The Wall Street Journal* (March 30, 1998): A18. (The market was at 8,782.12 that day.)

2. Go to www.barra.com for more details.

3. Charles Smithson, "Barings," *Managing Financial Risk*, Yearbook 1999 Appendix to Chapter 1 (New York: Canadian Imperial Bank of Commerce). http://www.schoolfp.cibc.com/home.htm

4. "Inn Trouble," *The Wall Street Journal* (March 4, 1999): 1.

5. John Labate, "Instinet: Electronic Traders Form Alliance," *Financial Times* (May 12, 1999).

Chapter 9 The Schism in Credit Risk Management

1. "The Banks That ISDA Forgot," *Risk* 11, no. 12 (December 1998): 21.

2. "OCC Bank Derivatives Report," Comptroller of the Currency, Second Quarter 1998.

Chapter 10 Credit Risk Management for Trading

1. Bank for International Settlements, *69th Annual Report* (June 7, 1999) Plus earlier Annual Reports. (BIS summarizes ISDA and Exchange volumes.)

Bank for International Settlements, *Central Bank Survey of Foreign Exchange and Derivatives Market Activity 1998* (May 1999). Triennial Survey performed in 1995 and 1998.

2. "The Banks That ISDA Forgot," *Risk* 11, no. 12 (December 1998): 21.

3. Bank for International Settlements, Monetary and Economic Department, *Central Bank Survey of Foreign Exchange and Derivatives Market Activity, 1998* (May 1999): 25.

4. Ottho Heldring, "Settle Down to Settling Up," *Risk* 11, no. 10 (October 1998): 46–49.

5. Bank for International Settlements, Basle, Table B-2, *Central Bank Survey of Foreign Exchange and Derivatives Market Activity 1998* (May 1999): 8. Available under publications at http://www.bis.org

6. "Settlement Risk in Foreign Exchange Transactions," (March 1996): 11. The Committee on Payment and Settlement Systems of Central Banks of the Group of Ten Countries. Section 3.1 "Duration of Foreign Exchange Settlement Exposures" (The Allsopp Report). Available under publications at http://www.bis.org

7. "CPSS Reducing Foreign Exchange Settlement Risk: A Progress Report," (July 1998): 16–20. The Committee on Payment and Settlement Systems of Central Banks of the Group of Ten Countries.

8. Clive Davidson, "Settlement Solutions," *Risk* 11, no. 11 (November 1998): 61–65.

9. More information is available from CLS Services Ltd. St., Alphage House, 2 Fore Street, London, EC2Y 5DA England or http://www.clsservices.demon.co.uk

10. Martin Mayer, "The Dangers of Derivatives," *The Wall Street Journal* (May 20, 1999): A20.

Chapter 11 Credit Risk Management for Traditional Lending

1. For more information: http://www.loanpricing.com

2. IFCA web site: http://risk.ifci.ch/SmartSearch.htm, type 1988 in the year box. This site has much more risk information.

3. Chris Matten, "The Role of Capital," *Managing Bank Capital, Capital Allocation, and Performance Measurement* Chapter 1 (New York: John Wiley & Sons, 1996).

4. "Credit Risk Models at Major U.S. Banking Institutions: Current State of the Art and Implications for Assessments of Capital Adequacy" (May 1998). Federal Reserve System Task Force on Internal Credit Risk Models. Available: http://www.us.kpmg.com/consulting/main.html, click on Publication Archive.

5. "Credit Risk and Regulatory Capital" International Swaps and Derivatives Association (March 1998). Available: http://www.isda.org/a5.html

6. "Basle: Reform or Reinvention?" *Risk* 12, no. 6 (June 1999): 29–31.

7. "Regulators Cool on Credit Models," *Risk* 11, no. 12 (December 1998): 6.

8. "A New Capital Adequacy Framework," A consultative paper issued by the Basle Committee on Banking Supervision (June 1999). Available: http://www.bis.org

9. "Credit Risk Rating at Large U.S. Banks," *Federal Reserve Bulletin* (November 1998). Available: http://www.bog.frb.fed.us/pubs/bulletin /default.htm

10. P. Halpern, M. Trebilcock, and S. Turnbull, "An Economic Analysis of Limited Liability in Corporate Law," *University of Toronto Law Journal* (1980).

11. F. Black and M. Scholes, "The Pricing of Options and Corporate Liabilities," *Journal of Political Economy* 81 (1973): 637–659.

12. "On the Pricing of Corporate Debt: The Risk Structure of Interest Rates," *Journal of Finance* 29, no. 2 (May 1974): 449–470.

13. Rebel A. Cole and Robert A. Eisengeis, "The Role of Principal-Agent Conflicts in the 1980s Thrift Crisis," *Real Estate Economics* 24, no. 2 (summer 1996): 195.

14. R. Miller, "Refining Ratings," *Risk* 11, no. 8 (August 1998): 97, 98, 99. Exhibit 11.6 is reproduced with permission of Dr. Ross Miller.

15. More information available: http://www.riskmetrics.com

16. More information available: http://www.csfp.csh.com/csfpfod/html/csfp_10.htm

17. More information available: NY McKinsey & Co. Office.

18. More information available with the Loan Analysis System at: http://www.us.kpmg.com/consulting

Chapter 12 Market Risk in Portfolios

1. More technical information available: Technical Documents under Research at http://www.riskmetrics.com

Chapter 13 Simulation

1. Till Guidimann, "The Monte Carlo Cookbook," *Risk* 11, no. 11 (November 1998): 59.

2. More information available: http://www.askari.com

3. "Converting Experts' Knowledge into Dynamic Variables Distributions for Monte Carlo Simulation," *Contingencies, American Academy of Actuaries* (January/February 1996).

4. SS & C Technologies at http://www.ssctech.com and Falcon Asset Management at http://www.falconasset.com

5. Anthony M. Santomero and David F. Babbel, "Financial Risk Management by Insurers: An Analysis of the Process," *The Journal of Risk and Insurance* 64, no. 2 (1997): 231–270.

Chapter 14 Risk Management: The Vision and the Reality

1. Chris Matten, *Managing Bank Capital, Capital Allocation, and Performance Measurement* (New York: John Wiley & Sons, 1996).
See also, Chris Dowd, *Beyond Value at Risk, the New Science of Risk Management* (New York: John Wiley & Sons, 1998).

2. Nicholas Dunbar, "The New Emperors of Wall Street," *Risk* 12, no. 3 (March 1999): 26–33.

3. More technical information available: Research at http://www .riskmetrics.com

4. "The Practice of Risk Management, A Day in the Life of a Risk Manager," *Euromoney Books* Chapter 1 (London: Goldman Sachs & Co. and SBC Warburg Dillon Read, 1998).

5. More information available: http://www.standishgroup.com

Chapter 15 The Global Risk Management Development Model

1. Robert C. Merton et al., *Global Financial Systems: A Functional Perspective* (Boston: Harvard Business School Press, 1997): Entire book recommended.

2. Ibid., Chapter 5 on The Allocation of Risk.

Chapter 16 Developing GRM: What Works, What Doesn't

1. "New Strategy Hits Chase's Asset Growth, U.S. Banks Aim to Lift Profitability," *Financial Times* (June 12, 1998).

2. Thomas G. Lebreque (speech to Federal Reserve Bank of NY), "Risk Management: One Institution's Experience," *Economic Policy Review* 4, no. 3 (October 1998): 237.

3. Timothy L. O'Brien "Taking the Danger Out of Risk," *New York Times* (January 20, 1999): C-1.

4. Ibid., New Strategy Hits Asset Growth.

5. "Chase CFO Puts the Emphasis on Productivity," *American Banker* 164, no. 12 (January 20, 1999).

6. Ibid.

7. "The Practice of Risk Management, A Day in the Life of a Risk Manager," *Euromoney Books* Chapter 1 (London: Goldman Sachs & Co. and SBC Warburg Dillon Read).

Index

For in-depth market information and news, visit Bloomberg.com which draws proprietary content from the BLOOMBERG PROFESSIONAL™ service and Bloomberg's host of media products to provide high-quality news and information in multiple languages on stocks, bonds, currencies, and commodities—at **www.bloomberg.com.**

Bloomberg L.P., founded in 1981, is a global information services, news, and media company. Headquartered in New York, the company has nine sales offices, two data centers, and 80 news bureaus worldwide.

Bloomberg Financial Markets, serving customers in 100 countries around the world, holds a unique position within the financial services industry by providing an unparalleled combination of news, information, and analytic tools in a single package known as the BLOOMBERG PROFESSIONAL™ service. Corporations, banks, money management firms, financial exchanges, insurance companies, and many other entities and organizations rely on Bloomberg as their primary source of information.

BLOOMBERG NEWS^SM, founded in 1990, offers worldwide coverage of economies, companies, industries, governments, financial markets, politics, and sports. The news service is the main content provider for Bloomberg's broadcast media, which include BLOOMBERG TELEVISION®—the 24-hour cable and satellite television network available in ten languages worldwide—and BLOOMBERG RADIO™—an international radio network anchored by flagship station BLOOMBERG® RADIO AM 1130 in New York.

In addition to the BLOOMBERG PRESS® line of books, Bloomberg publishes BLOOMBERG® Magazine, BLOOMBERG PERSONAL FINANCE™, and BLOOMBERG® WEALTH MANAGER. To learn more about Bloomberg, call a sales representative at:

Frankfurt:	49-69-920-410	San Francisco:	1-415-912-2960
Hong Kong:	852-977-6000	São Paulo:	5511-3048-4500
London:	44-171-330-7500	Singapore:	65-438-8585
New York:	1-212-318-2000	Sydney:	61-29-777-8686
Princeton:	1-609-279-3000	Tokyo:	81-3-3201-8900

James T. Gleason has been a risk-management consultant for more than fifteen years at firms that include Coopers & Lybrand and Arthur Andersen & Co. He has worked as an independent consultant to help implement risk management solutions at Citicorp, First National Bank of Chicago, ING-Barings (Netherlands), Rabobank (Netherlands), and other large companies. He is a contributor to *Risk* magazine. He is with IBM Consulting and resides in Darien, Connecticut.